The American History Series

SERIES EDITORS

John Hope Franklin, *Duke University*
A. S. Eisenstadt, *Brooklyn College*

Elliott Robert Barkan
CALIFORNIA STATE UNIVERSITY
SAN BERNARDINO

And Still They Come

Immigrants and American Society 1920 to the 1990s

HARLAN DAVIDSON, INC.
WHEELING, ILLINOIS 60090-6000

Library of Congress Cataloging-in-Publication Data

Barkan, Elliott Robert.
    And still they come : immigrants and American society, 1920 to
    the 1990s / Elliot Robert Barkan.
        p. cm. — (The American history series / Wheeling, Ill./)
    Includes bibliographical references and index.
    ISBN 0-88295-928-X
    1. Immigrants—United States—History—20th century. 2. United
    States—Emigration and immigration—History—20th century.
    I. Title. II . Series.
    JV6455.B18   1996
    304.8´73´00904—dc20   95-48992
                                        CIP

Cover credit: Cartoon by Chip Bok for the *Akron Beacon Journal* © 1994.
Used by permission of Chip Bok and Creators Syndicate.

Manufactured in the United States of America
03 02 01 00 99 3 4 5 6 7 TS

FOREWORD

Every generation writes its own history for the reason that it sees the past in the foreshortened perspective of its own experience. This has surely been true of the writing of American history. The practical aim of our historiography is to give us a more informed sense of where we are going by helping us understand the road we took in getting where we are. As the nature and dimensions of American life are changing, so too are the themes of our historical writing. Today's scholars are hard at work reconsidering every major aspect of the nation's past: its politics, diplomacy, economy, society, recreation, mores and values, as well as status, ethnic, race, sexual, and family relations. The lists of series titles that appear at the back of this book will show at once that our historians are ever broadening the range of their studies.

The aim of this series is to offer our readers a survey of what today's historians are saying about the central themes and aspects of the American past. To do this, we have invited to write for the series only scholars who have made notable contributions to the respective fields in which they are working. Drawing on primary and secondary materials, each volume presents a factual and narrative account of its particular subject, one that affords readers a basis for perceiving its larger dimensions and importance. Conscious that readers respond to the closeness and immediacy of a subject, each of our authors seeks to restore the past as an actual present, to revive it as a living reality. The individuals and groups who figure in the pages of our books appear as real people who once were looking for survival and fulfillment. Aware that historical subjects are often matters of controversy, our authors present their own findings and conclusions. Each volume closes with an extensive critical essay on the writings of the major authorities on its particular theme.

The books in this series are designed for use in both basic and advanced courses in American history, on the undergraduate and graduate levels. Such a series has a particular value these days, when the format of American history courses is being altered to accommodate a greater diversity of reading materials. The series offers a number of distinct advantages. It extends the dimensions of regular course work. Going well beyond the confines of the textbook, it makes clear that the study of our past is, more than the student might otherwise understand, at once complex, profound, and absorbing. It presents that past as a subject of continuing interest and fresh investigation. The work of experts in their respective fields, the series, moreover, puts at the disposal of the reader the rich findings of historical inquiry. It invites the reader to join, in major fields of research, those who are pondering anew the central themes and aspects of our past. And it reminds the reader that in each successive generation of the ever-changing American adventure, men and women and children were attempting, as we are now, to live their lives and to make their way.

John Hope Franklin
A. S. Eisenstadt

CONTENTS

List of Tables and Figures

(Tables found in the Appendix are given in Italics)

ACKNOWLEDGMENTS

There are many debts one always has at this stage. I owe a special debt of gratitude to Robert Warren, Michael Hoefer, and (now retired) Margaret Sullivan of the Statistics Section of the Immigration and Naturalization Service, in Washington, D.C., for providing over the years an immense amount of invaluable data from their records on immigrants and new citizens, so much of it never published. I would also like to thank for their comments on various portions of this manuscript Lawrence Fuchs, Leonard Dinnerstein, Ray Mohl, Walter Nugent, Donna Gabaccia, Sydney Stahl Weinberg, Maxine Sellers, Roger Daniels, David Reimers, Cheryl Greenberg, June Alexander, David Mauk, Gena Foisy, Gail Karpman, and especially the late (and much missed) George Pozzetta; the editors of this American history series, Profs. Abraham Eisenstadt and John Hope Franklin; the senior editor of Harlan Davidson, Maureen Gilgore Hewitt; and the two anonymous reviewers. Dean Julius Kaplan, of California State University San Bernardino, provided a valuable grant that helped cover a significant portion of the costs for the photographs included in this book. Finally, immensely and indispensably valuable have been the comments, suggestions, and remarkable forebearance of my frover, my bride, the source of my joy, Bryn Medrich Barkan.

Dedicated to
my in-house editor,
Bryn Medrich Barkan

One grand example of America's melting pot is this family photo from a wedding in 1995. The seated grandmother of the bride is full-blooded Chichimec Indian; the bride's mother was born in Mexico; and the bride's father is of Danish ancestry. The groom is of East European Jewish origin, and the other brothers- and sisters-in-law are of English, Irish, French, Swedish, Dutch, and German backgrounds. And all are Mormon.

INTRODUCTION

The well-known public figure exclaimed, "If America is to survive as 'one nation, one people,' we need to call timeout on immigration, to assimilate the tens of millions who have lately arrived. We need to get to know one another. . . . And we need soon to bring down the curtain on this idea of hyphenated Americanism." Written in 1920? 1924? No, Republican presidential hopeful Patrick Buchanan wrote it in October 1994, expressing a growing public sentiment of concern about the nation's immigration and refugee policies. Three months later, the Republicans, having won majorities in both houses of Congress for the first time in four decades, introduced bills to tighten curbs on illegal immigration, reduce legal immigration, and withdraw dozens of federal services from foreign-born noncitizens.

In some respects, public opinion appeared to be swinging back to the 1920s. Whether it would indeed come full circle and whether we would actually see restrictive legislation enacted was not yet certain by October 1995. One thing was clear: The presence of very mixed feelings about immigrants and refugees was not new. Nevertheless, the depth of the current anxieties about them, fueled by the clamor over illegal immigration in 1993 and 1994 and the general climate of economic uncertainty, had surprised many observers. It was not, for example, very apparent when I began this study in 1992, barely a year after the quite liberal immigration act of 1990 had taken effect.

The current trend brings to mind an early 1920s cartoon that depicted a carnival stage with a bespectacled white man sitting alone, blankfaced; the caption contained a poem describing this "last Yankee alive" in nineteen seventy-five. The concerns of the public at that time were bluntly stated by the man who would shepherd the restrictive immigration legislation of the 1920s through the House of Representatives, Albert Johnson, a Republican from Washington State: "The United States is our land. . . . We intend to maintain it so." Indeed, President Calvin Coolidge himself declared in his 1923 State of the Union Address that "America must be kept American." The nation agreed with the new Republican leadership and, in so doing, took itself off in a new direction.

This volume is, in one way, the story of that new direction in immigration policy and the many twists and turns it took before striking off in still another direction some forty years later. That revised policy would then be followed by more unanticipated convolutions before coming up against what may, in the 1990s, prove to be a tidal wave of demand that the nation once more enact a timeout period for consolidation, assimilation, and economic readjustment. In a second way, this book is also about the immigrants themselves and their children, their communities, and their struggles to find a place in American society. That, too, is a story with many paths taken by numerous groups toward diverse objectives. The outcomes of their various encounters with America have NOT been the same. Some peoples have been here for generations and millions of other people only for two decades or so. Moreover, the groups themselves have varied considerably in their backgrounds as well as by their places of settlement in America and by their own particular needs and goals.

During the past seven decades of immigration and ethnic adaptation, the nation itself has undergone enormous changes, vastly altering the setting into which these diverse peoples have had to fit. A major part of the transformation was brought on by the civil rights revolution of the 1960s and 1970s, which legitimized ethnic diversity in American life and reassured newcomers that they could openly preserve many traditions while ad-

justing to American life. And yet, as before, Americans remained
of two minds, acknowledging the ethnic pluralism while hoping
and expecting that the immigrants and refugees would hasten to
become "American." The theme, then, of this work is the way
American immigration and ethnicity[1] have been affected by—
and in turn have influenced—public policies, public sentiments,
public culture, and each other.

However, this book has no single story line—no *one* tale to
tell—because those policies have been complex and changing;
because the motives for migration have ranged from family to
famine, from work to war; because the nation's minority groups
have become so varied; and because the relationships between
the newer minorities and the older, native populations (especially those more directly affected by the new immigration, particularly African Americans) have been so different. And, it must
not be forgotten, despite the mood swings in America, millions
more are still seeking to come to the United States: In January
1994, 3.8 million persons were awaiting visas that would allow
them to migrate to the United States and remain. Even more
telling, just for the 1995 lottery involving the 55,000 "diversity"
visas (open to people from countries sending few emigrants),
8 million people applied.

Given all this, could there still actually be *an* American immigration story today, one overarching portrait, such as the one
historian Oscar Handlin attempted in his 1951 classic, *The Uprooted*? Could one thematic narrative render fairly the experiences of Chinese and Czechs, Filipinos and Finns, Cubans and
Cambodians? When nearly all of the nation's immigrants moved
west across the Atlantic, writers like Handlin thought they had
uncovered sufficient commonalities. Even though the later homelands lay in the farther reaches of eastern and southern Europe,
parallels were sought between "old" comers and "new" comers,
for though some were peasants and others townspeople, some

---

[1]Basically, I use "immigrant" and "immigration" to refer to newcomers, and
"ethnic" and "ethnicity" to apply to the communities and cultures they and their
descendants create in their new homeland. See bibliography.

farmers and others landless, they were all European and nearly all Judeo-Christian. It was considered somewhat irrelevant (or but a "strange interlude," to use one historian's phrase) to observe that Japanese were sailing eastward to America, Québécois were journeying southward, and Mexicans and Barbadians northward during the same years Germans, Italians, Poles, and Jews were embarking westward.

Therefore, if historians have learned anything since Handlin's Pulitzer Prize–winning study, it is that such epic stories read well but do not always provide an accurate portrait, failing, for example, to capture not only the range of immigrant types but also the broader, multidirectional, global nature of contemporary migration. In such a portrait, strokes of the brush that are too broad and sweeping can also all too easily blur distinctions between those who came by sea, or across land, or even criss-crossed both, and those who later flew over them. They can obscure the differences between those who fled pogroms, revolution, civil war, oppressive regimes and those who struggled to escape unrelenting poverty or the ravages of war. They can also gloss over the variations between those whose aspirations envisioned time in America as a means to achieving goals in their homelands and those whose talents and/or dreams simply could not find sufficient fulfillment in those native lands.

These complexities notwithstanding, there does remain at least one persistent thread through them all that ought not to be forgotten: Migration involves the choices and actions of individual men and women and their families. Even in the severest of circumstances there are those who take action and those who do not, those daring to uproot themselves and those remaining rooted. Mario Puzo, a second-generation American and author of *The Godfather*, captured this well when he referred to his parents' immigrant generation in words that span decades of American history and embrace multitudes of new Americans:

And all those old-style grim conservative Italians whom I hated, then pitied so patronizingly, they also turned out to be heroes. . . . How did they ever have the balls to get married, have kids, go out to earn a living in a strange land, with no skills, not even knowing the language? They made it . . . without even a dream. Heroes all around me. I never saw them. But how could I? They wore lumpy work clothes and handlebar moustaches, they blew their noses on their fingers and they were so short that their high school children towered over them. . . . Brave men, brave women. . . . Illiterate Colombos, they dared to seek the promised land. And so they, too, dreamed a dream.

Three final points: First, this volume is a sequel to Alan Kraut's fine study of immigration, *The Huddled Masses: The Immigrant in American Society, 1880–1921* (1982), in this Harlan Davidson series. The time frame of each volume has its own logic. *And Still They Come: Immigrants and American Society, 1920 to the 1990s* covers the eras from restriction to reform to possibly renewed restriction in this last decade of the century.

Second, the book is divided into three parts: 1920–40, 1940–65, and 1965–95. The initial part treats the interwar years, during which the nation retreated from a relatively open, international posture regarding immigration (except for Asians) to quotas and restrictions that became ever more rigid in the face of the Depression of the 1930s and the threat of renewed war. The second encompasses World War II and the onset of the Cold War, the quest for security at home and the nation's recognition that its world leadership position necessitated changes in favor of more sympathetic immigration policies. The two postwar decades, 1945–65, were marked by a struggle between the nation's nativist and humanitarian traditions; ultimately, the latter won out because of continuous refugee and other pressures. The third part, up to late 1995, details the impact of four major reform packages (1965, 1980, 1986, and 1990), the waves of new refugees and undocumented aliens from many continents, and the growing disenchantment with the nation's immigration policies.

The last point, to reiterate, is that this book is an examination of both the immigrant and the ethnic experiences across three-quarters of this century. On the one hand, there is a considerable degree of similarity in the ways that new groups have, in many respects, replicated the efforts of their predecessors and contemporaries to adjust to their new homeland. Nevertheless, circumstances have certainly altered some particular features of the immigrant patterns over the decades. On the other, in that very traditional ethnic struggle to negotiate what ought to be preserved in their traditions from what ought to be jettisoned, the immigrants' children and grandchildren have had to face equally great and novel challenges. An ever more rapidly changing America and American culture have been drawing ethnic group members ever more forcefully into the mainstream. They have commonly tried to refrain—at least, for a time—from entirely cutting themselves off from their past, and those cultural roots have sometimes been partially revived by newer waves of immigrants. However, the processes of integration have usually prevailed, although not at the same rate for all groups and especially not for peoples of color.

Meanwhile, with all this, native-born Americans have had their own dilemmas: struggling to accommodate to the old groups and then to the new ones and struggling to adjust to the heightened visibility of so much ethnic diversity. Many have enjoyed how that diversity has enriched the national culture; others have seen it as a threat to the nation's heritage and traditions. While Americans debate, immigrants acculturate and their children integrate.

The on-going struggles and dualisms among both ethnic groups and natives are at the core of the American experience—and the core of this book—and, as stated at the outset, its central argument is that there has been no one outcome. Besides, with so many millions of recent newcomers across the nation, far too many stories remain unfinished, their paces of change quite varied, and their ends by no means certain.

PART ONE

From Postwar
to the Eve of World War: 1920–1940

The waves of immigrants to America from the 1880s to the early 1920s were reduced to swells by the late 1920s and mere ripples in the 1930s. Hardened by social and economic uncertainties, widespread racism, persistent anti-Semitism, and dubious scientific theories about race and intelligence, the American public endorsed immigrant quotas in the 1920s and then repeatedly resisted a flexible response to refugees during the Depression of the 1930s. With reentry becoming more difficult, immigrants during the 1920s were confronted with a narrowing gateway that forced them to choose whether to leave the United States or to remain and settle. Ethnic communities—of immigrants and their children—groped for ways to hold on to their traditions while accommodating to a highly urbanized society and a rapidly modernizing national culture. Other challenges they faced included concerted opposition to labor unions; competition from Canadian and Mexican migrant workers as well as African Americans moving out of the South; and campaigns against political radicals and Asian newcomers. Even small town and rural America could not remain entirely immune to the changes.

When the Depression struck, many first- and second-generation Americans had to face the struggle of economic survival and continued cultural adaptation in many of the hardest hit areas of the nation. Although some groups gained through the various New Deal programs, others confronted hostility so severe they were forced to emigrate or face deportation. At the same time, more technological innovations appeared—especially involving the cinema, radio, and automobile—enabling the new mass culture to spread among immigrants and native born alike more rapidly and irresistibly. Certainly, ethnic group life would go on, but the pace of integration would accelerate.

CHAPTER ONE

The 1920s:
Halting the Immigrant
Floodtide

What dramatic developments convinced Americans to begin
turning away from their traditional open door for immigrants?
What prompted Congress to adopt a series of increasingly more
narrow and rigid standards for admission? Preservation of the
"traditional" northern European composition of the American
people was given as a principal goal, but the motives would prove
more complex than that. And, at the same time that Congress
was taking action legislatively, the U.S. Supreme Court was re-
affirming that American citizenship—the key to full participation in American society—was not available to foreigners of all
races. During the 1920s, the federal government both expressed
and reinforced the nation's anxiety-ridden concerns.

Adopting Quotas and National Origins

Students of American history assume that if any immigrant
could have effortlessly adjusted to America it would have been
a person from England. What must the process have meant for

all other newcomers if the British journalist S. K. Ratcliffe could observe in 1927 that, in fact, even a Briton would be quite shocked upon arrival, notwithstanding that he or she spoke English and was most likely familiar with urban life? "America must be to him a land of extraordinary strangeness," he wrote. "He has never seen anything like it. The scene . . . is something he could not have imagined. The external differences between England and America are altogether indescribable. And to begin with, there is the immense difference of scale. . . . Before crossing the Atlantic he thought, very likely, that Pittsburgh would be only Sheffield with an American accent. He finds that he has come, not only into a new country, but into a new and terrifying civilization."

Ratcliffe might have been equally surprised to discover that many Americans of the twenties also saw their country as a terrifyingly new society. They believed the causes lay not so much in the industrial, technological, and urban changes as in the great numbers of immigrants who were once more entering the country, most often crowding into cities already teeming with strangers from other lands. The Immigration Act of 1917, with its literacy test, had failed to halt the flow of hundreds of thousands of newcomers between 1918 and 1921. That one-half million also left the country seemed not to matter. Ellis Island, in New York harbor, the nation's principal center for processing immigrants, continued to be a "House of Babel," with multitudes of new immigrants filling its great halls with dozens of languages. Anxieties abounded across the nation, inflamed by strikes, race riots, and nativist warnings of the dangers being posed by "the yellow and brown races" as well as by inferior white "races," especially the "abnormally twisted" and "filthy" Jews. By early 1921, many Americans were convinced that they were under siege. Would the immigrants add to the labor unrest? Strengthen radical organizations with their imported Bolshevik doctrines and sympathizers? Increase Prohibition-related crime (often attributed to foreigners)? Aggravate unemployment problems? They feared the worst.

The overpowering conviction taking shape among many Americans was that the volume of immigrants had exceeded the nation's ability to absorb them. Many Americans believed that the programs to Americanize immigrants and promote citizenship had failed and, in fact, these new peoples were not assimilable. It was little understood how complex and unnerving the process of adaptation to a new homeland could be.

Still, the moves almost to shut the nation's doors were more than the consequence of the widespread postwar disillusionment, fears of unrest by foreign-born agitators, and growing isolationism. The increasing numbers of immigrants from Canada, Mexico, and the West Indies lessened the business community's need for European workers. Immigrant communities thus lost that important political voice on their behalf, one that might have counterbalanced the alarmists and nativists and reassured mainstream Americans. It was an influential voice they could not replace because so large a percentage of foreigners were not yet citizens and could not vote; they lacked political clout. No other powerful interest group arose to thwart the restrictionists, or to counter such remarks as those by Congressional leader Albert Johnson, in December 1920: "The welfare of the United States demands that the door should be closed to immigrants for a time. We are being made a dumping-ground for the human wreckage of the [world] war. And worst of all, they are coming in such numbers at a time when we are unable adequately to take care of them."

In May 1921, President Harding signed the Emergency Quota Act. It imposed a ceiling of 357,800 immigrants annually from outside the Western Hemisphere, with more than half set aside for northern and western Europeans (based upon 3 percent of the foreign-born population in 1910). Only about 1 percent was apportioned for non-Europeans. The nation would not again reopen the gates to unlimited immigration. Moreover, the law went beyond declaring that certain types of individuals were not welcomed, such as anarchists and prostitutes. It now deemed specific nationality groups less desirable than others. It also had the effect of validating the notion—if only for a short time—that nationalities were racial categories, possibly immutable ones. In the end, it was not simply the law that had changed. America had changed.

The immigration legislation of the 1920s, a clear turning point in American history, represented the heightened expression of the nation's fears and its urgent need to take stock of a half century of immense social, economic, technological, and cultural changes. Likewise, the laws compelled foreigners to make momentous choices. Many who had come with the intention of returning home, or had come and gone regularly ("birds of passage"), now had to decide whether to leave or to remain and, if to stay, how to bring over their families. With this settling down there soon appeared growing numbers of second-generation youngsters, American-born and America-oriented. In the cauldron of the twenties a new era of American immigration was taking form.

A year after the emergency quota law was enacted *Abie's Irish Rose* opened on New York's Broadway and began the longest run of any show up to that time, 2,532 performances in about seven years. In a city where three out of every four persons were foreigners or the children of foreigners, Jewish Abie, Irish Rose, and their twin sons offered a paean for tolerance, eventually winning over their priest and rabbi. "Catholics, Hebrews, Protestants alike," Father Whalen tells Rabbi Samuels regarding their World War I experiences, "forgot the prejudices and came to realize that all faiths and creeds have about the same destination after all."

Unfortunately, many Americans were not ready for that message. They were more likely to endorse the remarks made by Calvin Coolidge, soon to become president, that "Biological laws tell us that certain divergent people will not mix or blend." And they were more willing to accept the arguments of eugenicist Harry Laughlin on the inferior breeding stocks entering the country and polluting it. New immigrants, he claimed "objectively," had disproportionately more "inborn socially inadequate qualities." He periodically testified before Congress, and almost no one challenged him. A Tennesseean's warning to his congressman, J. William Taylor, may have well expressed a widespread and growing sentiment about the wrong path the nation had taken with its traditional open door: "Rome had faith in the melting pot as we have. It scorned the iron certainties of heredity as we do. It lost its instinct for race preservation, as we have lost ours." In fact, the president of Colgate University, George B. Cutten, made that precise point in 1923 regarding the direction America was going: "The melting pot is destructive to our race. . . . The danger the 'melting pot' brings to the nation is the breeding out of the higher divisions of the white race and the breeding in of the lower divisions." The implication? The temporary legislation of 1921 had to be made permanent.

The next legislative step was shaped by Albert Johnson in the House and David A. Reed (Penn.) in the Senate. Signed into law on May 26, 1924, the Johnson-Reed Act contained a number of pathbreaking provisions. Congress accepted the idea of basing permanent quotas on the total contribution of each nationality to the entire population, based on a special assessment of the 1920 census. Three years were initially set aside to develop this program of National Origins (finally launched in 1929). The interim plan called for quotas that would more closely reflect the nation's earlier "racial" distribution. The act pushed back the formula to 2 percent of the foreign born in 1890, with a ceiling of less than 165,000. Over two-thirds of the total were designated for Germany, Great Britain, and Ireland. Congress again exempted immigrants from the Americas, while almost entirely excluding Asians, a category of persons which the courts had recently reaffirmed as "aliens ineligible for citizenship" (see below, pp. 16–17).

In calculating the nation's national origins, almost ninety-five million white persons in the 1920 census were separated by whether their roots were in the colonial period or later, a procedure that very much weighted the results in favor of the English.[1] The revised guidelines set a limit of about 153,700, with 43 per-

---

[1]Sixty percent of white persons in 1790 were determined to have been of English extraction.

cent for Great Britain, 17 percent for Germany, and 12 percent for Ireland. The National Origins formula hurt many others: for example, Italians had averaged nearly 158,000 per year prior to 1920 but were given an annual quota of 5,802. An average of 17,600 Greeks had been admitted previously, while their quota was now merely 307.

America had effectively blocked the way of particular Europeans and others whom they deemed less desirable. As Tennessee Congressman William Vaile put it, "We would not want any immigrants at all unless we could hope that they would become assimilated to our language, customs, and institutions, unless they could blend thoroughly into our body politic." Thus, he continued, "we prefer to base our quotas on groups whose value has been established through several generations." With the various changes introduced in the 1924 legislation, particularly shifting the processing of prospective immigrants to the consulates abroad, the great days of Ellis Island passed. Over twelve million had been admitted there. Some would still arrive there first, but its main role was changed to more of a detention center for foreigners and it would eventually be closed entirely in the fall of 1954.

By the time the National Origins System became effective the heat of many of the worst racist passions had cooled. Even the Ku Klux Klan had fallen into disrepute. Ironically, it took Prohibition finally to galvanize many immigrant groups into promoting citizenship and encouraging voting. They wanted especially to support New York Governor Alfred E. Smith, the Democratic candidate for president in 1928 and the first Catholic ever nominated (and an opponent of Prohibition).

The nativist tide may have ebbed by the late 1920s, but by no means had it disappeared. In fact, the man who defeated Smith, President Herbert Hoover, gave vent to just such attitudes when he responded to a criticism expressed by an Italian-Jewish congressman from New York City (and its next mayor), Fiorello La Guardia. He wrote an astonishing attack on La Guardia for being "a little out of your class in presuming to criticize the President. . . . You should go back to where you belong and advise Mussolini on how to make good honest citizens in Italy. The Italians are predominately our murderers and bootleggers. . . . Like a lot of the foreign spawn, you do not appreciate the country which supports and tolerates you."

The Struggle Over American Citizenship

As that 1928 election campaign would demonstrate to immigrants, citizenship had been a vital aspect of their experience, although one too often overlooked by historians. Yet, having it or not, being eligible for it or not, has frequently been a major issue. It has been linked to the race, gender, and political views of immigrants and their spouses, often with significant consequences for their fortunes in America; all three could affect their legal status. For example, as improbable as it may appear, the Nationality Act of 1907 had stripped the citizenship from native-born American women who married noncitizens and denied eligibility to foreign-born women wed to such men. These women were thus deprived of the right to determine their own national allegiance, and they were, among other things, subjected to state laws barring aliens from entering certain professions, particularly teaching. They had been powerless to stop the legislation or to secure its repeal until 1920, when the woman's suffrage movement won them the right to vote through ratification of the Nineteenth Amendment.

Women's groups immediately campaigned to change the 1907 law. On September 22, 1922, President Harding signed the Married Women's Nationality Act (the Cable Act). The law declared that foreign-born women would thereafter need to apply for citizenship independently of their spouses and that American women would no longer be denied their birthright as a result of marrying a noncitizen. There remained a catch, however, for the act also declared that, if her spouse were ineligible for citizenship—in other words, were an Asian male—the American-born woman lost her citizenship for as long as she remained married! It would take another decade to get that inequity against women removed.

More enduring was the treatment of Asians themselves. The original nationality laws had limited the right to acquire citizenship to free white persons until, in 1870, this right was expanded to include those of African descent as well.[2] The Fourteenth Amendment, ratified in 1868, had also declared that *all* persons born in the United States and subject to its jurisdiction were citizens. These two changes left open the issue of other nonwhite immigrants. Consequently, there were inconsistencies in the application of the law. Over the years, some Asians were naturalized, including 420 Japanese and 69 Asian Indians. Nonetheless, the term "aliens ineligible for citizenship" had become a weapon for those determined to drive as many Asians out of the country as possible by depriving them of basic privileges, jobs, and economic opportunities. Asian immigrants resisted at every turn but won only limited battles. Lacking American citizenship, they were often forced to rely heavily on American lawyers or to resort to elaborate evasions of such measures as the alien land laws denying them the right to own or lease farm lands. The culmination of this powerlessness would be one of the most serious violations of civil rights in American history, the internment of Japanese Americans in concentration camps in 1942.

When the Asian citizenship controversy came before the U.S. Supreme Court during the 1920s, it firmly set the seal on Asians' inferior status. Takao Ozawa said that "at heart" he was "a true American," speaking English at home to his children, who attended church and public school. Having resided in Hawaii and California for twenty years, during which time he had been graduated from Berkeley High School and had attended the University of California at Berkeley, Ozawa felt fully qualified when he applied for citizenship in Hawaii in 1916. But he was Japanese, not white, and his application was denied. He appealed. In 1922, the U.S. Attorney General told the Supreme Court that Japanese should be denied the right of citizenship because they could never assimilate and, moreover, were a threat to American agri-

---

[2] The citizenship guaranteed Mexicans in the 1848 Treaty of Guadalupe-Hidalgo was reaffirmed by the Supreme Court in 1897.

culture. The Court unanimously concluded that Ozawa was "clearly" not Caucasian and, based on his racial origins, remained ineligible for citizenship.

The following year, the Court carried the matter one step further. A high-caste Hindu, Bhagat Singh Thind, had been granted citizenship in Oregon as a World War I veteran, but the Bureau of Naturalization sought to "denaturalize" him as an ineligible alien. Although conceding that Thind was indeed Caucasian, the Court did an about face and disregarded the racial origins position it had pronounced in its recent Ozawa decision. It declared that Thind was not white according to the "understanding of the common man" and thus did not meet the criteria for citizenship. The denaturalization was upheld.

In view of the legislation and decisions directed against so many groups, it is clear that Congress and the courts reflected and then reinforced the general mood of the 1920s: retreat, retrench, exclude.

Mounting anxieties arising from World War I and the postwar era had spilled over into the 1920s. A nation reeling from change called for some kind of a halt. But since Americans could not undo the changes by which the nation was being transformed, they could at least stem the flood tide of strange peoples and, in that way, regain some sense of control over their culture and society. In the process, the federal government went beyond defining different classes of aliens to establishing different categories of desirable immigrants. All this would represent both challenges and opportunities for immigrants and their children.

CHAPTER TWO

Adapting to America: The Interwar Years

The 1920s were turbulent years, marked by old fears and new freedoms. On the one hand, Americans strenuously maintained barriers against minorities and outsiders. On the other, they were also celebrating the great expansion in consumer goods, services, and conveniences that made their lives much easier. Meanwhile, immigrants continued to enter the country and to encounter the longstanding challenges so many newcomers have had to face: earning a living, settling in, and adjusting to a rapidly modernizing society that was steadily altering the life styles of all Americans, native and newcomer.

The Not-So-Roaring Twenties

Quite possibly, the 1920s was one of the worst decades in American history for "outsiders." In that era of Prohibition, Americans wanted to prohibit far more than just the consumption of alcohol. Immigrants and their children confronted racism, nativism, and exclusion, while continuing their efforts to build communities and adapt to America. Segregation laws directed against African Americans in the South were at their most severe (the era of "Jim Crow"). African Americans and others were being terrorized by the Ku Klux Klan, which had approximately three million members (including some half-million women) by its peak in the mid-1920s. Much like African Americans in the South, Mexicans, Filipinos, and Asians in the West were also being treated as racial minorities, encountering formidable legal barriers, discrimination, and, often, violent rejection. And Native Americans continued their struggles to save their remaining reservation lands and ancient customs from the grasp of landseekers and determined assimilationists.

Even white European immigrants were not exempt from bigoted treatment. In 1920, two immigrant anarchists, Nicola Sacco and Bartolomeo Vanzetti, were arrested for two murders in a bungled robbery in Massachusetts. Their trial became a lightning rod for the frustrations and antiforeign anger of Americans. At one point, the judge himself referred to the defendants as "anarchist bastards." For seven years the case dragged on, culminating with the defendants' execution in August 1927—in the face of conflicting evidence, violations of judicial procedures, and world-wide protests for clemency. About to be sentenced to death, Vanzetti declared in court that the Socialist Party leader and presidential candidate, Eugene Debs, "has said that not even a dog that kills chickens would have found an American jury disposed to convict it with the proof that the Commonwealth [of Massachusetts] has produced against us." Equally controversial had been the case of six Sicilians tried for the 1921 bank robbery and murder of a guard in Tangipahoa Parish, Louisiana. On May 9, 1924, all six were hanged for the single murder.

Although in these instances the hostility was overt, other types of discrimination continued to occur. The genteel forms of discrimination against Jews were well established by the early 1920s. Ivy League universities and medical schools began imposing quotas in order to limit Jewish admissions. Henry Ford embarked on an anti-Semitic crusade in his newspaper, the *Dearborn Independent,* publishing a known Russian forgery, a pamphlet concocted by the Czarist secret police, that claimed the existence of an international Jewish conspiracy.

In 1920, in a population of nearly 106 million, there were well over 36 million white persons in the United States who were either foreign-born or second-generation, as well as more than 185,000 Asians, most of whom were foreign-born.[1] In the principal urban areas of the Northeast, such as New York, Boston, Providence, and Pittsburgh, almost seven out of ten persons were foreigners or second generation, whereas few cities in the South had more than 10,000 foreign-born. Despite the public stereotypes, a majority of the foreigners and their children were northern and western Europeans, but because southern and eastern Europeans were so concentrated in the cities, their greater visibility unnerved native-born Americans.

Since almost half of the foreign born had not yet been naturalized by 1920, Americans were convinced that the newcomers were not adapting, not fitting in, not eager to become American citizens. This was especially thought to be the case when it was reported that the majority of the northern Europeans were naturalized, whereas only 28 percent of Poles and Italians and 16 percent of Greeks and Portuguese had obtained American citizenship. Americans did not recognize that it was not simply an issue of many among the most recent newcomers not making the decision to remain and/or switch citizenships; rather, so many of the immigrants were only relatively recent arrivals, and, as a major 1922 study made clear, they just needed more time.

Meanwhile, more immigrants were admitted; the laws had narrowed the gateway to America, not closed it. Over four million were admitted during the 1920s, although one million also left. But the new laws had their desired impact, for the average number of immigrants fell by half during the decade, and from southern and eastern Europe by three-quarters. Another important shift fell outside the provisions of the law: more than

---

[1]In addition, on the Hawaiian Islands in 1920 there were close to another 160,000 Chinese, Japanese, Filipinos, and Koreans, comprising more than three-fifths of the territory's population.

two out of five now entered from the Americas. (See Appendix, Table 2.1.)

Besides the issues of national origins, one of the most important changes at this time concerned female immigrants. In 1926, for the first time in American history, the total number of European females admitted exceeded that of males. During the early 1920s, ten nationalities had included a majority of women; in 1928, twenty sent more females, among them Finns, Irish, and a remarkable four-fifths of Greeks. Very many were young and married, and most were coming to stay. This was an important development, for it meant that many immigrant communities were indeed shifting from sojourning to settling. The presence of more married women undoubtedly affected how rapidly immigrant groups would create communities and networks and how full their adjustment to America would be, because, while the young, unmarried female immigrants would generally be out working (if they were not in school), married women generally were not. They represented permanence, commitment, family life, and important social ties. By contrast, the experience was much more difficult for the Chinese, among whom, due to the exclusion laws, the proportion of females was half that in most other groups (only 20 percent in 1930, up from 12.6 percent in 1920).

Taken all together, the foreign-born population by 1930—despite the laws—was higher than it was a decade earlier (14.2 million). This was principally a result of the increase among southern and eastern Europeans who had come in the early 1920s and Canadians and Mexicans throughout the decade. (See Appendix, Table 2.2.)

For all those who chose to remain, the whole process of fitting in required a good deal of time—and it was rarely ever easy. Some years ago, George Drossos, a Greek immigrant in Chicago, said, "It is a calamity, you know, for a person who leaves a country of birth and goes away. . . . He's a stranger *here*, and if he goes back he'll be a stranger *there*. So he's a man without a country." Were the immigrants faced with "calamity" or with the satisfaction that, for their having chosen to remain, their children born in the new land would be American? Their dilemma? How to cope with the mixed reception among Americans and how to balance traditional ways that gave meaning to their lives with the demands of a new society. And the actions and desires of the young children posed for their immigrant parents even more difficult choices in resolving the conflict between custom and the temptations of America.

For many, the solution clearly lay in the old country. As Paul Sturman, a Czech immigrant, put it in 1920: "Men would leave for America, spend a few years in the coal mines of Pennsylvania, or the iron mills in Pittsburgh, in Chicago in the slaughterhouses, save enough money to either buy himself a piece of land, [or] put his cottage into shape and live there. They wanted to get back. They would never feel good in America." But, for many more others, the goal was not to be found where they had been born. Walter Wallace, a Lithuanian immigrant who arrived in 1923, described the all-too-common reaction: "It was kind of bad for awhile til we got to know people and speak the language and quit being called greenhorns. People say, you ought to preserve your own heritage or something, but all we could think of was, we didn't want to be different, we wanted to be like the rest of all Americans."

Ultimately, there was no one resolution for the great diversity of newcomers. The presence of different generations in most ethnic communities meant that there were immigrants with different lengths of residence and different degrees of adjustment and a second generation (or more) with considerable age differences and degrees of acculturation. Experiences varied considerably. Old timers and new, youngsters and adults, immigrants and ethnics of various origins, all influenced one another in many ways, for all were having to deal with the challenges of the larger American society. In the small towns and rural areas, where there were often relatively more ethnically homogeneous communities such as in the Midwest and Northwest, the process of adjustment could be less demanding than in the cities. Indeed, in all places one could find immigrants, especially the women, who had succeeded in largely isolating themselves from the strange new world. For most, that was neither possible nor desirable.

Should the wives go out to work? Should the children remain in school? Should the parents insist on their language being used at home, or should they promote English? Should the teenagers be allowed "to date" and even choose their own spouses? Or, should the immigrant parents simply emigrate and avoid such difficult choices? So many issues. So many dilemmas. If indeed the idea adapted from historian Frederick Jackson Turner was valid—that the frontier was "the line of most rapid Americanization"—then such a line cut across many ethnic communities throughout America during the 1920s and 1930s, in the cities as well as the countryside. And, since exposure to the general culture more readily occurred in the cities, the increasing urbanization of nearly every group posed even more of a challenge than before. As the Norwegians put it, urbanization meant Americanization. Just under three-quarters of the foreign-born whites resided in urban areas. The least urban were the Mexicans, Finns, and Norwegians; among the most urban were the Poles, Italians, and especially the Russian Jews.

By no means, however, were cities the same in all places, although New York City, with over two million foreign born in 1920, set the stereotype of a foreign-dominated urban America. But even that New York scene, with its seemingly endless rows of dingy, side-by-side, four- and five-story tenements, is somewhat unrepresentative. Manhattan was unique, for no other city had more crowding or more large tenements. What is more, almost one-third of its foreign born in 1930 had arrived just since 1920, a number that exceeded the total foreign-born populations in every other American city except Chicago. Nonetheless, many groups of immigrants and their children were widely dispersed, shaping the character of many cities: the Irish and Italians in Boston and Philadelphia; the Poles in Detroit; the Germans in St. Louis, Cincinnati, and Milwaukee; the Scandinavians in Minneapolis and Seattle; and the Mexicans in El Paso and San Antonio.

In cities across the country ethnic influences were enduring because ethnic populations tended to remain in the general regions where they initially settled. Gradually, they would be drawn with others into common school, work, and religious settings (and eventually political ones, too). When they resettled out of their initial areas (such as out of Manhattan to other boroughs, or out of the near Westside of Chicago to communities to the north and west of the downtown area), interethnic group contact would become more commonplace. In fact, between the two world wars, urban settlement was already beginning to be followed by some suburban dispersal. Still, it was in those urban regions that most newcomers lived.

Earning a Living

Wherever the immigrants and their children settled, there was the basic necessity of finding and holding a job and, for most, supporting the family, either as parent or as contributing child. There were undoubtedly considerable group differences in the jobs they preferred, in the amount of education they would seek (or permit their children to obtain), and in the levels of their aspirations and goals of social mobility. For the immigrants, of course, cultural traditions and historical experiences shaped these attitudes, as did the skills and education they brought (or did not bring) with them. For the second generation, attitudes would be formed by a combination of inherited values, their own degree of acculturation and education, and the opportunities before them.

In some cases, for example among the Italians, Poles, Slovaks, and Mexicans, education was at first seen by immigrants "in terms of the peasant traditions" and not—as Jews, Greeks, Armenians, and Japanese saw it—as the avenue to economic and perhaps social mobility. As the Slovak mother told her sons, "School won't make you any money." Polish, Croatian, Serb, and Hungarian men in the mills and mines, slaughterhouses and meat processing plants provided "models of immobility" for their sons. They focused on the "realities" of working-class life—home, family, and job security. Others recognized the value of education—though not always at first—and were willing to make the sacrifices (mainly, doing without the children's incomes) to see them through school.

Conditions did begin to change, but mostly when the Depression struck. Those new circumstances underscored differences that arose between the generations. For example, in a recent study of Italian women, one finds that most Italians came to America with little appreciation for education as a worthwhile investment; children were to supplement the family income. However, the lack of job opportunities in the early 1930s forced them to modify their strategies for survival. One result was a significant jump in the percentage of high school aged boys and girls who remained in school. Adding to the scarcity of jobs would be the New Deal legislation ending child labor and discouraging employment work done in the homes. Along with rigorous enforcement of high school attendance requirements (until age sixteen), New York high schools began offering more clerical-oriented courses. Businesses and government agencies began opening up white collar jobs to Italian American girls and others of southern and eastern European extraction.

Of course, the effects of motivation, acculturation, and opportunity could be found in many places besides New York. In Cleveland lived an immigrant named Carmelo who had left his village in Messina, Italy, for America, married Nicoletta in 1911, and earned a living as a laborer. In 1920 he worked in a steel mill; a decade later he owned a grocery store and a home in Shaker Heights. He and Nicoletta had just two children, both of whom graduated from high school; the son took over the business in 1940. During that same time, Ioan, who had come from Rumania, opened a poolroom and coffeehouse in Cleveland. His two sons graduated from high school and college, with one becoming an executive in a Rumanian national association, while the second opened a funeral home for Greek Orthodox persons. In contrast, most of the Slovak immigrants in Cleveland did not open businesses but held blue-collar jobs, as did their sons. Many tried to be like Carmelo or Ioan, but more often than not they slipped back to blue collar jobs after their entrepreneurial adventures failed.

Many did not try that avenue at all but searched where they could for what they could; they had to adapt. Consider the extensive Montano family, which had entered Texas from Mexico in 1920. After the men worked for a time on a dairy farm, they learned about jobs in Michigan. They moved north and got work on sugar beet farms near Saginaw. Soon, they followed other Mexicans into Saginaw, and the men found employment in the General Motors foundry. Three years later, Maria Montano, recalling the time her father had travelled north, persuaded her husband to go to the Ford Motor Company in Detroit, where her father had worked years before. The day they arrived, Venturo was hired. Their relocation to the cities in quest of jobs typified a common experience then. Simply finding work represented success for most immigrants.

Even if success for many immigrants was modest, it usually more than fulfilled the dreams they had carried with them, especially for those who got beyond the factories and farms and into business. Many businesses that immigrants founded eventually targeted the broader, general markets, but more immediately it was in the ethnic communities themselves that one would usually find the greatest number and array of business people. They provided the full range of goods and services that immigrants and their children sought—from shoemakers, butchers, bankers, morticians, and journalists to saloon keepers and pool-hall proprietors. Eventually, even a variety of professionals appeared (who were more often than not second generation), including lawyers, physicians, dentists, and teachers. But, out of all these efforts, people came to recognize considerable differences in the ways members of certain ethnic groups specialized. They concentrated in certain businesses, sometimes as a result of prior experiences in their native lands and often as a consequence of newfound opportunities. Quite frequently, immigrants went into business as a result of the networks of their compatriots who had already pioneered in those particular types of enterprise, had been at least somewhat successful, and usually were willing to assist the newest venturers. Germans started bakeries and breweries; Greeks opened confectioneries and restaurants; Italians operated groceries, fresh-food stores, and barbershops; Japanese concentrated on garden nurseries and markets for fruits, vegetables, and flowers; and Jews went from tailoring and tinkering to a whole array of manufacturing, wholesaling, and retailing.

There were certainly some whose fortunes soared, sometimes by their taking risks in whole new industries. Luck and good timing figured in, too. So, Spyrous Skouras, Louis B. Mayer, Carl Laemmle, Samuel Goldwyn, and Charlie Chaplin were great successes in the new film industries of Hollywood. Spectacular success was rare, however, compared to the struggles and limited mobility that were the experience of most. Simple dogged perseverance was all most immigrants could count on. While Norwegians, Germans, Japanese, and Punjabis continued to till the soil, Italians carved out subway tunnels in New York, Mexicans worked the railroad tracks from Kansas to California, and Poles and Slovaks labored in the steel mills, automobile assembly plants, and stockyards of the Midwest.

So often the dreams they nurtured were not for themselves but for their children, their children's opportunities, their children's security. The results could be seen by 1920. True, immigrant men and women were disproportionately providing the brawn for America's factories, mines, and farms, and most of their children were doing the same. But the percentage of second-generation men in manufacturing was substantially less, and more than twice the proportion of second-generation men held clerical, professional, or other white-collar jobs by 1920 than among the foreign born. Among the women, more than one-third of the foreign born were domestics compared with less than one-sixth among the second generation. The shift to white-collar jobs was very apparent for women, too.

Because most were starting at the bottom, immigrants and their families struggled to survive by adopting various household strategies to make ends meet. A major factor was the extent to which women continued to work, for marriage was commonly the great dividing line. "A woman's ethnic group determined her values, relationships to her family, facility with the city and English language and the ratio of men she was exposed to," as well as her likelihood of working and where she would seek that employment. If they were not allowed to remain in school, the immigrants' unmarried daughters were permitted to go out to work along with their brothers (or were simply told to do so). Married women were generally expected not to work outside the home, and the vast majority for most of this period—probably two-thirds or more—apparently did not. They were the family financial managers; they often took in boarders and provided meals; and many did work at home such as finishing parts of garments and making ties, bows, buttons, and artificial flowers. However, as the Depression deepened in the 1930s, wives often found they could get outside employment more readily than could their husbands, and the household strategies (and gender roles) needed to be modified.

While few of the immigrant/ethnic groups felt as compelled by necessity to have their wives and mothers work as did African Americans, sometimes circumstances proved more compelling than the group's cultural traditions that disapproved of their employment outside the home. A Mexican man in Chicago spoke about his wife obtaining work in a meat-packing plant: "We were getting quite desperate as my funds were getting low. My wife resolved to go to work even though in Mexico she had never, never worked. I felt at first very ashamed . . . because I was not able to support her . . . , [but] economic circumstances in this country are different from Mexico. . . . Sometimes she works six hours a day, sometimes eight and sometimes ten hours."

Given the cultural constraints, only a minority of immigrant wives worked outside the home, but they were more likely to do so if it were a family business or farm—as did the Jewish, Italian, Japanese, and Korean wives. Or, it could be a firm where relatives or the whole family were employed (or, at least other women of the same ethnic group), as in canneries and other food-processing and packing-house companies that employed Italians and Mexicans during peak seasons and in the Detroit cigar-making firms that predominantly used Polish women. Josephine Costanzo, who came from Italy in 1923, remembered her mother working in a Lawrence, Massachusetts, textile mill. "It was unusual. In Italy there were no jobs for women. In fact, people that heard about it back in the village didn't like the idea of the women working. But my mother felt she was doing no different from all the other women, so she was going to work. Make some money."

It was also not uncommon for some wives to continue working if their husbands launched businesses that could get them out of the factories and on their own, or if they agreed that the women should work in order to hasten family efforts to acquire property or a home. For example, Italians in Tampa saw rolling cigars as a means to an end. Alex and Josephine Scaglione met while doing just that. He then opened a grocery store. She continued working after they wed to insure an adequate income while the business was growing. Their son stayed in school and eventually became a high school principal and college president. But traditions did not give way so easily for most, and Italians in general appear to have held on with particular firmness to the notion of wives remaining at home. That preference continued into the second generation. A 1925 study of an Italian section of Buffalo reported that, whereas the second-generation daughters were employed, not one mother or wife worked outside the home and only 12 percent of second-generation wives did so.

Whatever the cultural preferences, multiple wage earners were still essential for most immigrant families to survive. If only one-fifth to one-quarter of the wives were employed, it fell to the children to fill the income gap. In 1920 nearly two-thirds of the sixteen-year-old immigrant boys and half the girls that age were out working. For their second-generation counterparts, over half the boys and two-fifths of the girls were employed. Those daughters, along with the young, single immigrant girls, would follow friends and relatives into, for example, food-processing plants, candy factories, clothing firms, cigar-making establishments, and especially—as did Irish, Mexican, and Swedish girls— into domestic work. If education were pursued, as among Jewish, Finnish, and Japanese girls, then more would seek sales and clerical jobs, or go into teaching, nursing, and social work. This move into white-collar positions became more commonplace for other second-generation women by the late 1930s and 1940s.

All these struggles were taking place in an American economy that continued to change with remarkable speed, especially as it moved toward greater consumerism and a mass culture. Unavoidably, it profoundly affected ethnic communities and their businesses. Already by the late 1920s, many of them were beginning to be hurt by department stores, chain stores, and supermarkets. Local newspapers found themselves competing with mainstream ones that were introducing special ethnic sections. The children of the immigrant owners would end up seeking jobs in the same firms that were undermining the family businesses. As one observer put it, "the sons and daughters of self-employed tailors, shoemakers, and peddlers became sales people and clerks in those department stores and supermarkets, or automobile and insurance salesmen working in language worlds outside the experience of their parents."

But not all immigrants or second generation persons found legal avenues for mobility—or even survival. This was especially the case during the crime-plagued 1920s and 1930s. Arnold "The Brain" Rothstein allegedly fixed the 1919 World Series and built the largest gambling empire up until then. He also kept his ethnic ties. When the predominantly Jewish garment manufacturers in 1926 turned to Jack "Legs" Diamond to break the unions and the Jewish labor leaders went to Arnold's father for help, Arnold prevailed on Jack to pull out. Shortly thereafter, Arnold was murdered over a gambling debt. Louis "Lepke" Buchalter went in for extortion and was involved in organizing The Syndicate during the 1930s as well as the infamous Jewish hit squad known as Murder, Inc. However, since that group also helped break up pro-Nazi Bund rallies, it was sometimes popular among Jews. Half-a-dozen years later, Louis was executed for murder. While, it is said, Jake "Greasy Thumb" Guzik was providing the real brains behind the Capone gang, Harry "Pittsburgh Phil" Strauss was out killing twenty-eight people and lamenting that he was only ranked by the FBI as Public Enemy No. 6.

Most certainly, only a tiny percentage of persons ever participated directly in such criminal activities, but the media exploited the exploits and cultivated stereotypes that would endure—especially regarding Italians. And it was precisely those images that affected many people. An Italian living in Chicago recalls that there were the "men in large cars, with boys and girls of the neighborhood standing on the running board. I saw them come into the neighborhood in splendor as heroes. Many times they showered handfuls of silver to youngsters who waited to get a glance of them—the new heroes—because they had just made the headlines in the newspapers." During Prohibition, Italians with a penchant for fast dollars, like Al Capone and Johnny Torrio in Chicago, moved to dominate the bootlegging of liquor and soon expanded into other illicit areas. Many of them had begun their careers with gambling, extortion, prostitution, and the like within their own ethnic communities. In a few instances community leaders united to drive out crime when lucrative, legal alternatives became available. For example, narcotics, prostitution, and gambling were widespread in the Chinese bachelor society, such as that in San Francisco, triggering violent clashes between competing secret societies known as tongs. As Chinatown tourism grew in popularity by the 1920s and the bachelor population steadily declined, community leaders finally succeeded in suppressing the tong wars and at least driving crime out of sight. Nonetheless, this criminal image remained part of the mystique of Chinatowns and was exploited to lure tourists seeking the exotic.

Another route some turned to besides crime was entertainment. Not a few immigrants began (or resumed) careers in ethnic theatres, went on to vaudeville, and became stars of American stage and screen, including Al Jolson, Fanny Brice, Danny Kaye, Jack Benny, and Bob Hope, as well as Irving Berlin, George Gershwin, and Mary Pickford. A little later on, so, too, would Anna Maria Italiano, Margarita Cansino, Doris von Kappelhoff, and Bernard Schwarz—better known as Ann Bancroft, Rita Hayworth, Doris Day, and Tony Curtis.

The other nontraditional avenue of mobility was sports, in which ethnic succession has long been a reality. But, it also meant more than that. For many, sports has not only been a path for mobility but also a major form of acculturation. Newcomers and their children could identify with these public achievers, read their exploits in the press, cheer for them, and try to emulate them on the streets and sandlots of America. As one historian recently put it, "The road to Americanization led through Yankee Stadium, the Polo Grounds, and Fenway Park."

In the late nineteenth century, Irish boxers were prominent, especially with the likes of John L. Sullivan and Jim Corbett. Prior to the 1920s, the Irish had already been challenged by some African Americans, such as Jack Johnson. Now they were seeing Jewish competitors emerge, too, among them Benny Leonard and Barney Ross. In fact, the interwar years were the golden age of Jewish athletes, many of whom were second generation Americans. Besides boxing and football, there was baseball and the beginning of the Hank Greenberg era, "the first Jewish athlete to cross over from ethnic to national favorite." Basketball likewise proved to be immensely popular among ethnic groups. In 1937–38, forty-five of the ninety-one persons in the professional American Basketball League were Jews—for instance, Nat Holman, one of the most influential players and coaches "in basketball history"—but, during the 1930s, there were also the Lithuanian and Polish Roman Catholic Championships and such professional teams as the Detroit Pulaskis, the (Irish) Brookyln Visitations, and the Buffalo Germans.

Ties that Bind: Homelands and Ethnic Institutions

Many factors influenced the extent of people's ties to their homeland; few immigrant groups remained indifferent to it. That significantly affected their actions in America and Americans' perceptions of them. In his 1937 novel, Younghill Kang wrote that "Koreans thought of themselves as exiles, not as immigrants," a sentiment others expressed, too. Though a small group, the Koreans were intensely committed to the liberation of their homeland from the Japanese. The women organized the Korean Women's Patriotic Society as part of this effort. Some Koreans established quasi-military training programs in California and later organized boycotts of Japanese products ("DON'T BUY THE JAP'S SOY SAUCE"). One exiled leader in America, Syngman Rhee, would become president of the liberated South Korea in 1948. The Chinese supported the Kuomintang when it was established in Nanking in 1927, and, during the following decade, also raised substantial sums to fight Japanese aggression.

A great number of Europeans also remained active in the politics of their homeland. Until the early 1920s, Poles worked intensively to secure an independent Poland, and over 100,000 returned between 1920 and 1923. Greeks were caught up for years in the domestic politics of Greece, which spilled over into feuds regarding the leadership of the American Greek Orthodox Churches and in the rivalry between the two principal Greek American associations, both established in the 1920s, the American Hellenic Educational Progressive Association (AHEPA) and the Greek American Progressive Association (GAPA). Meanwhile, Italians' interest in their homeland soared, as many viewed with pride the achievements of Benito Mussolini. Like many other groups, the Italians looked to a strong homeland as a means of enhancing their status in America. Italian radicals, however, fiercely opposed Mussolini, as did others. Because of Mussolini, in 1928 Amadeo Giannini changed the name of his Bank of Italy to Bank of America.

In contrast, severely traumatized by their experience during World War I, most Germans shunned ethnic organizations and open displays of German culture, or contented themselves with American-oriented ones, such as the new Steuben Society. Ludwig Dilger, who had migrated in 1881, wrote regularly to his brother in Germany about conditions in America. In March 1930, he explained that he most certainly had taught his children German. "But they don't teach German in our schools," he added, "and in general, since the war, not much German is spoken here, and the children forget German very quickly. And by the way, my wife was born and brought up here, and I only speak English with her." Nearly four years later he could tell his brother that "Your Hitler is hated a lot here and all over America, but not the German people. . . . I am proud of my German heritage, but American from head to toe." While such sentiments were apparently widespread, the 1930s would see the formation of small pro-Nazi groups, the Friends of New Germany and the German American Bund, most of whose support would come from postwar German immigrants. The interwar period is filled with such contrasting responses. Some, among them the Japanese immigrants (*Issei*), for example, sent second-generation, American-born children (*Nisei*) back home for an education; they returned as *Kibei*, imbued with Japanese nationalism. Other Issei focused on their new homeland, preferring to emphasize their children's acculturation in America. By 1940, even second-generation Mexican Americans in Chicago, noted one historian, had "little interest in Mexico."

But it did not matter how explicit one's attachment was to the homeland. The immigrants' cultural baggage contained numerous items from the old country, many not readily abandoned. A Russian mother wrote to Abraham Cahan, editor of the Jewish *Daily Forward* and its novel "advice column," the Bintel Brief: "I . . . want to express my opinion that Russian Jews and Hungarian Jews should not intermarry, a Russian Jew and an Hungarian Jew are in my opinion two different worlds and one does not and cannot understand the other." Of course, such Jews could and they did. And they even "intermarried"—among themselves! That they were all Jews was, to this mother and many other Jews, less important than other factors of culture, language, occupation, and status, which divided those who shared the same faith. Differences regarding religious practices would persist, and already before 1940 the question of Zionism—the creation of a Jewish homeland in Palestine—would become an equally contentious issue, splitting the Jewish community.

Few groups lacked such factionalism, quite often the legacy of Old-World conflicts. A good example of the impact of religious diversity within a single nationality group concerns Carpatho-Rusyns, whose homeland stretched from Poland to the Ukraine. Portions of this people were Greek Catholic; others joined the Byzantine Ruthenian Rite Catholic Church. In 1929, many split with Rome over doctrinal and administrative issues (local control), and thousands joined Russian Orthodox parishes and then established their own Carpatho-Russian Orthodox Church in America. A few years earlier in New York, various segments had formed the Russian Orthodox Greek Catholic Church. Since old-world communities were rarely if ever homogenous, there was little reason to expect communities in America to be free of factions and tensions. Thus, Finns were split by whether one spoke Swedish or Finnish, belonged to the Suomi Synod, the Apostolic or National Lutheran Churches, or the Congregationalists, or preferred the Finnish Socialist Federation.

While one could multiply these illustrations, there is the other side of the issue. In most communities people retained strong, primary attachments to village, province, or region of origin, and in America the organizations they initially participated in would directly reflect those roots. Many were invaluable for ethnic community development, such as the churches, parish schools, hometown clubs (like the Greeks' *topika somateia*), newspapers, and social and recreational programs. Almost always the early mutual aid and fraternal and women's associations represented the locales from which they had come, including the Japanese *kenjinkai*, Jewish *landsmanshaftn*, Norwegian *bygdelags*, and Mexican *mutualistas*.

Of course, as immigrants and their children became more acculturated, they recognized the good financial sense and other advantages that lay in constructing a more inclusive ethnic community. Among the organizations resulting from these many efforts at a broader, more inclusive representation were the Sons of Italy, Union St. Jean Baptiste d'Amérique (French Canadian), the League of United Latin American Citizens (LULAC), and even such organizations as the Filipino Federation of Labor, the Chicago Swedish locals of the International Brotherhood of Painters and Allied Trades, and the Chinese Hand Laundry Alliance.

A number of these organizations were specifically created by second-generation men and women and almost uniformly echoed the sentiments of the Dante Club, formed by Italians in Chicago Heights and committed to "disseminating American principles" as well as promoting fraternal life and social intercourse. Most required citizenship for one to be a member, including the LULAC, the Japanese American Citizens League (JACL), and the Greeks' AHEPA. Not only was the involvement of the second-generation women in these activities a break with the past, but that most organizations created by the second generation were focused on America rather than the old country also readily conveyed their greater integration.

Language, Culture, and the Second Generation

Most immigrants arrived with notes attached, addresses of their destinations, and they believed they were on their way to a neighborhood or community where their language would be spoken. Valeria Kozaczka Demuz recounts that when she arrived from Poland in May 1926 at the age of sixteen, she and her eighteen-year-old sister were quite frightened. Stopped in New Bedford, Connecticut, before reaching their parents in Providence, Rhode Island, they saw a policeman beside the train. "He's talkin' English to us and I got so mad. I was bewildered, I figured that everybody would talk Polish because we never heard any other language but Polish. I looked at him and figured that he should speak Polish and I said, "Mow po Polku?" [Don't you speak Polish?] . . . And with that he started laughing worse. And then he sees that I'm really put out with him, and he started to talk Polish." Not all experienced such fortunate coincidence.

Insofar as they could, immigrants would learn some English, and insofar as it was practicable to do so, they would also strive to retain their familiar and reassuring language and customs. The culture defined their peoplehood. And what about their children growing up in this America? Did the adjustment get easier for the second generation? Betty Smith caught a sense of some of the challenge and adventure in the generational change in her 1943 best-selling novel, *A Tree Grows in Brooklyn*, about an Irish American girl, Francie Nolan:

At the beginning of the term, Teacher called the roll and asked each child her lineage. The answers were typical.

"I'm Polish American. My father was born in Warsaw."

"Irish American. My Fayther and mither were born in County Cork."

When Nolan was called, Francie answered proudly, "I'm an American."

"I know you're American," said the easily exasperated Teacher. "But what's your nationality?"

"American!" insisted Francie even more proudly. . . . "My parents are American. They were born in Brooklyn."

All the children turned around to look at the little girl whose parents had not come from the old country. And when Teacher said, "Brooklyn? Hm. I guess that makes you an American all right." Francie was proud and happy. How wonderful was Brooklyn, she thought, when just being born there automatically made you an American!

Not uncommonly, the children saw many matters differently from their parents and often felt especially embarrassed by their parents' foreign manners and accent. It was that condemning taint of foreignness they tried to avoid.

In his 1943 autobiographical novel, Jerry Mangione explained the somewhat exceptional environment in his home.

Another unpopular rule [my mother] vigorously enforced was that we speak no other language at home but that of our parents. Outside the house she expected us to speak English and often took pride in the fact that we spoke English so well that almost none of our relatives understood. Any English we spoke at home, however, was either by accident or on the sly. . . .

My mother's insistence that we speak only Italian at home drew a sharp line between our existence there and our life in the world outside. We gradually acquired the notion that we were Italian at home and American (whatever that was) elsewhere.

The immigrants may have created institutions that emphasized the native language or dialect, but fierce battles ensued over its continued usage as the second generations matured, frequently far from fluent in their parents' language. Often, it was already becoming Americanized; often, the children simply resisted using it. Eugene Boe recalled that his grandfather, Osten, was concerned that his grandson was not learning Norwegian not just because they would be unable to communicate but without the language his grandson "could not be confirmed in Norwegian at the Bethlehem Lutheran Church." But, Boe added, "to be able to speak Norwegian . . . meant you were going to speak English with a Norwegian accent. And that would be fatal. To speak with an accent of any kind was to invite the mockery and abuse of one's peers—a punishment far outweighing all possible benefits." The mixtures were sometimes inescapable, and Edna Ferber, in a 1926 story, described a young Finnish girl who had been going to public school in New York City and whose "English accent turned out to be a mixture of early Finnish and late Bronx."

Foreign languages changed, not surprisingly. Italian was well known for adapting terms from English: *visci, pichnicco, grosseria, barra, giobba, carro, storo, loya* (for whisky, picnic, grocery store, bar, job, car, store, lawyer). American English likewise incorporated numerous words from the immigrants: For example, the German suffix "fest" (songfest, slugfest, bookfest); many Yiddish words, phrases (kibbitz, chutzpah, schnook, shlep; I should worry), and rhyming slang (Oedipus-schmoedipus, so long as he loves his mother!); Spanish terms (fiesta, siesta, peon, rodeo, silo, incommunicado); and a host of Italian food words (ravioli, pizza, pasta).

Some groups fought fiercely to maintain their language, particularly French Canadians, Poles, and Slovaks. Others shifted rapidly to English, among them the Finns, Rumanians, and Russian Jews. It was, of course, not just the public schools or the Catholic Church that were responsible for the language transition during the 1920s and 1930s. Fewer newcomers arrived from the old country; others moved from their first homes and communities in America in search of better housing or job opportunities. But far and away the main cause could be found in the irresistible appeal of the radio, phonograph, mass-circulation newspapers with special sections to attract ethnic readers, and the cinema—especially as filmmakers during the 1920s broadened their products' audience appeal and introduced the "talkies" in 1927.

Along with the whole variety of media came mass advertising, the appeal of consumerism, then chain stores, installment buying, and "supermarkets"—and, with it all, the exposure to American culture and values, dress and manners, aspirations and fantasies, lifestyles real and fancied, idealized role models of heroes and heroines, and new standards of femininity. The novel

Hollywood star system seemed to embody the glitter of this modern culture. All were powerful competition for traditional cultural heritages. And it could begin so early! Jens Trygve Nilssen was but five years old in the fall of 1923, when his mother wrote to her family in Norway that he "does not go to kindergarten anymore. He went for two weeks, but apparently the children laughed at his Norwegian clothing. . . ." Later she observed that "He keeps a sharp lookout that he has clothes like the others."

Of course, no overnight transformation occurred, for those living in ethnic communities continued to prefer using the local stores, speaking to merchants in their mother tongue, listening to programs directed at their nationality or religion, and attending the neighborhood movie houses. Some groups actually added features of the American culture to shore up their own cultural boundaries. Chinese, Italian, Hungarian, and Yiddish theatres flourished; Yiddish films and Polish, Ukrainian, Italian, and Czech radio programs were popular. In fact, in Los Angeles, market prices of fresh produce were being aired on the radio—in Japanese.

The new mass culture also introduced second generation Americans to the latest fashions and fads, which became one of their means for asserting their own independence. Their growing numbers quickened the cultural transition of the immigrant communities, which were focused on the old ways, into ethnic communities that looked ahead, seeking their place in American society. Adding to that adaptation was the fact that, during the 1920s, among one-third of the white, American-born children of foreigners, one parent was a native-born American. This does not necessarily mean one spouse was of a different ethnicity, but it would be fair to assume that by 1930 these 8.5 million children were more likely to be exposed to more elements of the American culture than children whose parents were both foreigners.

In view of the ever more prominent place of American culture in the lives of immigrants and their children, it is ironic how many of them actually played important roles in the nation's cultural transformation. They included the editor and publisher

Joseph Pulitzer; radio network pioneers David Sarnoff (RCA, NBC) and William Paley (CBS); Broadway show producer Florenz Ziegfeld; composer George Gershwin; performer Al Jolson; Hollywood movie producers Sam Goldwyn, Louis B. Mayer, and David O. Selznick; movie chain owners Spyros Skouras and Alex Pantages; and such movie stars as Chaplin, Pickford, and the Marx Brothers.

But the battle of cultures and generations was not confined to movies and music. Accommodations were continually being worked out concerning foods, rituals, holiday observances, family customs and values, and even marriage preferences. One telling example of tradition-with-adjustment was the establishment of the kosher certification services by Orthodox Jews, using names like "OK Laboratory" (for Organized for Kashrut!) and subtly labelling kosher products with a "u" in a circle (for Union of Orthodox Jewish Congregations), so as not to dissuade Gentile customers.

All these transitions were by no means easy, for immigrants found themselves unavoidably caught between two worlds: Living in but not yet a part of the new society, especially in the cities. It could still be seen quite readily in the long stretch of St. Claire's Avenue in Cleveland, which was so thoroughly Slovene that, it was said, "English was a foreign language"! At the same time, more immigrant and second generation writers began to publish works describing their immigrant and ethnic experiences, including Ole Rolvaag, Louis Adamic, James Farrell, Pietro DiDonato, Anzia Yezierska, Henry Roth, Edward Bok, and Mary Harris "Mother" Jones.

Leadership, Citizenship, and Ethnic Politics

Stanley Nowak arrived in Detroit in 1924 at the age of twenty-one. He became the editor of a Polish socialist newspaper and, in 1936, a successful labor organizer for the United Automobile Workers. Two years later, he capitalized upon that to win election to the Michigan State Senate, where he served for a decade. Most immigrants did not go so far politically, but there can be little doubt that a vital factor in ethnic group life was the quality of leadership that emerged within the community. Most often, it was provided by the middle-class businessmen and professionals, as well as the grocers, saloonkeepers, and others important in the daily lives of the people. The clergy often played important leadership roles, too, at times competing for influence with leaders of secular organizations and those active in politics and unions.

Many men and some women sought political roles within and then beyond their immediate ethnic community. In some cases they were immigrants but quite commonly more acculturated second-generation persons. During these interwar years, individuals of various ethnic backgrounds emerged into the political limelight. They began by competing with representatives of earlier groups that had begun to disperse from their own initial communities, notably the Irish, Germans, and Swedes. The newer generation included mayors Fiorello La Guardia (Italian-Jewish, New York) and Anton Cermak (Czech, Chicago) and labor leaders like Luisa Moreno (Guatemala) and Rosa Pesotta (Italian). From coast to coast new spokespersons moved up in government, as did Governor (later Congressman) James Michael Curley (Irish, Massachusetts), Congressman Andrew Volstead (Norwegian, Minnesota), and Senators Felix Hebert (French Canadian, Rhode Island) and Dennis Chavez (Hispano, New Mexico). And, using a different strategy, there was the Jamaican immigrant, Marcus Garvey, who founded the first Black mass action movement with the Universal Negro Improvement Association.

Harry Roskolenko tells of the time his father informed his mother that he had become a citizen and now "must" vote. She asked, how much does this citizenship "cost that you don't have? Is God a citizen?" When she then asked for whom he would vote, he mentioned Meyer London, the enormously popular Lower East Side Jewish Socialist. "'Not for Dickstein?' said my mother. 'He wears glasses, too, Berel.'" Obviously, added Roskolenko, London's "glasses made him a great man in our eyes. He had some special vision, we thought. . . ." Furthermore, Roskolenko appended, "It was hard to conceive of a Jew who was a Republican. . . ."

Not surprisingly, political leaders like Dickstein, London, and La Guardia built local ethnic bases, relying upon their ethnic communities or coalitions of ethnic voters. Consequently, the proportion of foreign born holding American citizenship would become vitally important if the political influence of the group were to be strengthened. In particular, once the reality of immigration restrictions set in there was a sharp increase in the number of people seeking citizenship. Between 1925 and 1930, over 1.1 million persons acquired it, one-fifth of whom were Italian and one-in-six Polish. (See Appendix, Table 2.3.) By 1930, a majority of the foreign born held American citizenship. Those from nearby homelands and those among whom many had just arrived had the lowest percentages of naturalized persons, notably the West Indians and Mexicans (for example, only 6.4 percent of Mexicans). Many immigrants continued to put off the decision to apply, either because they still hoped to return home, or because they felt, as did numerous Greeks, that switching citizenship was "tantamount to betrayal of the homeland."

In the final analysis, people with political ambitions worked to convince immigrants of the value of citizenship and the right to vote. During the 1920s, growing numbers of Jews, Italians, Poles, Czechs, Slovaks, and Russians began voting, setting the stage for Governor Al Smith's 1928 campaign for president. The Democrats attracted many of these urban voters but had no monopoly on them. Even the Jews remained divided, with many of them, like the Midwest Germans, Finns, and others, favoring Socialist candidates.

The Democrats' new multiethnic coalition—the ethnic political revolution of the era—was completed by Franklin Delano Roosevelt, but historians trace its origins to the 1928 presidential campaign of New York governor Al Smith. "Before the Roosevelt Revolution," observed a major political analyst, "there was an Al Smith Revolution." Being a New Yorker and Catholic, Smith left many Americans quite suspicious. They saw him as "a representative of an alien culture . . . of a foreign potentate [the Papacy]." One of his ardent defenders wrote a spirited defense, appealing to those who feared Smith: "There is no reason why the back alley cannot produce as good moral, spiritual, mental and physical timber for politics as the backwoods." The issue, of course, was that he was a wet (anti-Prohibitionist), urban, New York Catholic Irishman.

The South went Republican, and Herbert Hoover won. But, significantly, Smith had won in the twelve largest cities—where ethnic groups were now most concentrated. Four years later, Roosevelt built on Smith's gains and advanced the political revolution that had begun in 1928: In New York City, for example, four-fifths of the Italians, three-fifths of the Germans, and well over 70 percent of Jews and the Irish supported him. By 1936, six million more voters had been registered, and five-sixths of them supported Roosevelt. That completed the New Deal coalition, which would largely endure for three decades. Even Norwegians and Swedes abandoned their traditional Republicanism for FDR in 1936.

The struggles of the foreign born and their children to come to terms with America were complicated by laws that reduced the influx of new members to the ethnic communities. Those who did not return to their homelands had to make the hard choices about remaining permanently and bringing over their families or finally starting ones in America. They, their children, and their communities then faced a whole set of challenges presented by the rapid and dramatic changes taking place in American culture. Preservation of traditional cultures and ties to the old countries proved to be more and more difficult, if not simply less desirable. Immigrants strove for a balance; their children strove for balance. Almost unavoidably—in the schools, workplaces, streets, cinema, dance halls, and polling places—those balancing efforts would often tip in different directions. The immigrants understandably held on to as much of the old customs and values as possible, while the second generation increasingly found themselves drawn to American ways.

CHAPTER THREE

The Thirties in Crisis: Repatriation, Refugees, and the New Deal

Many images loom in the memories of the 1930s, dominated as they were by Depression, defiance of Prohibition, dust-bowl migrants fleeing west, and the determination of organized labor to gain recognition. It was Roosevelt's New Deal experiments that provided hope to Americans by launching extensive work programs and massive construction projects, agricultural assistance and urban renewal, sweeping economic reforms and regulations, and long-overdue measures designed to provide people with security against future economic disasters. Given the conditions, it is not surprising that fewer immigrants chose to come to America, and others preferred to leave, seeking relief and security in their homelands. The darker, often understated, sides of the immigrants' woes of the 1930s involved those who elected to stay and were forced out and those who sought to enter and were kept out.

The stock market crashed in October 1929, and the economic crisis soon discouraged people from migrating. Over one-quarter million people had entered in the year prior to the crash, but President Hoover ordered more rigorous examinations of prospective immigrants in order to bar anyone "Likely to become a Public Charge."

For the whole of 1931,[1] just 97,100 newcomers arrived, and 61,900 others left. The next five years, between July 1931 and June 1936, marked the lowest level for that length of time in American immigration since record keeping began in 1820: Only 159,400 persons were admitted, whereas 297,800 emigrated, a net out-migration of 138,400 persons.

Congress reacted quickly to the crash. Some called for a temporary 90 percent reduction in all immigration. Others wanted to extend the quota law restrictions to the Americas, especially Texas Congressman John Box, who detested Mexicans. He had referred to them as a "blend of low grade Spaniard, peonized Indian and negro slave [which] mixes with negroes, mullatoes [sic], and other mongrels, and some sorry whites already here." Professor Roy Garis, of Vanderbilt University, had reported to Box that the minds of Mexicans "run to nothing higher than animal functions—eat, sleep, and sexual debauchery.... These people sleep by day and prowl by night like coyotes...." Many in the Southwest of that time would have concurred.

Repatriation: Mexicans and Filipinos

Coercion soon became commonplace. Officials sought ways to get rid of the unemployed. Mexicans and their American born children were transported to the border and abandoned, often starving, forcing the Mexican government to provide emergency aid. Pedro Gonzalez and his wife and four children had come in 1923 and later moved to Detroit. Laid off and then rehired by Ford in 1931, Gonzalez was again let go in March 1932. The Dearborn Welfare Department began threatening him, urging the family to return to Mexico. Then the police came, dragged

---

[1]These were fiscal years, July 1 to June 30.

them out of their home, and forced them into an ambulance that took them directly to the Detroit train station. Pablo Guerrero, of Mexicali, had first come in 1904, working since that time and raising five American-born children. He, too, would be shipped out from Los Angeles in 1932. Two years later, he sought to return, appealing to officials that his family be permitted to reenter "so that they may be educated in the schools of your country and not in Mexico." His request was denied.

Over 459,000 Mexicans had been recorded entering during the 1920s. Tens of thousands had fled the political and civil strife of the Revolution, and others had resumed their search for jobs. Northern industrialists and farmers in the North Central States had begun hiring Mexicans to replace Europeans. By 1928, for example, Mexicans constituted 11 percent of 65,700 workers in fifteen major industrial plants in the Chicago-Gary area. Thousands of others lived and worked in St. Louis, Detroit, and Pittsburgh.

The decades of negative attitudes and discrimination toward nonwhites in general and Mexicans in particular bore ill fruit when the Depression prompted officials to look for unemployed groups that might be targeted for removal. The press inflamed public opinion. Thousands of Mexicans and Mexican Americans were rounded up and detained, while those without proper papers were sought out for deportation. From the cities of the Midwest down to Texas and west to Los Angeles, one of the most tragic episodes of civil rights violations in American history commenced.

In Detroit, in the summer of 1932, the renowned Mexican artist Diego Rivera (working on a splendid mural there) and the local Mexican consul supported a voluntary repatriation effort. By December over one thousand people had returned, many of whom were U.S.-born children. But the experience proved so disastrous—they were virtually abandoned and left without resources or assistance—that Rivera and the consul reversed themselves and urged Mexicans to remain. Local government agencies were also offering free transportation to the border, without informing people that by accepting it they would probably be disqualified from reentering the country.

Industries laid off workers and refused to rehire those without citizenship. They were taking their cue from the federal government's requirement in several New Deal programs (especially the Works Progress Administration) that only citizens and those with "first papers" be hired.[2] Simultaneously, desperate Americans fleeing the dust bowls of Oklahoma and elsewhere in the Midwest made their way to California, nearly doubling the migrant labor pool and driving wages down. They displaced Mexicans, compelling many to return to Mexico. Any differences between deportations and such induced repatriations were hardly meaningful in terms of their end results. In their various forms, deportation and repatriation were employed to get rid of between 500,000 and 600,000 persons of Mexican ancestry during the 1930s, more than half of whom, it is estimated, were American citizens. By 1940 the foreign-born Mexican population had plummetted from 639,000 to 377,400.

The efforts to curb Filipino migration were not very subtle either, although, as nationals, they were entitled to admission into the United States. Their numbers on the mainland had risen nearly ninefold in the 1920s, to 45,200. Their job competition, labor militancy, and disregard for the unwritten rules of race etiquette (against mixing and marrying with Caucasian American women) sparked violent reprisals, especially in California. In 1934 the Supreme Court declared them ineligible for citizenship. In that same year the Tydings-McDuffie Act established the Philippines as a commonwealth, with independence to come in ten years. A limit of fifty immigrants annually was imposed, and all Filipino nationals were reclassified as "aliens." With that, Filipinos were immediately disqualified from relief and New Deal work

---

[2]*First papers* refers to the Declaration of Intent, which, prior to 1952, had to be filed before formally petitioning for naturalization. Declarations could be submitted after two years' residence, the petition for citizenship usually after five years.

programs. Congress then offered Filipinos free transportation home; the price was surrendering the right to reenter. Only 2,190 Filipinos accepted.

Culture, Politics, and the Labor Movement

As conditions deteriorated and unemployment reached the unprecedented level of 25 percent, people became more desperate for jobs and welfare (public relief). Besides the businesses that had started requiring new employees to be citizens, or at least to have their first papers, local relief agencies also began imposing similar requirements for welfare. Not surprisingly, in 1936 began a dramatic rise in the number of persons applying for naturalization. Between the first and second halves of the 1930s, there was nearly a 47 percent increase in the number of Europeans given citizenship, particularly among Italians (45 percent), Poles (53 percent), and Czechoslovaks (84 percent).

For those already employed, the solution seemed to lay in reversing the setbacks of the 1920s by pushing for collective bargaining and union recognition. Organized labor had experienced serious setbacks and a wave of antiunionism following the sometimes long and sometimes violent strikes between 1919 and 1922. Many businesses attempted to impose open (nonunion) shops. Others exploited the division among various ethnic groups by offering workers company unions and benefits—"welfare capitalism"—in order to weaken existing unions and undermine workers' reliance on the organizations of their individual ethnic communities. While the unions were in retreat during the 1920s, the companies' schemes eventually backfired, for they were bringing workers together across ethnic, racial, and skill lines, laying the foundation for more concerted labor action later on.

In the midst of the Depression a group of union leaders in the American Federation of Labor (AFL) pushed for organizing workers by industry rather than by craft or skills. A Committee of Industrial Organizations was established by the AFL in 1935. Three years later it became an independent entity, the Congress of Industrial Organizations (CIO). Organizers of different races and language backgrounds were sent out to mobilize the rank and file. Steel, auto, rubber, meatpacking, electrical appliance, and textile factories and food canneries were among the major industries that then faced strikers seeking union recognition. With the right to organize protected by the 1935 National Labor Relations Act, over two thousand strikes took place in 1935; in 1937 more than forty-seven hundred. Millions participated—immigrants, second generation, and other native-born Americans.

The lines dividing races and ethnic groups, and the barriers of language, were regularly crossed. For example, in a 1937 meeting of steelworkers, the CIO provided speakers in Polish, Lithuanian, Russian, Serbian, and Croatian. The Steel Workers Organizing Committee was said to resemble a coalition of ethnic fraternal societies. The International Ladies Garment Workers Union frequently used Yiddish and Italian, and other unions relied on still other combinations of languages. And women as well as men were in the forefront. Earlier in 1937, prior to the sitdown strike in the automobile plants of Detroit, two thousand women employees (mostly Poles) had launched the longest sitdown strike in labor history in pursuit of union recognition. The Depression proved to be a turning point, "a culminating moment" for the immigrant working class. Supported by ethnic newspapers, radio programs, and fraternal organizations, they demanded recognition, security, and "incorporation" into American society. By 1941, organized labor included 23 percent of all nonagricultural workers (farmworkers had not been covered).

Second-generation Americans played a vital role in this success, and that was only part of the transformation brought on by the Depression years. If the Twenties had introduced many ethnic Americans to the emerging American mass culture, the 1930s completed the transformation process. Like other Americans, they, too, came to accept the prevalence, usefulness, and desirability of the chain stores, supermarkets, movie theatre chains with their upscale "palaces," and nationally linked radio networks (already six hundred stations by 1925). Radio, in particular, universalized the working-class experience for all generations of

Americans. Along with sports, films, and music, radio programs in the 1930s became the elements of a shared mass culture, building familiar cultural bridges that reinforced the experiences being shared in the factories, shops, and even in the fields. Union "brothers" and "sisters" emphasized labor's "culture of unity."

Still, neither the great union campaigns nor the mass culture flowing across the nation had entirely dissolved the cultural and other institutions of the 11.5 million foreign-born and 23.5 million second-generation Americans (1940) or their ethnic loyalties. Change was persistent, yet much remained unchanged.

Anti-Semitism and the Refugee Question

A 1938 public opinion poll reported that 60 percent of Americans objected to the presence of Jews in America. Other polls between 1938 and 1941 found that one-third of the respondents would approve an anti-Jewish campaign and nearly another third would not object to it. Jews were seen as the greatest menace to the nation. No major leaders condemned the anti-Semitism, and these attitudes regarding Jews blended with those concerning immigrants in general. Earlier American concern about immigration now became fear, and that fear expressed itself in an inflexibility toward foreigners.

The Depression prompted many nations to close their gates and minds. The rise of fascism in Germany and Italy gradually created a refugee crisis, as Jews and other opponents and potential victims fled Hitler and later Mussolini. Many encountered a survival nationalism in neighboring countries, while the United States, despite its tradition of asylum, preserved its walls of quotas and but the smallest doorway for refugees.

In 1939, a symbol of their desperation captured the media's attention and almost moved hearts to action. The steamship *St. Louis* arrived in Havana harbor on May 13, with 936 passengers—930 of them Jews seeking refuge. Most were denied entry. Over 700 of them had been approved for admission to the United States and were awaiting their turn in the monthly number permitted to enter the country. Twenty-eight were permitted to enter Cuba; the remaining 900 were sent away. As the *St. Louis* steamed northward along the American coast—"the saddest ship afloat today," as the *New York Times* then described it—no country would accept the refugees. While the ship was returning to Germany, American Jews arranged with Jewish organizations in Europe to provide financial guarantees on behalf of the passengers. Only then were Great Britain, France, Belgium and the Netherlands persuaded to accept them. Within a year three of those nations would be invaded by German troops. Many from the *St. Louis* would perish.

In 1937, Roosevelt had finally allowed the rules for screening immigrant applicants to be relaxed, and, between July 1936 and June 1941, there was a huge jump in the number of Europeans admitted and a significant drop in the number of persons leaving the United States. The generally accepted figure for European refugees allowed into the United States between 1933 and 1944 is approximately one-quarter million persons, the majority of them Jews. But only two-fifths of the German quota had been used, closing off escape for thousands. Why did nearly 60 percent of the German quota go unused, especially when Avra Warren, U.S. State Department Visa Division Chief, found in 1939 that "more than 300,000 persons had applied for visas under the German quota"? Afterall, for the 1932-41 period, just over one-fifth of the quotas for all Europe were filled. The evidence is overwhelming: The failure to save more refugees, to use even the available visas, lay rooted in the hatred and fear of Jews: Pervasive anti-Semitism was at the core of the misfortune.

In March 1938, at about the time Hitler took over Austria, an American poll revealed that 41 percent of the people polled thought Jews had too much power. Two months later a poll showed that one-fifth wanted to drive the Jews out of the country in order to reduce their power; one-fourth would keep them out of politics. During that spring another poll reported 82 percent opposed the admission of any large number of Jewish exiles. Given the continually negative polls, Roosevelt would not overtly challenge that public opinion. He did use a loophole in the law to extend the visitor visas of some twelve-to fifteen-thousand Germans already in the country; yet, when announcing this, he hastened to say that they were "not all Jews, by any means."

The Germans did all they could to hamper the exodus. U.S. laws also created rigid and complex requirements, and their difficulties were made worse by the officials responsible for carrying them out. Assistant Secretary of State Wilbur Carr, head of the Consular Division, had earlier written to Congressman Albert Johnson that Russian and Polish Jews "are filthy, Un-American and often dangerous in their habits." Another Visa Division official, C. Paul Fletcher, had written in 1933 that, "if ships begin to arrive . . . laden with Jewish immigrants, the predominant Gentile population of the country will claim they have been betrayed through a 'sleeping' State Department."

Meanwhile, factionalism badly divided the Jewish community, weakening their political influence. *Most crucially, however, public opinion remained unwavering in its anti-Semitism and anti-foreignness because neither the president nor the press demonstrated any willingness to lead or reshape public sentiments until the war enveloped the nation and victory seemed more certain.*

Roosevelt's actions remained essentially cautious, politically expedient. On the one bill that might have challenged the public and saved children's lives—the Wagner-Rogers Bill—he chose to remain silent. In February 1939, Senator Robert Wagner and Congresswoman Edith Nourse Rogers introduced a bill to admit twenty thousand German children as nonquota immigrants. It was supported by the AFL but opposed by the Daughters of the American Revolution and the American Legion. A *Fortune* poll taken in April showed 83 percent against any increase in the quotas. No strong congressional contingent fought for the bill, and it died in House committee.

But the U.S. government did not entirely fail, for among the quarter-million refugees from Europe would come some two dozen Nobel Laureates, over five thousand physicians, and more than fifteen hundred lawyers and other professionals. Among them were physicists Enrico Fermi, Edward Teller, and Albert Einstein; conductors Arturo Toscanini, George Solti,

Eugene Ormandy, and Eric Leinsdorf; theologian Paul Tillich; and philosopher Hannah Arendt. And came other men and women in the thousands who would, in smaller ways, vastly enrich their new homeland.

The Thirties carried forward trends from the Twenties. First, the national mass culture was more evident in ethnic communities by the end of the 1930s, accelerating the Americanization process within them but still not erasing those communities or their cultures. Along with that, ethnic group members became accustomed to looking to the government for some of the assistance for which they had previously relied upon their own groups. Second, the setbacks suffered by organized labor in the 1920s were significantly altered now by the federal recognition of its right to organize. The successes of labor would bring to many immigrants and especially second-generation Americans both greater security and extensive involvement outside their ethnic communities. Third, the Depression generated an actual net outflow of migrants and triggered movements to expel unwanted foreign workers—and their American-born families. The public's fears and prejudices also lent support to the government's refusal to use at least the maximum number of visas available in order to save the lives of those fleeing fascism. As a result, many thousands of applicants for those visas perished.

PART TWO

From World War to Cold War: 1940–1965

The quarter century between 1940 and 1965 was a critically important stage between two of the nation's great eras of immigration. In this middle period, the nation grappled with a second world war, a cold war, and then a new world view that repeatedly called for exceptions to the restrictive immigration laws. Because of these policy shifts and the radically changed conditions in many sending countries, immigration between 1945 and 1965 differed in several vital ways from the prior patterns. For millions of people, rescue and hope would again be found in America. In fact, over 4.8 million immigrants were admitted (fiscal years 1946–65), and over 2.1 million acquired American citizenship.

A number of ethnic communities experienced renewed support and yet additional stress from the newcomers, while other groups were first taking root. Many immigrants and refugees differed considerably from their prewar predecessors, such as the large number of widely scattered, newly settled, foreign-born spouses of U.S. military personnel. Nevertheless, because the generations of newcomers and native born generally overlapped, the new immigrants' adaptation coincided with the patterns of assimilation among those living in America for decades.

This era was much influenced by a series of developments. First, there were in 1940 more than 11.5 million foreign-born persons—over 63 percent of them naturalized citizens—and well over 23.3 million second generation children (plus another quarter million persons of Asian and Pacific Islander ancestry in Hawaii). Many were fully involved in the war effort and then eagerly partook of the opportunities for mobility in postwar America. Yet, the nation's prewar anxieties about foreigners were intensified by insecurities during World War II and the Cold War. Although conservative measures reflecting those anxieties were enacted, domestic and international political considerations also spurred a reemphasis on the traditions of tolerance and humanitarianism, which likewise promoted changes in public opinion and national policies. In that context, continuing transportation innovations (especially in air travel) and rapidly changing local conditions in many countries throughout the world prompted people to develop new migration strategies. The result was a startling and unexpected shift in the composition of migrant populations. The United States and other receiving nations moved closer to a rimless world: fully global exchanges of people, products, cultures, and technology.

Finally, at the same time that European immigrants and their children continued to wage their struggle for acceptance and incorporation into American society, various racial groups began in earnest their own battles for equality and incorporation. The civil rights movement that surfaced in the 1940s and 1950s significantly influenced the lives of the more racially diverse immigrants who had begun to arrive in ever greater numbers. All these developments ultimately necessitated the abandonment of America's quota system, precipitating a racial revolution in American immigration.

CHAPTER FOUR

Waging War—At Home and Abroad

War in Europe compelled the U.S. government to increase security and determine how best to deal with the presence of five million foreign-born noncitizens, one-fourth of them nationals of the Axis powers, principally Germany (and Austria), Italy, and Japan. The State Department moved to control further immigration by imposing severe restraints on visas; Congress enacted a program to monitor resident aliens through compulsory registration; and, alleging military necessity, officials used a presidential executive order to sanction the internment in concentration camps of Japanese Americans living along the West Coast, thereby violating the civil rights of nearly an entire ethnic group.

Regulation, Registration, Internment

Riccardo Massoni, who arrived from Italy in 1939, recalls that "we found out that people here were terribly ignorant of what was going on in Europe. And so were the newspapers. They seemed to have no idea what Nazis were, or Mussolini." Massoni had grasped the fact that Americans did not know because many did not wish to know. As mentioned, polls in 1938 and 1939 reported overwhelming opposition to any breach of the immigration laws; two-thirds of those polled had preferred that refugees be kept out.

The war in Europe began in September 1939. Fears of spies and saboteurs prompted more barriers to immigration. Admissions from Nazi-occupied countries were reduced by 75 percent. A new, four-foot-long visa application form was introduced, with questions on both sides. Roosevelt remained unwilling, as one historian put it, to expend "valuable political capital on a doomed cause," namely modifying immigration policy. During the period in which the United States was at war in Europe, only 10 percent of the available quotas were allocated, leaving 190,000 visas unused. At the same time, internal barriers were erected. In August 1940, Congress approved the Alien Registration Act. All aliens fourteen and older (and not naturalized) were to register with the government. By the end of 1940 over five million persons had done so. Over half resided in the northeast. A half-dozen nationalities accounted for six-sevenths of the total: British, Italian, German, Polish, Mexican, and Soviet. Naturalization requirements were also tightened, and, in 1941, the Smith Act authorized the president to deport any alien where such action would be "in the interest of the United States."

Japan bombed Pearl Harbor on December 7, 1941, and war was declared against the Axis powers of Japan, Germany, Italy, and their allies. Severe problems immediately confronted those ethnic populations in America, for they were soon classified as enemy aliens. About one million Italians, Germans, and Japanese had registered in 1940. By June 1942, thousands of other enemy aliens had been apprehended. (For some, like sixty-five-year-old Martini Battistessa from Italy, the treatment came as an overwhelming shock. A resident of California for twenty years, he was expelled from his home, and, in despair, threw himself in front of a moving train.) Of the newly classified enemy aliens, nearly 400,000, who had earlier begun the process of citizenship by taking the necessary first steps, now rushed to submit their petitions for naturalization. Three-tenths of them were Italians.

The sheer size of the German and Italian foreign-born populations and the fact that they were mostly long-time, well-integrated residents made removing and/or detaining them quite impractical. Not only were few Germans known to be sympathetic to Hitler or active in a pro-Nazi organization, but American sympathies had also shifted toward Germans and Italians. This was in part because notable Americans were of those ethnic extractions, including baseball star Joe Dimaggio and 1940 presidential candidate Wendell Wilkie. The formidable number of German and Italian American voters likewise made Democratic policy makers quite reluctant to alienate them. Still, while foreign-born Italians were informed in October 1942 that they would no longer be classified as enemy aliens, Roosevelt refused to do the same for Germans, telling his attorney general, "I don't care so much about the Italians. They are a lot of opera singers, but the Germans are different[;] they may be dangerous."

Persons of Japanese ancestry posed one set of problems in Hawaii, where Pearl Harbor was bombed, and another on the mainland. In Hawaii, they made up 37 percent of the population. Following the attack, Japanese who were thought to be community leaders were quickly interned there. Military rule was imposed, and the strict controls prevented anti-Japanese American hysteria from developing. At the same time, the military governor, General Delos Emmons, resisted orders to evacuate Japanese based on their ancestry, emphasizing their economic roles and the absence of any sabotage.

On the mainland, the forty-seven thousand foreign-born Japanese were less fortunate. As aliens ineligible for citizenship and able to play a far less critical economic role due to their small numbers, the Issei were politically powerless and vulnerable. Most of their children were also too young to vote. Kyoko Takayanagi, recalling her youth in rural California, spoke of going to public school on the Monday following the Pearl Harbor attack and hearing repeated references to "Those damn Japs."

"It was all of this, and you were part of it. There were those who included you, that you were responsible, too, because of your Japanese descent, was the feeling we got.... I began to feel guilty—that I had to take the blame because it was Japan and my parents are from Japan."

The debate on what measures to take quickly centered on *all* persons of Japanese ancestry. Decades of deeply rooted public fears were not easily soothed, for there were the beliefs that loyalty to the emperor was an inherited Japanese trait and that "pride of race" had made them resistant to assimilation. Although the FBI uncovered no evidence of Japanese American espionage or sabotage, hysteria and scapegoating were allowed to go unchecked. *Life* and *Time* magazines ran illustrated stories on "How to tell Your Friends from the Japs," pointing out specific features and characteristics that distinguished Chinese from Japanese. Not everyone bothered with the fine points. Mary Paik Lee, a Korean immigrant, recalled that on December 7 she was threatened in the Whittier grocery store of Hannah Nixon—mother of Richard Nixon—who interceded on her behalf: "You have known Mrs. Lee for years," Mrs. Nixon told the other customers. "You know she's not Japanese, and even if she were, she is not to blame for what happened at Pearl Harbor." Lee observed, "They just assumed that all Orientals were Japanese."

By early January 1942, the media, newspaper columnists, "patriotic" organizations, agricultural interest groups, and then the politicians began to demand that some action be taken against the Japanese. Several key government officials, along with the head of the Western Defense Command, Lieutenant General John DeWitt, developed plans, alleging the grounds of military necessity, for the mass evacuation from the West Coast of all persons with as little as one-sixteenth Japanese ancestry. They prevailed upon President Roosevelt to authorize action. On February 19, he signed Executive Order 9066, conferring upon the Department of War unprecedented powers to exclude "any or all persons" from military areas.

Almost two-thirds of those Japanese Americans removed, detained, and relocated without any charges (approximately

70,000) had been born in the United States. Close to 111,000 persons were first placed in fifteen assembly centers and then transferred to ten quickly constructed concentration camps under the jurisdiction of the War Relocation Authority, most in isolated Western areas. However, in early June, before the transfer to the camps had hardly begun, the defeat of the Japanese navy at Midway Island ended any possibility of an invasion. *There was no military necessity for continuing the relocation and internment, and key government officials knew it.* When Gordon Hirayabashi and Minoru Yasui challenged the West Coast curfew and Fred Korematsu defied the evacuation orders, they were convicted and appealed to the U.S. Supreme Court. The Justice Department argued the cases on the basis of military necessity. The Court, demanding no proof, concluded in the Hirayabashi case (June 1943) that it could not "reject as unfounded the judgment of the military authorities and of Congress that there were disloyal members of the population whose number and strength could not be precisely and quickly ascertained." One dissenting judge pointed out that the case for collective guilt had been "based upon the accident of race or ancestry." Other decisions were similarly upheld. By the time the camps were ordered closed, in mid-December 1944, 120,000 Japanese Americans had been held for various periods of time in the camps. Almost four decades later, researchers discovered that the Justice and War Departments had suppressed, altered, and destroyed important evidence, thereby deceiving the Supreme Court.

Congress' Commission on the Wartime Relocation and Internment of Civilians (CWRIC) concluded in its final report in 1983 that "the broad historical causes which shaped these [evacuation and internment] decisions were race prejudice, war hysteria, and a failure of political leadership. . . . A grave injustice was done to American citizens and resident aliens of Japanese ancestry. . . ." The evacuees had experienced serious losses—financial and emotional—due to the wrenching disruptions their families, communities, cultural institutions, farms, and businesses had had to endure. Jeanne Wakatsuki Houston recalled her family's return from the Manzanar camp in October 1945 to Terminal Island, in Los Angeles Harbor:

Mama picked up the kitchenware and some silver she had stored with neighbors in Boyle Heights. But the warehouse where she'd stored the rest had been unaccountably 'robbed'—of furniture, appliances, and most of those silver anniversary gifts. Papa already knew the car he'd put money on before Pearl Harbor had been repossessed. And, as he suspected, no record of his fishing boats remained. This put him right back where he'd been in 1904, arriving in a new land and starting over from economic zero.

Initial compensation of $31 million under the Evacuation Claims Act of 1948 proved to be far too little. The CWRIC in 1983 calculated that Japanese American income and property losses may have been as high as $370 million in 1945 dollars and approximately $1.5 billion in 1983 dollars—and, with interest, twice that or more. For many, the greater losses were psychological—the deep sense of having been betrayed by their own government—and those emotional scars had remained largely hidden for a generation. In mid-1994, community activist Miya Iwataki could still observe that "the camp experience represented a collective experience that seared the consciousness of every Japanese American, born in the camps or not."

Nevertheless, many Japanese Americans wanted to prove their loyalty explicitly. Thousands of Nisei in the camps volunteered for military service or were later drafted. About 23,000 Nisei, men and women, served in the armed forces, including nearly 4,000 in the Allied Translation and Interpreter Section in the Pacific theatre.[1] Approximately half were from Hawaii, and their 100th Battalion was merged with the new all-Japanese 442nd Regimental Combat Team. The 18,000 soldiers in it suffered nearly 9,500 casualties, including 600 killed, and won over 18,100

---

[1]While many writers use the figure of 33,000, Selective Service records indicate that 25,500 were processed for induction, and over 22,000 were actually inducted. Along with those who had enlisted, the figure comes to approximately 23,000 who served.

decorations and more Presidential Citations than any other unit in American history.

In this respect, members of many other ethnic groups were also among the twelve million men and women who eventually served in various military branches during the war, including well over sixteen thousand Chinese, about a third of a million Spanish speaking Americans and a like number of Poles, and an estimated half-million Italians. What is more, nearly 110,700 aliens serving in the military were naturalized between 1942 and 1945. Besides Germans and Italians, among the most prominent were Mexicans and Filipinos.

Waging War on the Homefront

The war accelerated changes already under way and brought to a boil long-simmering social strains. Both substantially reshaped ethnic America. The very fact that a total of twelve million American men and women were uprooted for military service and that fifteen million others moved in their pursuit of wartime jobs could not help but profoundly affect communities throughout the nation. (Consider that under the 1940 registration program, 814,000 aliens filed address changes just in 1943!)

Serge Nicholas, for example, a Russian who had come from Manchuria in 1938, referred to his years in the army as "a university of Life for me. It was an environment where from early morning until late at night, I had to speak the language and take orders in English. I *had* to communicate. I had been living in the Russian ghetto [in San Francisco], and if it hadn't been for the war I might not ever have had any reason to leave. It's so easy for the immigrant to become part of that community." A Polish immigrant recalled the kind of episode that so often has been legendary in the American military: It was, he said, "the best break in my life, as far as learning English. . . ." In one instance, "somebody tells me 'Throw the butt out,' and if you don't know slang, how do you know what *butt* means? So everybody threw the cigarette away, while I was standing smoking. For this I used to go on latrine duty and clean until midnight."

The government mobilized to achieve unity at home as well as victory abroad. All Americans had to ration many items and were urged to contribute to the scrap metal and war bond drives. People saw the bonds as a patriotic way of saving, and that would contribute to the enormous postwar consumer boom. Second-generation Slovak American Elsie Firka recalled that "war bonds helped us. John [her husband] got the bonds at the mill, and that helped with the down payment on our house and on the things we bought." On another level, in an effort to proclaim America as the "bastion against persecution," government spokesmen explored and proclaimed the multiple sources of American unity, identity, and character, even if what they pronounced contradicted reality.

Thus, President Roosevelt approved the drafting of Nisei from concentration camps where their parents and younger siblings remained, declaring—rather remarkably—that "Americanism is a matter of the mind and heart; Americanism is not, and never was, a matter of race and ancestry." Somewhat more realistic about whether America had become a nation of democracy and freedom, Eleanor Roosevelt did acknowledge that "we have not yet achieved it; we are far from it in many ways, but we know that is what we must achieve." Thanks to the unremitting efforts of the Slovenian American journalist Louis Adamic, the Statue of Liberty became more than ever the country's symbol of a nation with many roots in its immigrant peoples, enabling Americans to connect the culture of newer Americans with the country's civic principles. Cultural pluralism in a democracy was pronounced the key to the brotherhood of mankind and a legitimate American ideal. Embracing it now constituted part of the national loyalty.

As a Rhode Island textile union newsletter put it in 1944, such a definition of democracy was essential "so that the soldiers of every race, creed, and color—the Colin Kellys and the Meyer Levins and the Dorie Millers, the black man and the white and the yellow, the Catholic, the Protestant, and the Jew— 'SHALL NOT HAVE DIED IN VAIN.'" Plays, novels, movies, documentaries, and government public relations efforts (propaganda, in effect) all nurtured the themes of a shared "Common Ground," the name of a World War II play. Many war movies had a "typical" American platoon: an Irish Catholic, a Pole, an Italian, and a Jew, together with an officer (usually southern) who would inevitably, in the crisis of battle, come to appreciate the value of his diverse group. A widely publicized, true-life symbol of the unity being promoted came from the sinking of the S.S. *Dorchester* in February 1943, with the loss of 678 lives. Four Army chaplains of different faiths gave up their life preservers that other men might live and they stood together as the ship went down. In many ways, the war would prove to be "a culminating moment" for a large percentage of foreign-born and second-generation Americans, who had been struggling for years to obtain union recognition, job security, and respectability—in essence, "incorporation" into American society.

And women were as much as men at the forefront of the wartime effort. In fact, the leap in the proportion of working women—from 9 percent to 22 percent of union members—included thousands of immigrant and second-generation women. In particular, married women took advantage of the employment opportunities to supplement family income or take the place of husbands and other family members who had entered military service. Their having to support their families and handle all matters in the absence of their husbands profoundly affected cultural patterns and gender roles of family members among many ethnic groups (as well as other Americans).

Many women found work they would not otherwise have been able to get. For some, it was a matter of far better opportunities. Dr. Eva Carey, a Polish American who had become a radiologist during the 1930s, recalled that "World War II made the difference for women in medicine. Before the war, a woman could stand on her head and wiggle her toes and they wouldn't give you a job. Then, when male doctors were away in the service, hospitals were critically short of help."

Meanwhile, and quite understandably, European immigration between 1941 and 1945 fell by three-fourths. Newcomers from the Americas comprised nearly two-thirds of those admitted. Among the longer resident foreign born there began an accelerated drive to acquire American citizenship. Besides those who wanted to avoid the designation of enemy aliens, others acted in response to the alien registration program and to the widespread pattern of employers insisting that those hired have American citizenship, although that had not been legally required for most jobs. All told, over one and a half million persons were naturalized between 1941 and 1945, a 74 percent increase over the prior five years. Among them, despite the hostile treatment they had received, were well over one-quarter million Mexicans, nearly 8,400 Filipinos, 7,700 Chinese, and even 556 Japanese. In the peak year of 1944, 441,979 individuals took the oath, a record number that would stand for exactly the next five decades.

The figures on new citizens highlight a watershed change in American immigration history. A prelude had come in 1940, when—for reasons of goodwill—naturalization rights were extended to "descendants of races indigenous to the Western Hemisphere." Then, in December 1941, China and the United States became allies, and proposals were introduced to repeal the exclusion laws and extend to Chinese the right of citizenship. In December 1943, Roosevelt signed into law a quota of 105 Chinese per year and, most important, the right of Chinese immigrants to receive American citizenship—the beginning of the end of the category of "aliens ineligible for citizenship." Indeed, Filipinos soon objected to being disqualified, exclaiming that "Filipinos are good enough to die under the American flag on Bataan and Corregidor and good enough to pay taxes in Hawaii—but not good enough to vote, hold public office, practice law or medicine." In July 1946, similar privileges were extended to Filipinos and natives of the Indian subcontinent.

The Dilemmas of Ethnicity in Wartime

The quest for American citizenship was part of more substantial changes underway. The upheavals, population movements, and wartime media campaigns inevitably weakened some ethnic communities by eroding their isolation, opening up leadership opportunities for veterans, and exposing many members far more directly to the dominant society and culture. That led, for example, to a sharp drop in foreign language radio stations (from 205 in 1942 to 126 in 1948), a 15 percent decline in foreign language publications, and a quickening of the shift to English in many parochial schools.

Yet, such developments by no means meant that ethnicity was disappearing, or that activities on behalf of old homelands were entirely evaporating. Numerous ethnic communities strove to assist compatriots who were experiencing the wars, invasions, and extermination programs. Among the many that were so involved stood the Croatians, Czechs and Slovaks, and Ukrainians. In 1944, for example, two thousand Polish American delegates from twenty-two states met in Buffalo to establish the Polish American Congress in order to lobby against Soviet influence in a postwar independent Poland.

The most complex involvement concerning events overseas involved American Jews. Various factors before 1940, especially conflicts between people for and against zionism and the widespread anxieties about anti-Semitism, had "adversely affected" their ability to act collectively. They were unable to construct a coalition to pressure the president into acting sooner on behalf of European Jewry. At a news conference on November 25, 1942, a leading American rabbi, Stephen Wise, presented concrete data that two million Jews had already been killed (which the U.S. government already knew but had not disclosed). In January 1944, Roosevelt at last relented and established the War Refugee Board. Five months later, he acceded to one other gesture, when he authorized temporary haven for a small number of refugees. In August, 982 persons from seventeen countries (mostly Jews) arrived and were confined to a camp in Oswego, New York. At the end of 1945, President Harry Truman approved their admission. Nonetheless, while the feuding had severely hampered the Jewish organizations, in the final analysis, it was Roosevelt's unresponsiveness that proved to be far more serious. Perhaps, as has been argued, his inaction was a consequence of a "realistic" assessment of the hostility in Congress and the public and his unwillingness to take on additional political risk. For three years he failed to act and when he finally did it was out of "considerations of strategy and propaganda." "In the end," concluded David Wyman, a leading scholar of these events, "the era's most prominent symbol of humanitarianism turned away from one of history's most compelling moral challenges."

The massive wartime changes in American society did not extinguish existing inter-ethnic strains; indeed, some were seriously aggravated by them. While Italian, Irish, and German opponents of U.S. entry into the war moved quickly to demonstrate their loyalty once war had actually been declared, in the 1940 election significant numbers of these voters had abandoned Roosevelt for Wendell Wilkie. His condemnation of Hitler and Mussolini and support for Great Britain had angered them. Elsewhere, in districts with such groups as the Poles, whose homelands had been invaded by the Germans, Roosevelt's votes shot up. Roosevelt won in 1940 and 1944 because many such urban ethnic groups remained behind him.

More explosive were the outbreaks of violence in Detroit in 1942 and in Mobile, Detroit, and Los Angeles in 1943. A number of other cities were embroiled in lesser conflicts. The clashes were most often a consequence of the uprooting of millions, who were then thrown together for the first time. Housing, jobs, and access to recreational areas were among the immediate sparks of the white (often white ethnic) and African American clashes. The white reaction (for example, among Detroit Poles) was frequently an expression of their resistance to changes that were perceived as threatening the existing ethnic communities. Such anti-Black violence would resurface in many cities after the war, as white veterans and workers struggled to preserve their economic gains, their shrinking communities, or their new suburban havens. As one historian put it, in the minds of whites, life, liberty and the pursuit of happiness meant jobs, homes, and the choice of one's neighbors.

Equally telling were the outbursts in Los Angeles. On August 2, 1942, a young Mexican American was found dead near a gravel pit, known as the Sleepy Lagoon. Although he was not a gang member, over twenty members of one gang were arrested. In the trial that followed, Mexicans were labelled as inherently criminal and violent. Their civil rights were routinely violated. The local media sensationalized the case. Although the convictions would be overturned in 1944, public attitudes had been inflamed by the press, as they had been against Japanese Americans earlier. Los Angeles exploded in June 1943. Friction between sailors and young Mexican Americans had intensified. Then, for five consecutive nights, rampaging through East Los Angeles, prodded by racist news reports, sailors and then soldiers, too, attacked the young *pachucos*, ripping off their elaborately oversized "zoot suits" and beating them up.[2] The police arrested the Mexican Americans, and Rear Admiral D. W. Bagley declared that the sailors had only acted in self-defense!

In this chapter we have seen how the government responded to the perceived need for security by taking actions that were both reasonable and irrational, measured and yet extreme. European immigration was curtailed; resident aliens were required to register; and millions of ethnic Americans were drafted into military service. At the same time, wartime hysteria and the legacy of racism also stirred government officials to intern nearly all Japanese Americans living along the West Coast—on the basis of ancestry not evidence of disloyalty, out of racism not military necessity. Even so, some twenty-three thousand Japanese Americans would serve in the military, along with two million or more other immigrants and children of immigrants. And, in record numbers, the foreign born applied for American citizenship. Meanwhile, millions of others, men and women across the country, endured the sacrifices and the rationing and joined the labor force in defense plants and other industries as well as in an ex-

---

[2]Zoot suiters had copied clothing and hair styles popular then among African American musicians and jitterbug dancers in the East. The zoot suiters were young, usually second-generation Mexican American teens who were searching for their own identity and resisting the pressures to conform and assimilate. In the popular Mexican slang, they identified themselves as *pachucos*, or *chukes* for short.

panded array of federal jobs. Finally, notwithstanding government efforts to promote ethnic toleration and incorporation into the mainstream, interethnic conflicts occurred. The confrontations represented more than wartime social strains; they were also manifestations of the clashes that often occur when significant societal changes uproot populations and undermine traditional patterns of social and economic relationships.

CHAPTER FIVE

Breaking New Ground: War Brides, DPs, and Refugees

It was the autumn of 1945; the victories were complete. The United States had emerged as the leading power. Roosevelt had died in April, and his vice president, Harry S. Truman, had carried the wars to completion. Now, new issues pressed for attention. The tens of thousands of military personnel who had met and married while serving abroad wanted their new spouses to come to America as quickly as possible. Visual reports detailed the unfathomable horrors of the Holocaust—Hitler's Final Solution. Millions of traumatized survivors needed new homes and new lives. Americans were gradually persuaded to accept a whole new classification of immigrants—Displaced Persons (DPs)— and then waves of desperate refugees. Nonetheless, there remained many defenders of the National Origins System, those who insisted that the basic law needed only some modifications, not an overhaul. The McCarran-Walter Immigration Act of 1952 reflected the new set of anxieties arising not from hot wars (though the Korean War beginning in June 1950 showed that they were still likely) but from a Cold War with the Soviet Union and the expanding number of Communist governments. The United States would struggle with one hand to preserve the fabric of its racially and ethnically biased immigration system and, with the other, to unravel it in the face of inescapable global and domestic events.

Innovations: War Brides and DPs

Before Congress adjourned in December 1945, it enacted the War Brides Act, providing for a three-year period during which the spouses and children of U.S. citizens in the military could more easily apply for nonquota visas. However, extending the law to Asian wives, who were ineligible for citizenship (except the now admissible Chinese) would take six more years. According to the Immigration and Naturalization Service (INS), 119,700 persons (mostly brides) entered with War Brides Act visas between 1946 and 1950. They came from fifty countries, half from the United Kingdom, Germany, and Italy—and 5,000 from China.

Most of the 5,000 Chinese married Chinese American soldiers. In other cases Chinese and Asian Indian men used the Act to reunite with spouses left behind as much as thirty years earlier. Another not uncommon scenario occurred in the story of G.I. Frank Pfeiffer, who arrived in Yokohama, Japan, in September 1945 and two months later met Sachiko Sekiya. "They dated, although she spoke no English and he did not understand Japanese. Frank proposed in January 1946 by pointing to Sachiko's heart and then his own. The wedding ceremony followed." But actually rejoining one's U.S. spouse in America was no simple matter, for, said one war bride, "Going to America then was like going to the moon!" And, recalled Mary Coffman of Bristol, England, she had "come to realize what a tremendous amount of courage it took for my father to embrace me on the Bristol Railway platform for possibly the last time in his life. People did not fly back and forth between America and Europe like they do today."

In December 1945, Truman took a second step that opened the way to dramatic policy changes. In the aftermath of the war some 8 million survivors had been uprooted. By late summer 1945, almost 1.9 million Displaced Persons remained in camps in Europe. In response to complaints about camp conditions, Truman sent Earl G. Harrison, dean of the University of Pennsylvania Law School, to investigate. Walking through the Bergen Belsen concentration camp, tears streaming down his face, Harrison whispered to a survivor, "But how did you survive and where did you take your strength from?" His report to Truman led to immediate orders to Gen. Dwight D. Eisenhower to improve camp conditions and undoubtedly convinced the president of the need for urgent action.

The president waited until the day after Congress had adjourned, December 22, 1945, to issue his Presidential Directive. In it, he urged that consular facilities be rapidly established in the U.S. occupation zone within Germany in order to facilitate the more rapid admission of DPs to the United States. Truman's public explanation was enormously symbolic. "I consider that common decency and the fundamental comradeship of all human beings requires us to do what lies in our power . . . to reduce human suffering." By so doing, he went on, the United States would "set an example for the rest of the world. . . ." Over 41,300 refugees were admitted before the Directive was replaced by the Displaced Persons Act (June 1948).

One particular beneficiary of the Directive was Werner Michael Blumenthal. He and his family had fled Germany in 1938, making their way to Shanghai because no visas were required to enter there. In July 1947, he was one of those fortunate enough to obtain a U.S. visa. Two months later, he arrived in San Francisco, twenty-one years old. Within a decade, motivated by the opportunities for education and employment, Blumenthal earned his Ph.D. in international economics from Princeton University and soon became vice president of a holding company. In 1961, the Kennedy administration offered this former refugee a position as deputy assistant secretary of state. He then invited to lunch in the reserved dining room the puzzled foreign service officer who had approved his visa in Shanghai fourteen years earlier. Blumenthal showed him the tattered visa with the man's own signature, and "he was truly speechless." "This was," said Blumenthal, "probably one of the proudest moments of my life." Two years later, he was appointed a U.S. ambassador and in 1976 became Secretary of the Treasury under President Jimmy Carter.

The December 1945 Directive and the 1945 War Brides Act set the stage for other changes. News reports on conditions in Europe and the increased role of voluntary agencies in the resettlement of refugees (VOLAGS, as they were called) finally made possible some policy reforms. Various religious and social organizations devised more sweeping strategies to reshape public opinion in support of a broader refugee policy. The principal group behind this effort was the nondenominational Citizens Committee on Displaced Persons, chaired by Earl G. Harrison. The end result was a string of Congressional compromises that Truman reluctantly accepted.

The Displaced Persons Act of June 25, 1948, has been described as "the first piece of legislation in American history that set *refugee policy* as opposed to immigration policy." But it was imperfect. It provided for 205,000 visas over a two-year period—half the number requested. They were to be charged against the various nations' quotas, although half of future annual quotas could be "mortgaged"—borrowed against. Supporters sought to avoid any hint of the act being too pro-Jewish and imposed many restrictions on who could qualify. And all adults had to have jobs, housing, and sponsors—a role many VOLAGS were to fulfill.

In June 1950, Congress extended the law for two more years, increased the total number of visas to 415,700, and opened eligibility to more diverse refugee groups. Overall, of the 1 million Displaced Persons resettled in 113 countries between the end of 1947 and mid-1952, 409,700 were admitted by the United States. Of the latter, approximately 47 percent were Catholic, 16 percent Jewish, and 35 percent Protestant or other. Over 4,000 were orphans. Almost 356,000 visas had been mortgaged for them, including half the quotas of several countries beyond a lifetime: Greece to the year 2,017 and Latvia until 2,274! And yet, it was already apparent that a refugee policy was required that applied across more than one ocean, for in 1949, after the fall of Nationalist China to the Communists, over 1,600 visas were given to Chinese students and professors then in the United States.

Raveling and Unraveling National Origins

The quota system was being subverted by the consequences of war and now, as the U.S.S.R. consolidated its control over Eastern Europe, the politics of the Cold War. Fear of Communism was intensified by the fall of Czechoslovakia in 1948 and China in 1949 and by the alleged threats to Turkey and Greece. Public anxieties were whipped up by Senator Pat McCarran's investigations of foreigners in the Communist Party, by Senator Joseph McCarthy's charges of "Commies and queers" in the State Department, and by the outbreak of the Korean War in June 1950. Fear of Communism replaced "the old fear of ethnic invasion." It seemed loyalty counted for more than the race or nationality of the immigrants.

Victor Machinko, a Ukrainian who had managed to escape the Soviet Union during the war and later make his way to Cleveland, expressed a fitting sentiment in this regard: "I haven't met any Americans as really patriotic as I am because they don't realize what they have, and I do. They don't appreciate it. You've got some Communists even, you know. I'm working with one. They don't know what it is like. . . . You just can't beat America."

The McCarran Internal Security Act of September 1950 posed a further threat to the nation's immigrants. Membership in any subversive organization could now constitute grounds for exclusion, deportation, denial of citizenship, and even the loss of citizenship. Ominously reminiscent of legislation that had sharply altered the Japanese American experience, the McCarran act authorized the president, in a national emergency, to round up and detain persons suspected of threatening the national interests.

Besides pursuing security issues, Senator Pat McCarran fought any liberalization of the immigration laws, warning that "we have in the United States today hard-core, indigestible blocs which have not become integrated into the American way of life but which, on the contrary, are our deadly enemies." He worked with Congressman Francis Walter, Chair of the House Un-American Activities Committee. The resulting McCarran-Walter Immigration and Nationality Act, June 27, 1952, represented the most complete codification of the immigration and naturalization laws up to that time. It retained the basic national origins formula because, as a Senate report put it, that remained "a rational and logical method . . . to best preserve the sociological and cultural balance" in the nation's population. President Truman viewed the law as biased, a slur on ethnic Americans, for it carried "over into this year of 1952 the isolationist limitations of our 1924 law." In 1953, a presidential commission severely criticized the law as discriminatory, punitive, and distrustful of "all aliens." They predicted that it would be "in some respects unworkable."

To begin with, although the law preserved the quota system, it shifted the preferences according to which persons could be admitted. (Figure 5.1 compares the 1929 and 1952 preferences.) Second, the act defined a huge Asia-Pacific Triangle, providing just two thousand visas for all countries within it. But while other quotas were applied according to country of birth, these were ancestry categories (such as Chinese, Korean, Japanese); Asians born anywhere had to qualify under those limited categories. Third, the law now made persons of all races eligible for naturalization and it eliminated the initial step of filing "first papers." Finally, the law provided an option that would ultimately constitute the backdoor of American immigration for almost three decades: It gave the Attorney General, in emergencies, the power to "parole" temporarily into the country an individual lacking a visa.

During the decade that followed, Congress and the president did not abandon the national origins systems. Rather, in piecemeal fashion, they unraveled it. Within fourteen months, Congress approved "the first major breach" of the whole system. With the Displaced Persons Act having expired, the new

Figure 5.1	Basic Preferences of the 1929 and 1952 Immigration Laws

1929 (Cap: 153,714)	1952 (Cap: 154,657; later 156,487)
NONQUOTA: Wives and minor children of citizens; current husbands of citizens; professors, students, and clergy; inhabitants of Western Hemisphere.	NONQUOTA: Spouses and minor children of citizens; clergy; inhabitants of the Western Hemisphere
FIRST: Parents and adult children of citizens; husbands subsequently wed to citizens*; and skilled agriculturalists. 50% of quota	FIRST: Urgently needed skilled workers. 50% of quota
SECOND: Spouse and minor children of resident aliens. Remaining quota visas	SECOND: Parents of citizens. 30% of quota
NONPREFERENCE: Any remaining after Second Preference	THIRD: Spouse and unmarried children of resident aliens. 20% of quota
	NONPREFERENCE: Siblings and older children of citizens. One-fourth of remaining visas
	"New Seed." Any remaining visas
	(In 1959 there were some changes made: siblings were shifted to Second Preference)

*Wed as of a certain cut-off date. The cut-off date was periodically advanced.

president, Dwight D. Eisenhower, immediately urged further refugee legislation. As Supreme Commander of Allied Forces in Europe, he had visited the Ohrdruf concentration camp and witnessed a scene from the Holocaust himself. In August 1953, the Refugee Relief Act was passed, providing for 214,000 nonquota visas for refugees from Communism as well as from Italy and Greece, for Dutch fleeing Indonesia, and for several thousand other persons from Asia and the Middle East. With the Refugee-Escapee Act of September 1957, Congress further undermined the racially based quotas: Unused visas from 1953 were reallocated independently of national origin; backlogged visa applications were converted to nonquota ones, although the applicants were not related to U.S. citizens; the mortgaged quotas used for DPs were simply erased; and more than 11,000 refugees were admitted from Asia, the Middle East, and Africa, further disregarding the 1952 ceilings.

The outbreak of the Hungarian Revolt in late October 1956 led to a mass exodus of over 150,000 refugees to Austria. Eisenhower seized upon the 1952 "parole" provision and used it for the admission of 15,000 Hungarians. Eventually, over 30,600 were paroled in and given permanent residence after two years of residence. In 1958, Dutch persons were expelled from the former Dutch colony of Indonesia, a non-Communist country, yet Congress authorized 11,500 visas for them. In fact, the same act of 1958 provided for the admission of nearly 4,000 Cape Verdeans from the Azores, following earthquakes and volcanic eruptions on Fayal Island in the Azores.

Three other measures also set the stage for the 1965 reforms. First, with the Cuban Revolution of January 1959 Fidel Castro came to power. Cubans were able to enter the United States with visas until diplomatic relations were broken on January 1, 1961. President John F. Kennedy, building on Eisenhower's policy, established the Cuban Refugee Program and, over the next eighteen months, paroled in over 62,500 Cubans. Between 1959 and the missile crisis in October 1962, some 215,000 Cubans entered. Second, Kennedy also responded to famine in China and the exodus to Hong Kong by authorizing, in May 1962, the parole of approximately 15,000 Chinese refugees from Hong Kong. Finally, of great symbolic importance, the Act of September 26, 1961, had declared that visa forms would no longer request the applicant's race and ethnicity.

The many special executive and legislative actions outlined here concerning refugees had made possible the admission of

734,000 persons between 1946 and 1965.[1] These actions represented significant and repeated measures to exempt groups from
the elaborate set of preferences and quotas that were at the heart
of the original National Origins formula. The fate of the system
established in 1929 and reaffirmed in 1952 was virtually sealed—
unable to withstand the diplomatic pressures of a Cold War, the
resurgence of humanitarianism, the leadership of three presidents, and the political reality that many ethnic groups in America
had become a force that could no longer be easily ignored.

America's Migrants: With and Without Papers

Undoubtedly, for many (if not most) newcomers, moving into
American society continued to be a startling experience. Leida
Sorro, arriving from Estonia, well remembered 1951:

From Ellis Island we took a train through the Middle West. I remember
being on the train and seeing these kids . . . playing with money. We
didn't know it was play money. . . . There's all this money falling around,
and all we had for the five of us to eat on the train for three days was
twenty dollars. Finally, Evie picked up a piece of the play money and we
looked—twenty dollars! We thought it was real. And here were these
children playing with all that money. We thought, "My God! It really is
true; Americans really are rich."

Yet, the 4.83 million persons legally admitted (1946–65[2]),
came with many motives for their migration. Most conspicuous
were the refugees from wars in Europe and Asia; those fleeing
the establishment of Communist governments in Eastern Europe, Asia, and Cuba; and those escaping political turmoil and
civil struggles from Haiti to Indonesia. There was also the impact of American armies stationed abroad, and the socializing
that inevitably occurred with local men and women, first recognized with the arrival in the United States of thousands of war

---

[1]If one includes Cubans and Hong Kong Chinese parolled in but not yet
given permanent residence, the full figure exceeds 800,000.

[2]Because of the Federal fiscal years, this actually covers from July 1, 1945,
through June 30, 1965.

brides and grooms. Religion was sometimes a factor, as with the Tongans who converted to Mormonism and then migrated to Hawaii. The most common motive, however, continued to be economic hardships, from Greece to Mexico and the West Indies. Professionals were lured by more lucrative opportunities, too, for example, those from Norway, England, and Canada—in particular Canadian engineers, doctors, and nurses.

In fact, Congress had continued to exempt most Western Hemisphere immigration from the quota system, and the gradual deepening of migration channels from the West Indies, Central America, Argentina, Colombia, and Ecuador fostered greater information networks.[3] Immigrants from the Americas, who accounted for one-sixth of the U.S. total in 1940, rose to two-fifths in the mid-1950s, and edged up to just over half of all newcomers in 1965. For the 1945–65 period, 36 percent of the nation's immigrants had been born in the Americas. By 1960, Mexicans constituted one in six of the nation's noncitizens, and Canadians the second largest alien population. This did not escape the attention of Congress.

In reality, little of what occurred in American immigration during the postwar years followed the lines set out in 1929 or 1952. Between 1946 and 1965, only 57 percent of all immigrants admitted to the United States were from Europe; the percentage was well below that by the early 1960s. Due to the various refugee laws, more southern and eastern Europeans were admitted than was provided for under the quota system, while Ireland and Great Britain (with 56 percent of the allotted quotas) failed to use about three-fifths of theirs. Even allowing for emigration, the years between 1946 and 1965 added over 2.5 million

---

[3]This was true, too, for Puerto Ricans, but they have been American citizens since 1917 and, therefore, are not among the foreign-born immigrants covered here. However, their migration patterns and mainland communities have many similarities with those of other Latinos, who are classified as foreign-born. Puerto Rican migration to the mainland also rose after the war, due to the same combination of factors and facilitated by the availability of inexpensive air routes between Puerto Rico and New York City.

Europeans to those American ethnic groups, just as Western Hemisphere migration contributed some 1 million persons to the Latino and West Indian communities.[4]

And even Asians benefitted from the legislative changes, for the gradual removal of the racial barriers to immigration and citizenship profoundly affected Asian migration even before 1965. In the late 1940s, Asian and Middle Eastern immigration[5] represented less than 3 percent of the total; in the early 1960s, over 7 percent. A key role in the escalation of Asian immigration was the American military presence in the Philippines, Japan, numerous islands in the Pacific, and then in Korea. Between 1946 and 1965, two-fifths to three-quarters of the principal Asian groups consisted of the wives of U.S. citizens. (And American women were socializing, too, for they sponsored over sixteen thousand husbands.) Overall, a majority of all Asian immigrants were family members of U.S. citizens.

Among other factors responsible for the changes were the growing number of students and professionals (particularly Asians) who chose to remain in America. After 1952, all Asians were at last eligible for citizenship. Besides the longtime residents who now applied, newcomers (especially Koreans) did so more rapidly than did all others, which then enabled these Asians to sponsor other family members. Finally, by the late 1950s, increasing numbers of Middle Easterners began migrating to the United States, including Iranians, Syrians, and Lebanese, etching newer migration streams.

In contrast to the highly publicized war brides and DPs, much of the nonrefugee migration of the 1950s and early 1960s was nearly invisible, in particular the millions of Mexican *braceros*— the temporary farm workers—who supplied the brawn and the

---

[4]Canadians are omitted here because, except for the French Canadians (who comprised 25 percent of the Canadian foreign stock population in 1950 and were largely concentrated in New England), Canadians have been among the weakest to establish ethnic communities in the United States, with only some few local exceptions.

[5]The INS' published annual reports after 1945 combined Asia and the Middle East.

backs for the great agribusinesses. The farm workers were concentrated primarily in the Southwest and parts of the Midwest and were usually migratory. Undocumented Mexican aliens commonly followed the migration paths of their legal compatriots, and the lines often blurred between them, for both groups filled many unskilled and semiskilled positions that Americans paid little mind to, except to rely upon such labor for cheaper services and products.

An agreement between the United States and Mexico in June 1942 enabled almost 168,000 *braceros* to work in twenty-one states. Many were later employed by canning and packing houses and on railroads. Growers continued to use these temporary agricultural workers after the war but without contracts. Meanwhile, the apprehension of undocumented aliens increased almost seven fold between 1945 and 1951. Huge numbers of these illegal aliens, often called "wetbacks" or *mojados* (from crossing the Rio Grande), were "dried out"—that is, given legal status to work rather than being sent back. The outbreak of the Korean War led to the renewal of the *Bracero* program in 1951, which then continued through December 1964. During that time, 4.24 million temporary workers were recruited, most of whom were Mexican. But by the 1960s, the political climate was already changing. Domestic labor groups attacked the program. Greater agricultural mechanization reduced many growers' dependency on such large pools of labor. At the same time, Congressional sensitivities were heightened by the civil rights movement. The Democratic administration was persuaded to let the program die in December 1964.

Just as the *Bracero* program had hampered agricultural union efforts for two decades, so its demise set the stage for the successful unionizing efforts of Cesar Chavez (National Farm Workers of America) and Philip Vera Cruz and Larry Itliong (Agricultural Workers Organizing Committee). They merged their organizations in 1965 into the United Farm Workers Organizing Committee. Cutting off the legal channels of entry for *braceros*, however, also sharply intensified the influx of undocumented aliens. Transportation improvements within Mexico had eased the access to the northern regions, while the 30 percent increase in population and the scarcity of jobs heightened the pressures to seek work across the border. Decades of chain migration had forged networks of information regarding the availability of jobs and higher wages in the United States. American products that workers brought home and the houses they built and goods they purchased with their U.S. earnings also encouraged others to go *al norte*—even for a short time.

Apprehensions of undocumented aliens jumped from a half million in 1951 to over 865,000 two years later. With that, Eisenhower appointed retired Lt. Gen. Joseph Swing as Commissioner of the INS in order to restore control of the border. He organized Operation Wetback, from California eastward to Texas, beginning in June 1954. The INS quickly apprehended more than one million undocumented Mexican persons and nearly one-quarter million more the following fiscal year. With an agreement between growers and the government in 1956 that substantially expanded the *Bracero* program, the decade of 1956–65 would see the fewest apprehensions of illegal migrants for the entire half century since 1945—with merely 29,651 in 1960. The 1955 INS annual report had concluded: "The border has been secured." For that next decade, until economic and political conditions changed, it appeared to be true.

The postwar decades compelled Americans to address a world they could not have envisioned during the 1920s and 1930s. As many had said, on the day of its passage (over Truman's veto) the McCarran-Walter Act of 1952 was already out-of-date. The United States was confronted with political and humanitarian considerations that could not be dealt with within the confines of the National Origins System, requiring, for example, legislative and executive actions to admit unprecedented numbers of refugees. Their diversity differed significantly from the composition intended in the original 1920s legislation. The newcomers during the middle period would be later seen as leading edges of the waves of new peoples who would immigrate after 1965. The increasing numbers of Latinos, West Indians, Asians, and Middle Easterners illuminate the fact that, while postwar Europe was rapidly recovering, other regions were experiencing more turmoil and pressures on their populations to migrate, temporarily or permanently. But the story of immigrants and American society did not stop at the border or the shoreline, or the airport tarmac.

CHAPTER SIX

Immigrants and American Society at Midcentury

In the decades after 1945, the children and grandchildren of the earlier wave of immigrants grappled with the challenges, opportunities, and social and cultural attractions of postwar America. Meanwhile, the myriad groups of refugees, war brides and war grooms, long-separated Asian spouses, and several million other new immigrants faced their own challenges as they adapted to new lives in the United States. In the midcentury decades, ethnic America was at no single stage of sociocultural evolution, or integration, for there were present within specific groups multiple generations that spanned all ages and vastly different lengths of time in the country. Some groups were dispersed, others quite concentrated. They could be found in diverse social and economic environments and with rather uneven degrees of unity and networking. They also varied in their educational and occupational attainment, gender roles, participation in nonethnic associations, and rates of intermarriage, among other things.

Long-standing generalizations about the transformation and decline in the viability and cohesiveness of European ethnic

groups mask significant exceptions during this period. Important developments were then taking place among new ethnic
communities, even within the Northeast but especially in the
Southwest and Pacific regions. The 1944 Servicemen's Readjustment Act, popularly known as the G.I. Bill, opened opportunities to returning military personnel for training they would likely
not have otherwise had available; it also changed attitudes and
opened new avenues for mobility. Between 1945 and 1952, 7.8
million soldiers took advantage of this legislation. By the end of
this quarter century (1940–65), retirements by persons from the
North into what became known as the Sunbelt (not just the moves
to nearby suburbias), the Cuban Revolution, and the launching
of the momentous civil rights movement would profoundly affect many of the nation's immigrants and their descendants, not
least of all Europeans—both those long present and those but
recently arrived.

An Overview: Immigrants and Ethnics

Already by the early 1960s, when Presidents Kennedy and
Johnson were proposing immigration reforms, only 42 percent
of the nation's immigrants were coming from traditional European sources (1961–65). How, then, had the nation's ethnic
group members—immigrants and the recent descendants of immigrants (the second and third generations)—been responding
to the momentous changes that followed the outbreak of World
War II?

There were many new immigrant voices in the 1940s and
1950s, some expressing the same struggles as earlier generations,
echoing the continuity of the immigrant experience, at the same
time that the children of the earlier waves were finding their
own places—even in suburbia. Consider Judith Flack, a third-
generation Italian American born during the war, who grew up
in Pittsburgh, on Magu Street, where the people "were most Italians—in fact, they were all Italians—and there were lots of children." Her grandfather had tried to teach her Italian, but "I know
only the bad words. He used to listen to the Italian stations on

the radio, the Italian hour on Sundays." "We followed a lot of Italian customs when the grandparents were with us, but as we got older and the grandparents passed on, it sort of slackened off." Her first marriage to a second-generation Italian failed, and she wed an old Irish American friend, Ronnie. Upon reflection, she observed that "Being Italian is much less a part of my life than when I was a child. Then, I was Italian and everything I did and all my friends were Italian; I went to an Italian church and school. Now, outside of making Italian dishes for Ronnie, I can't think of anything. . . . None of our neighbors are Italian, none of them are Catholic. Ronnie isn't Catholic. I don't belong to any Italian groups, and I don't go to a Catholic church. . . ." Her mother, Lydia Pofi, had stayed more involved in the community, commenting that she and her husband had joined ISDA—Italian Sons and Daughters of America—and "a group called the Fifty-Plus Club. We're almost all Italians." Many were members of a high school club that broke up as the girls moved to the suburbs, "but we've always stayed in touch."

Sometimes one did not need to wait a generation or two to move out of the group or to blend in to the larger society, especially if one were rather young at the outset. Anton Tamsaare (a pseudonym) was born in Estonia five years before Judith Flack. At the age of ten, he and his family, refugees sponsored by a Lutheran VOLAG, settled in Arthur, North Dakota—population one hundred! While they continued to speak Estonian at home, Anton said, "People kind of forget that you've come recently. You live just like everyone else." And about the time he graduated college in 1961, he could say, "I don't think in a conscious way that being an immigrant play[ed] any role anymore. In a way the story kind of ends there, or maybe it ended when I was fifteen. . . . I've adopted some sort of Anglophile way of life."

In most instances, one sees the process of adaptation beginning with the immigrants, but not always. Not all were receptive to change. Ilse Kienzle came with her husband from Germany in 1955. "I didn't want to come. Why should I go there [America]? Why should I go to a country who bombed our whole city for nothing?" She lived in Jersey City, New Jersey, but, despite having children born in the United States, "I just didn't want to learn English. I tried to find every German store I could." In West New York, she added, there was "almost a German neighborhood. There was a German church, there was a German butcher, there was a German furniture store, and there was a bakery where they talked German. So I didn't need English." She had one wish: "I never want to be buried here." A similar attitude was expressed by war bride Frieda Ross, who came in 1948. Her marriage began with a splash: The wedding ceremony was broadcast on that new medium of communication, television, on "Bride and Groom." Yet, the marriage was soon failing: "We drifted apart. I met alot of German people, and I sort of palled with them . . . drifted with the German people. . . ." She remarried, but said years later, although she realized things had drastically changed back home, "I still keep the apartment [in Germany], just in case anything happens to Mike [her husband]."

Adaptation was neither automatic nor always easy for immigrants—that is, for most immigrants. A young Welshman, Tacwyn Morgan, a war groom living in Detroit, had the exceptional advantage of language, education, and skills and never regretted his move to America. "No, my home is here. I like Americans. I like their freedom. It might be a little bit of this feeling that in England I was a Welshman. . . . That's how I was known. In America you don't have that feeling." In the final analysis, his wife was a major factor: "And it's difficult for me to separate the United States from Louise. It's Louise to me."

For those without a Louise, though educated and urbane, coming to America could be a bewildering encounter. Denise Levertov, an Englishwoman of Russian Jewish ancestry, arrived as a war bride in 1948. On her first day, out walking in Brooklyn with her husband in "a bourgeois Jewish section," she saw "women with fantastic hairdos, very full, long skirts—it was the after-the-war fashion—lots of makeup." She commented to her husband that "anywhere in Europe, a neighborhood like this wouldn't have tarts on the street, and they certainly wouldn't be walking around in broad daylight!" They were only high school girls, he told her. "These were just girls dressed up for a Saturday evening . . . perfectly respectable," she realized. "I think I had a severe case of culture shock. . . ."

Within this range of responses marginality has often lurked below the surface for many newcomers, as it did for Klara Zwicker, who arrived from Germany in 1957. "I like to go home to Germany. I get all excited, and after a while then I've got to come back. Got to see everybody, you know, and see what's going on. And then when I'm there I feel like I should come back here. It's always such an in-between, you know. I like to go home, yet when you're there you're somehow disappointed, because you always figure when you left everything's going to stay like that—but it doesn't. And I feel like an outsider." She was an outsider in the new home and then in the old one, as well.

And there was a marginality that compounded the initial struggles to adapt. Mary Paik Lee had come from Korea in 1905 as five-year-old Kuang Sun Paik. She and her husband, H. M. Lee, gave up truck farming and moved to Los Angeles in 1950. She recalled how hard it was in the early 1950s for women to get jobs as domestics because of the language. "Although not being able to speak English was a big problem, after long hours of hard labor, no one had the time or energy to study English." A more specific episode illuminated an aspect of the Asian immigrant experience fewer of their European counterparts would commonly know: imposed marginality.

Once an American lady asked [recalled Lee] if I was going to vote that day. I said I was too busy and couldn't get away. She started to give me a lecture about my civic duty. I looked at her in wonder. She considered herself well educated and thought she knew everything. Yet she didn't know that the reason I didn't vote was that Orientals were not allowed to be citizens, so we didn't have the right to vote [before 1952]. She became very angry and said, 'That's not so! Everyone in America has equal rights.' But she came back a few days later and said a lawyer friend had told her I was right. We remained good friends anyway.

In 1960, after fifty-five years in America, Kuang Sun Paik and her husband became American citizens. At that point, she did what many new Americans have done, she changed her name.

The arrival of over 5.5 million people between 1931 and 1965 (see Appendix, Table 6.1), even allowing for the emigration of some 1 million people, provided a multitude of ethnic communities with considerable numbers of additional persons with cultural, emotional, familial, and sometimes even political ties to their homelands. And there is reason to believe that many of the emigrants left their mark, too, before completing their sojourn in America. Thus, overlaying the transition of "immigrant America" to "ethnic America"—the progressive integration of the second and third (and later) generations—was an ethnic persistence and even ethnic resurgence within many communities, particularly as a consequence of this new immigration. With that also came expanding channels of migration and networks that would shape much of the next great tide of immigration after 1965.

Immigrants and Ethnics: Urban, Suburban, Rural

These changes in ethnic America were inseparable from the transformation of America itself that followed the war, especially with the convergence in many cities of newcomers, ethnic communities, and African Americans and whites from the South. Old Americans and new, white and of color, found themselves clashing, struggling to co-exist in their mutually new environments. The decay of the inner cities, the decline of manufacturing in many areas of the North, and the shift to a more white collar and service-oriented economy soon compounded the pressures on all groups. Outmigrations to suburban rings, "the crabgrass frontier," defined the postwar era.

During the 1950s, while central cities grew by 11 percent, suburbs expanded by 46 percent. A "home-ownership revolution" was taking place, symbolized by huge, novel tract-home developments. These suburbs tended to attract families of roughly comparable incomes and backgrounds. As one historian put it, "The very poor did not live in the new suburbs, and neither, as a rule, did the very rich. . . ." And the suburban migration was "an ethnically selective process," for it was the second and third generations that were most able to afford the homes and more eager to leave the old neighborhoods. For them, it "was moving into America"—although, researchers have noted, "the new suburbanites were very much like the friends and neighbors they had left behind. They didn't drop their ties or ethnic organizations or abandon the Democratic party," even if they did prefer a Republican president in 1952 and 1956.

Yet, on the one hand, many people did remain tied to their existing communities and were reluctant to uproot, perhaps because of their age and/or for religious and communal reasons (the Orthodox Jews, for instance) or because they already owned homes there (as did many Italians and Poles). On the other, expansion by African Americans and other minorities (particularly Puerto Ricans and other Latinos) into these areas created local crises and even violent confrontations, prompting residents in the existing ethnic neighborhoods to relocate and often recluster farther out from the cities. Still others joined the march of retirees to the Sunbelt, with ethnic concentrations reappearing in some areas there, too, especially in Florida.

Thus, while many succumbed to the "suburban effect" and others used it simply to escape unwanted neighborhood transformations, there were not only those in the older urban centers who tried to resist the "softening" of traditional ethnic ties but groups outside the metropolitan cores that did so, too. For example, considerable numbers of Wisconsin Norwegians remained quite rural and, as did communities of Midwest Czechs, Dutch, and Danes, as well as Mexicans in the Southwest, continued to value and preserve those ethnic communities. If they did move, they tended to recluster elsewhere.

To set these postwar transformations affecting immigrant and ethnic America in a larger perspective, consider four significant developments. First, geographic: Between 1940 and 1960 the foreign-born population in the New England, Mid-Atlantic, and East North Central areas fell by about one-fourth and substantially increased in the South and Pacific Coastal sections, indicating a partial shift in where the centers of immigrant and ethnic activities would be found. Second, demographic: In 1940, half of the foreign born had already been in the country at least twenty-five years. By 1960, their median age was over fifty-seven. Despite the fact that over 3.5 million immigrants were admitted during the 1950s (and only 418,600 left), the total foreign-born population fell by almost one-fifth (to 9.3 million, 1960). Even the second generation (23.7 million) was an aging population, for in 1960 their median age was almost forty-three. The third and later generations of the pre-1930 immigrants were about to move to the forefront. Third, gender: The preponderance of male immigrants before 1930 was followed by female majorities thereafter. In fact, nearly two-thirds were women in the three main years when war brides were arriving (1946–48). For the whole period 1946–65, over 55 percent of all those admitted were females. In 1960, for the first time, a majority of all foreign-born Americans were female. The dynamics of ethnic communities, families, and labor-force participation were likely to be affected by this migration pattern. Fourth, second-generation parentage: Between 1940 and 1960, mixed marriages involving foreigners (mostly foreign-born women) and native-born persons increased significantly. The number of second-generation children with one native-born and one foreign-born parent rose by one-fourth. As suggested before, the integration of the children of such mixed backgrounds was more rapid, and, along with the emerging third generation, they would come to be the bridge between their ethnic communities and the larger society.

Despite the efforts of those who remained determined to hold fast to their traditions and communities, the geographic and demographic alterations make it clear that this was an era in great flux. The relocation to suburbia symbolized much of what was changing. Given that, a recent observation by a historian regarding American Jews applied to others as well: "In the compacted Jewish neighborhood of the cities, Jewish identity was absorbed by osmosis. In suburbia, it had to be nurtured." The fact that churches, synagogues, and other ethnic institutions sometimes followed, if not accompanied, the suburban settlers proved invaluable. Religious institutions adapted their programs, services, and styles of communication to fit the land of little street life, of the two-car, single-family homes. Many became, in suburbia, the principal social centers, organizing a host of such things as clubs, sports leagues, and study groups.

Those accommodations reflected others under way: The diminishing use of foreign languages and the continued shift to English in religious services; the declining number of foreign language publications, festivals, and religious services (and the appearance and growth of English publications—for example, the *Chinese Digest* and the *Nisei's Pacific Citizen*); the drop in the number of Catholic nationality parishes (from 2,006 to 1,848); the growth of Jewish Conservative and Reformed congregations; and the realignments and consolidation of some Protestant denominations. (For example, Danes and Norwegians Americanized their church names and later joined with Germans to create the Lutheran Church of America in 1962.) Paralleling these developments, new organizations with more of an American focus, such as the Bosnian American Cultural Association, the German American National Congress, and the (Mexican American) G.I. Forum, joined those formed before the war by second generation men and women, including the League of United Latin American Citizens and the Japanese American Citizens League.

The dramatic decrease in anti-Semitism by the early 1950s and the virtual disappearance of anti-Catholicism, symbolized by the 1960 election of John F. Kennedy as the first Catholic President, suggest that attitudes as well as institutions were in flux during these years. Indeed, affirmation of ethnicity by focusing more on religion than nationality had become the popular means of proclaiming one's Americanness. In his famous 1955 study of the religious revival of the 1950s, *Protestant, Catholic, and Jew*, Will Herberg reported on findings that appeared to show a triple melting pot among second- and third-generation Americans. Protestants, Catholics and Jews were marrying others of their own religion, and smaller percentages were also confining their choices to their nationality subgroups. Herberg declared that religion had become Americans' principal form of identification and that the religious community was their primary one.

Even more specifically, he declared that "being a Protestant, Catholic, or a Jew is understood as the specific way, and increasingly perhaps the only way, of being an American and locating oneself in American society." Not being one of the three was "not to be anything, not to have a *name*. . . ." Powerful consensus attitudes were at work during the 1950s.

Clearly, if mobility was contributing to the institutional changes and new attitudes towards identity and religious affiliation, it was also increasing interethnic contacts and various types of intermarriage. Discussions centered mostly on religious intermarriages, with the argument being made by some that it was not uncommon for such marriages to occur within the same nationality, or for the spousal preferences to be within the regional groupings (for a Northern European to prefer another Northern European, even of a different faith, for instance). Other studies did reveal a strong trend, however, among younger siblings of the second generation toward the selection of partners beyond nationality boundaries but within religious ones. Marriage variations by generation and birthplace abounded, accompanying the growing numbers of other religious communities, including the Orthodox, Muslim, and Hindu.[1] Certainly, the arrival of over a half-million foreign spouses of U.S. citizens, well over two-fifths of whom were married to military personnel, underscored the significance of intermarriage as a path to integration for foreigners—especially for the vast majority of the 126,400 Asian immigrant spouses (1946–65). It likewise highlighted the larger issue of racial intermarriage. As state laws banning such marriages declined from about thirty to fourteen states—before being entirely ruled unconstitutional in 1967—those unions also increased.

If the shifts described here reflected some of the larger changes in American society as well as the broadened aspirations and attitudes of significant segments of ethnic America, then the recasting of their attitudes and identities—measured,

---

[1]The Mormon Church, with its roots uniquely in America, was also continuing to grow at this time and included many immigrants.

for example, by the greater number and percentage of intermarriages—could also be seen as a consequence of still other important patterns, such as the higher levels of education, greater labor force participation by women, and more job mobility. There was, by this time, a general recognition among more ethnic groups that education did indeed represent an important (and viable) avenue for mobility. By 1960, the median years of education for second-generation males (10.9) exceeded that for all native born males (10.6). For women, the native-born and second generation figures were the same (11.1). (See Appendix, Table 6.2.) Although the variations among groups (they were less evident but still present) represented in large part the effects of both urban-rural and religio-cultural backgrounds, among virtually every one of the sixteen nationality groups listed in the 1960 census, second-generation females surpassed males in median years of education. It is also clear that most females were not expected to go beyond high school, for double the percentage of males had completed college. Nonetheless, the real sign of the transition in values and opportunities lay in the intergenerational leaps, the sizable differences in median years of education between immigrants and their children, for example, Lithuanians (5.2 vs. 12.0) and Italians (5.9 vs. 10.9).

Paralleling the greater interest in acquiring more education were the shifting attitudes regarding women in the labor force and occupational aspirations. More second generation women were out working (about 32-38 percent among the various groups), although cultural factors—if not situational ones (including childbearing)—persisted in defining some of those differences. For example, half the Polish women held jobs, though their median age was about forty-two, but only three-tenths of Mexican women did so, despite a median age of merely twenty-three years. (Although part of the reason may have been that the Mexican women were in an earlier stage of parenting their small children, Mexican men—like many others—tended to interpret their wives' working outside the home as a negative reflection on their manhood and a threat to the family unity.) A similar combination of generational change and ethnic variations could be seen in terms of occupation. (See Appendix, Table 6.3.) By 1960, two-fifths of second generation males and three-fifths of females held white-collar jobs, compared with one-third and two-fifths, respectively, among the foreign born. Nevertheless, as with their parents, specific second generation groups varied in terms of how many and how quickly they moved up to such employment. Higher percentages of people with British, Irish, and Swedish family backgrounds attained white-collar work than those of Italian, German, and Polish descent. The highest percentage of white-collar work, however, was secured by Russian Jews. With Mexicans, too, one saw signs of change, despite their small proportion holding white-collar jobs: One-third of the foreign-born males were in agriculture (mostly as farm laborers) but only 12 percent of the sons of Mexican immigrants were.

As striking as the shifts involving education, occupation, and even religion were the greater political integration and maturation taking place, as Dalip Singh Saund illustrated. Saund had come from India in 1919, married a Czech immigrant, farmed land leased under his wife's name, and campaigned for the right of Asian Indians and Pakistanis to acquire citizenship, which was legislated in 1946. A decade later he was elected to the U.S. House of Representatives. Hiram Fong and Daniel Inouye were both seasoned Hawaiian politicians by the time Hawaii became a state in 1959, for Asians had figured prominently in territorial politics since the 1920s (which may have dissuaded some white mainland Congressmen from approving statehood sooner). Fong was elected Hawaii's first U.S. senator and Inouye one of its first congressmen. A few years later, Inouye also became a senator, and Spark Matsunaga and Patsy Takemoto Mink were elected the state's two members of Congress, a dozen years before the first Japanese American was elected on the mainland.

Across the continent, meanwhile, Republicans in New Haven, Connecticut, decided, with the war over, that an Italian candidate for mayor would no longer offend people. Italian voters, who felt shut out of the Democratic Party by the Irish, threw their support behind William Celentano. He won, was reelected three times, and Italians there remained loyal to the party. In

New York City, Paul O'Dwyer, the Irish American (Democratic) Tammany leader, returned from service in Washington to be elected mayor, but Carmine deSapio replaced him as head of the party in 1947. Within the decade, an Italian succession had taken place there, too, and City Council President Vincent Impelliteri, running as an independent, was elected mayor in 1950. John Pastore became the first Italian American governor, when he was elected in Rhode Island in 1946, and the first Italian American U.S. senator four years later. By 1948 there were already eight Italian American members of Congress. While the Irish under Mayor Richard Daley continued to dominate Chicago politics for another generation, Slovenian American Frank Lausche was elected mayor of Cleveland in 1940, governor of Ohio, and in 1956 U.S. senator. Across the country, Mexican Americans struggled for recognition. Following a series of government maneuvers to harass and thwart their efforts during the late 1930s and 1940s, they established both MAPA (the Mexican American Political Association) and PASSO (Political Association of Spanish Speaking Peoples) in the 1950s and Viva Kennedy in 1960.

Kennedy's election, of course, was a culmination of the postwar ethnic politics. He largely defused the Catholic issue by proclaiming that he would act "without regard to outside religious pressure or dictate" and, if that were not possible, he would resign. He did receive 80 percent of the Catholic vote and at least that much of the Jewish vote; but only 38 percent of the Protestant vote, losing some areas where anti-Catholicism strongly persisted. It was a narrow victory but an ethnic triumph.

Overall, given the presence of different generations, there were undoubtedly those who had begun to emphasize religion more than nationality, to express a more symbolic or token ethnicity, and to embrace a "New Trinity" of Americanism, consumerism, and mass culture. Perhaps they were taking their cues from such popular television programs as *Father Knows Best*, *Leave It to Beaver*, and *Ozzie and Harriet*, with their idyllic portrayals of American life. And not without great irony, for, at the very time that immigrants were coming to be viewed as the archetypical Americans—classically portrayed in Oscar Handlin's epic history, *The Uprooted* (1951), and reaffirmed in the heightened reverence for the Statue of Liberty—many second-generation Americans were distancing themselves physically, emotionally, and culturally from those very homeland roots. No longer depicted as a social and cultural threat, immigrants and their children were now being seen more benignly, even sympathetically; no longer threatened and excluded, they themselves were now freer to realize their own American dreams.

So many changes were taking place; so many commentators were concentrating on the rush to the suburbs and what seemed like a flight from nationality to religion as the core of people's ties and identity. One could easily overlook the extent of ethnic persistence, which made less of a splash in the media and was less compelling news to outside observers. Even relocation from ethnic enclaves and neighborhoods to outlying areas and suburbs did not simply represent a divorce from one's ethnic group. In the socialization patterns between parents and children (and beyond them, with kin, peers, and community members, too)— what one historian called the "texture of life"—many ethnic-related attitudes, values, behaviors, priorities, family patterns, child-rearing styles, gender roles, religious orientations, food preferences, and even employment, friendship, and political choices continued to be transmitted or modeled. Networks of kin and compatriots were not all severed. Visits were often made to the old neighborhoods to attend church, see relatives and old friends, purchase favorite foods, and participate in traditional festivals. New organizations such as sports leagues and the Scouts mirrored those in the general community but were frequently composed of members of the same racial, religious, or nationality group.

In addition, the fact that the foreign-stock populations of most major cities still ranged from 30 percent to 50 percent of their total serves as a reminder that in many of those urban neighborhoods ethnicity undoubtedly endured. If, for example, one considers the "old" communities of the Dutch, such as in Grand Rapids, Michigan, and those who moved nearly *en masse* from

Chicago's Douglas Park and Lawndale west to Cicero, Berwyn, and Oak Park, one finds "clannishness even among the fifth and sixth generations." In fact, noted one historian in the late 1970s, it was still "possible for Dutch Americans to proceed from cradle to grave without leaving the primary associations of that ethnic community." In several New England cities, French Canadian communities also persisted; perhaps they were not as all-inclusive as those of the Dutch but they remained quite viable. Likewise, Polish Americans had "created one of the densest and most complete complexes of ethnic institutions of any group in America." Before the Second World War and after, they, too, could yet live their entire lives "in a Polish milieu."

In the early 1960s, from the older Jewish and Italian communities remaining in New York City to the Armenians in Fresno and the Japanese and Chinese in Honolulu and Hilo, there were ethnic communities that did not all "go the way of the suburbs"—that is, change residentially or culturally and lose much of what had made them distinctive. And many had no desire to do so. Maiu Sorro Espinosa, who fled from Estonia with her mother and arrived in 1951, observed, "One of my friends says that he feels that Estonia is like his mother, and he will always love his mother; but America is like his wife, and he wants to take care of her and dedicate himself and his energies to her. That is how I feel. . . ."

New Immigrants, New Americans, Old Issues

Unlike most new immigrants, who have searched for friends or relatives usually living with or near compatriots—not infrequently persons from the same place in the homeland—the foreigners who wed U.S. military personnel commonly joined those spouses in their communities throughout the country. These communities were not usually ones comprising persons of the immigrants' own ethnicity. Large numbers of European, Asian, and Australian women (and men) went through this particular kind of dispersion. Consequently, isolated and needing to acculturate rapidly, they not only had scarcely any impact on the ethnic communities of their own countrymen and women but they also often experienced greater stress than did other immigrants who were not so scattered.

Italian Ines d'Angelo married an Italian American, but when she met her in-laws, she reports, "I could not understand [them], either their English or their Italian, because they spoke a dialect that to me was a completely strange language." Even Isabel Heely, of Australia, found that "it was as hard to go from Australian English to American English as from a foreign language." In some cases, German and Japanese war brides met with hostility held over from the war. In others, the problem was the antimiscegenation laws, or the cultural shock of encountering the poverty of rural living, as happened to Lisa Slaughter, who left Hamburg for a Tennessee home that had no electricity, plumbing, or running water. Besides the many cultural differences and the absence of ethnic institutional support, "homesickness was a war bride's worst enemy," concluded researchers who had interviewed these women. Many marriages did not survive the personal and cultural strains that surfaced. Colette Montgomery was a French war bride who arrived in 1946, believing that nothing could be worse than was her family life at home. Instead, even she soon found reason to be homesick: "I didn't speak any English and my husband turned out to be an alcoholic. The marriage was a disaster, a total disaster. I had a brand-new baby and I was totally alone. I was living in Brooklyn with a baby, an alcoholic husband, and some hostile inlaws."

Even the comparatively rapid assimilation of (non-French) Canadians, English, Australians, and others with the cultural and personal resources to do so should not obscure the fact that not all migrants—or war brides, or refugees—did well or chose to remain. Many experienced poverty and problems of juvenile delinquency; suicides were not a rare phenomenon. Despair, of course, could be very real for those who came with education, training, and high expectations only to find them of little use in America. Paul Maracek and his family fled Czechoslovakia after the Communist takeover in 1948. They arrived in Detroit in 1949. He recalls his father's experience: "My mother and my father both had been guaranteed work . . . [But] even though he was a Doctor of Law, that was not recognized and even would not be equivalent to a bachelor's degree. . . . He tried getting a job, just as a dishwasher, and then he got a job at a Ford assembly plant." Eventually, he became an accountant, but "it was hard. . . . hardest for my father because he left his native country and his profession, his friends, and everything he had."

Notwithstanding the difficulties that were almost indistinguishable from the process of resettlement, tens of thousands of postwar refugees and immigrants entered their own ethnic communities, as did many Armenians, Greeks, Jews, Lithuanians, and Ukrainians. With others, for example, Colombians and Haitians, communities were being shaped by the new arrivals. In a few instances, as happened with the Serbs and Croats, the new meshed reasonably well with the old because the newcomers provided a leadership and community revitalization admired by the old-timers. In many other cases, as with the Greeks, Poles, and Chinese, the differences led to considerable friction, and the new members rather promptly established their own institutions.

Sometimes the source of the problem was that the postwar groups were better educated, more urbane, and often more politically active than the early arrivals. Other times it was a matter of significant religious differences, such as between the older Syrian Christians and the newer Arab Muslims. In the case of the small, prewar communities of Asian Indians, three-fifths of which were in California, they were made up principally of Punjabi Sikhs, along with those of other religions; but, due to their scant numbers, their differences had hardly been emphasized. The splitting up of Pakistan and India in 1947 carried over to America, where separate Pakistani and Hindustani organizations were soon formed. Most postwar migrants (1946–65: 6,371) simply bypassed the older communities. In the case of the Chinese, ideological differences were frequently reflected in the dialect differences between the older Cantonese-speaking generation and new Mandarin-speaking migrants. Another quite significant instance concerned the growing population from the West Indies, more than half of whom resided in New York City. Despite their color, there was limited racial unity with the existing African American community; religious and cultural differences divided them. They established separate communities, networks, and organizations and infrequently mixed or married with non-West Indian blacks. This was particularly true of the upper- and middle-class Haitians who began arriving in larger numbers during the late 1950s and 1960s to escape dictator François Duvalier.

In effect, one finds repeated examples where the gulf between the pre- and postwar migrants proved unbridgeable. Bitter exchanges and accusations divided the communities, and the newcomers felt compelled to create "a society within a society." Polish Americans were rather indifferent to the wartime experiences of the DPs and resented their lack of gratitude for the assistance Polish Americans provided. The new immigrants were nationalistic, anxious to restore their lost status, and somewhat condescending toward second generation Poles. They went their separate ways. Ukrainian refugees were no less set on creating their own institutions. But while they were less aloof than their Polish counterparts, they did not adapt well to American society, nor could they shake the conviction that they were only "communities in exile."

For many such peoples a vital part of their adjustment was their rapid involvement in public affairs tied to homeland issues, not at all unlike that by others after World War I. Among some, notably the Chinese and Portuguese, divisions over old-world issues not only carried over into postwar American communities, but those homeland governments actually intervened in them. Such was the case with the Kuomintang's efforts to solidify support in the Chinatowns and with the Salazar government's continuous propaganda directed at Portuguese in America. In contrast were those groups that actively campaigned to overthrow governments in their homelands, most often Communist ones, as was the case with those from various Eastern European states and the Chinese and Cubans. American Jews, on the other hand, were in the unique situation of not having come from the homeland they sought to establish and then secure, in Palestine. Jewish organizations raised an extraordinary $100 million in contributions in 1946 to aid Jewish resettlement there and an even more impressive $200 million two years later when the newly created state of Israel was fighting for survival. Not only did the new nation instill pride in American Jews but some five hundred per year acted upon that pride and emigrated to settle in Israel.

Immigrants and American Citizenship

The laws and court rulings discriminating against various non-white immigrants were gradually repealed between 1940 and 1952. With the shift to color-blind citizenship, the national government now recognized three classifications of persons (besides nationals residing in U.S. possessions): aliens, naturalized citizens, and native-born citizens. It had become very clear to foreigners during the previous decades that the alien status was increasingly a barrier to employment and eligibility for public relief. However, it also became quite evident to many during World War II and in the postwar era that a naturalized citizen was not quite equal to a person born in America. The Internal Security Act of 1950 and the McCarran-Walter Immigration and Nationality Act of 1952 had declared membership in an allegedly subversive group to be grounds for denaturalization and deportation as well as exclusion.

Perhaps Congress had the case of William Schneiderman in mind. A member of the Communist Party, he had become a citizen in 1927. In 1940, the government moved to denaturalize him on the grounds he lied at the time he applied. It lost on appeal in 1943, after efforts by J. Edgar Hoover to frame him. The Supreme Court ruled that mere membership was insufficient proof of a "clear, unequivocal, and convincing" danger. Since the Constitution did not enunciate a specific political philosophy, the Court added, any political statement—even a foolish one—was legitimate so long as it did not advocate violence. Then, in a 1950 decision, the Court reaffirmed the sovereign right of the government to determine the precise grounds for excluding applicants seeking admission: "Whatever the procedure authorized by Congress is, that is due process as far as an alien denied entry is concerned." Two years later, the Court went further, asserting that the right of an alien to remain was at the pleasure of the government, "which could terminate his stay at will." The repatriation movement of the 1930s and Operation Wetback certainly made that very clear.

Many immigrants felt exceedingly vulnerable because it was now apparent that acquiring citizenship was no certain protection against a government that was overreacting; it was, wrote legal scholar Milton Konvitz in 1953, "citizenship with strings," "neither free nor secure." These were expressions of a "restrictive nationalism"—a narrow conception of the national community. Nevertheless, in two areas a victory did take place for aliens during this period. In 1929, a well-known pacifist, Rosika Schwimmer, age forty-nine, had been denied citizenship because of her conscientious objections, her refusal to say that she would bear arms to defend the nation. Seventeen years later, in *Girouard vs. United States* (1946), the Court adopted the earlier dissenting view: Given that religious beliefs or those of conscience did not disqualify one for public office, they ought not, therefore, to disqualify an applicant for citizenship. The 1952 Immigration and Nationality Act included provisions for alternative service. In the second instance, decisions upholding Alien Land Laws in 1923 had caused great inconvenience and losses to Asians, as had other laws denying privileges and rights to "aliens ineligible for citizenship"—such as California's law denying them commercial fishing licenses. The Court struck that down in 1948. In that same year, in *Oyama vs. California* (1948), the Court disallowed California's confiscation of property that Frank Oyama had bought in his son's name. However, while declaring the Alien

Land Law "outright racial discrimination," it did not actually invalidate it. The category of ineligible aliens was eliminated by Congress in 1952.

Possession of citizenship as a qualification to engage in many occupations was another persistent problem for immigrants that continued through these years. For example, the fact that in Arkansas by the 1950s a person had to be a citizen to work as a barber, masseur, or peddler underscored the broadly based reality that citizenship could be essential for all kinds of substantial matters, including many types of employment—sixty-five different ones in 1946 and eighty-one in 1967. Many states required attorneys, physicians, pharmacists, dentists, and especially liquor dealers to be citizens. Likewise, Virginia imposed a citizenship prerequisite on pawn brokers, Louisiana on lobster fishermen, and New York on tree experts.

It was evident to many immigrants that there were certainly advantages to American citizenship. Sometimes, it was just a personal wish. Colette Montgomery "got very interested in the American political campaign of 1956. Actually that's why I became an American citizen, because I wanted to vote for [Adlai] Stevenson. . . . I became an American citizen on the fourteenth of July! That was my last Bastille Day as a French citizen. I was happy but at the same time, I was very nostalgic. I felt very peculiar." More generally, some groups continued to respond to the question of citizenship in rather consistent patterns. Mexicans and French Canadians, from contiguous homelands, consistently had lower rates of naturalization. Lower levels of education, the severe trauma of the repatriation, and a strong vein of patriotism stemming from the Mexican Revolution continued to dissuade most Mexicans from applying. Only 26 percent were naturalized in 1950, and, as of 1955, Mexicans had an average waiting period of nearly thirty-four years before acquiring American citizenship. On the other hand, refugees were one group usually eager for citizenship, especially if the probability of returning home were slim. In 1955, for example, two-fifths of all those naturalized were persons from countries falling under the Displaced

Persons Act of 1948, and the average waiting time for many of the nationalities was a mere six and one-half years. War brides were another category of persons particularly interested in citizenship. As spouses of citizens, they had only to wait three years rather than the usual five. Between 1949 and 1952, more than half of all those naturalized were spouses of U.S. citizens. One other group consisted of military personnel, who were again made immediately eligible for citizenship during the Korean War. Some 24,000 took advantage of that provision. Finally, there were those who had long waited, having been disqualified because of race. Compared to just 40 persons in 1952, 6,750 Japanese were made citizens in 1954 and 7,593 in 1955. They had an average waiting time of over thirty-eight years. Among the 538 Koreans naturalized in 1954–55, the average time was nearly forty years.

Overall, naturalized foreigners steadily increased from 47 percent of all foreign-born persons in 1920 to over 63 percent on the eve of war, and 74 percent in 1950. Between 1946 and 1965, over 2.15 million persons acquired American citizenship. The Germans, British, Italians, Poles, Russians, and Baltic peoples accounted for over 47 percent of those naturalized. In general, the lowest percentages of naturalized persons were among those from the Americas. (See Appendix, Table 6.4.)

In the final analysis, such numbers should not obscure the pride many felt when they acquired citizenship. Anna Laver recalled the judge saying to the others waiting for their final examination, in effect [and in her English], "'You see this woman? This woman just come from the old country but two years [?], and some of you come twenty years, and you don't know nothing. She pass. Okay, everything correct.' I got citizenship papers. Well, everyone look at me—that's true. I was bigger than a prize fighter."

This chapter has examined the state of immigrant and ethnic America at midcentury. We have seen that many who had survived the Depression and wartime eagerly took advantage of the postwar opportunities, often compromising their ethnic traditions in their quest for social mobility and respectability. Yet, moving to the suburbs did not always entail such a price, and children of immigrants did not simply drop their immigrant heritage at the city line. Moreover, many prewar immigrants still retained their culture, though modified over time, and many postwar newcomers brought with them a strong determination to build (or rebuild) ethnic communities. What one sees at midcentury, therefore, is an array of ethnic communities still spanning the spectrum of the immigrant ethnic experience: If there were those who were moving away from it, there were many others firmly holding on. Any portrait of immigrants in American society must recall all of these, just as it should note those newcomers eager for American citizenship and those more reluctant to switch nationalities.

To appreciate some of the impact on America of immigrants and their children across these middle years, one has only to recall how America came to a halt on Tuesday evenings in the 1950s so as not to miss Milton Berle's Texaco Hour; how many Americans were enchanted by Lucille Ball and her Cuban husband, Desi Arnez; how many swooned to the sounds of Frank Sinatra, Tony Bennett, Maria Callas, and Ezio Pinza—Italians all—or laughed at the antics of Jerry Lewis, Danny Kaye, or that Englishman Bob Hope, or later followed the TV life of the Lebanese American Danny Thomas; how many thrilled to the music of Aaron Copeland, or the conducting of Arturo Toscanini, George Szell, and Bruno Walter; or how many were mesmerized by the writings of Arthur Miller, Eugene O'Neill, and William Saroyan; how many were astonished by French Canadian Grace Metalious' *Peyton Place* or were drawn into the Beat Generation by the works of another French Canadian American, Jack Kerouac, or discovered identity crises through Erik Erikson, or childhood psychology with Buchenwald survivor Bruno Bettleheim. In all the arts and entertainment, as in the sciences and medicine, education and literature, immigrant and ethnic Americans were significantly enriching the nation between 1940 and 1965.

Ellis Island was closed on November 12, 1954, and the last detainee, a Norwegian seaman named Petersen who had missed his ship, was released; in actuality, the old sea ports had been replaced by airports. The following year an international conference of economists concluded that a revival of large scale emigration was unlikely and would not be a relevant solution for the problems of underdeveloped countries. Nevertheless, amidst the fragmentation, confrontation, and reformation of the 1960s, the next great era of American immigration was about to begin.

PART THREE

America in a Rimless World:
1965–1995

A recent teenage Soviet émigré living in Brooklyn reflected on the rainbow of ethnic groups there: "Where are the Americans is all I want to know? I haven't met any yet." A refugee from Ethiopia, Tesfai Gebremarian, commented on the irony he found in the astonishing diversity of peoples encountering each other in America. Following his arrival in August 1984, he obtained a job caring for patients in a Washington, D.C., hospital. "In Eritrea, for many years, my wife and I were fighting for our freedom against Cuban soldiers. Now that we have freedom in this country, I am taking care of Cubans. And even though I didn't have time to take advanced English classes, I was sent to Spanish classes by the hospital."

Who make up today's American diversity? A portrait of contemporary American ethnicity would include: Soviet Jews co-existing with Brooklyn's Irish, Italians, African Americans, and Puerto Ricans; Portuguese and Colombian factory workers crossing paths in Rhode Island; nonunion Chinese and Mexican women—legal and illegal immigrants—eking out a living as garment factory workers in Los Angeles; Nicaraguans carving out a Little Managua not far from the Little Havana of Miami; Hmong refugee families learning to farm Wisconsin land adjacent to long-resident Norwegians; and Asian Indian computer programmers creating software in the Silicon Valley near San Francisco, where other immigrants assemble the hardware.

America and American immigration policy have had to adjust to world events that have gone from postwar to postcolonial to post-Soviet. The appearance of new nations in the Caribbean, Africa, Asia, and the South Pacific, the collapse of the Soviet Union (1991), and the rapid end to the Cold War have constituted geopolitical events of immense magnitude. Global economic changes have brought postindustrial conditions to the United States and

Europe. Elsewhere, they have triggered expanding urbanization and disruptions of local economies due to modernization, the growth of new manufacturing centers, and the enormous movements of peoples and goods. Transportation and communication systems now encircle the world, redefining the realities of national borders and the dynamics of migration and immigrant networks. Worldwide telephone, FAX and electronic mail links have become the newest immigrant letters. These developments have taken the populations of more than 185 nations into regional economic systems and brought those systems beyond the Pacific and Atlantic rims to the threshold of a rimless world.

The price for such innovation has been a pace of change faster than many local political, economic, and social systems have been able to accommodate. Many displaced workers, including professionals and skilled workers underemployed or unemployed in their own homelands, have been compelled to migrate—frequently with the encouragement and assistance of their own governments. Tens of thousands of immigrants send home remittances that globally amount to billions of dollars, which support their families and, in turn, stimulate local economies. In relocating they have created communities connected to each other and to their homelands by trade, transportation, tourism, and technology—multipolar centers sustaining the movements of temporary and permanent newcomers. Yesteryear's birds of passage have become today's flocks of commuting and circular migrants.

Meantime, modernization has also made American culture virtually ubiquitous, acquainting peoples on every inhabited continent with the (supposed) incomparable opportunities of advanced capitalism in America. But the United States has not itself been left untouched by dramatic changes: That same ubiquitous culture has continued to exert enormous influence over many ethnic groups in the United States, inescapably reshaping their cultures and cohesiveness, for few can resist its pervasive presence. The expanding, technologically driven and more service-oriented economy has generated sustained demands for skilled and professional workers, affecting both the job prospects of newcomers and their children and the decisions of those still considering mi-

gration. The political maturation of more European, Latino, Asian, and now West Indian ethnic groups has altered the politics and policies of many local and state governments as well as expanded their presence at the national level. And the civil rights revolution has enabled many groups of immigrants and their children to be beneficiaries of advances originally designed to resolve great inequities in the lives of African Americans. American ethnicity near the end of the twentieth century remains as dynamic an unfolding story as it was at the beginning of the century.

CHAPTER SEVEN

In the Era of the Cold War and Beyond: Immigrants and Ethnics

Challenged by dramatic domestic and international developments, the United States embarked upon a series of immigration reforms as profound in their impact as those of the 1920s. First, Congress abandoned the National Origins System in 1965. Second, in response to the fall of Vietnam in 1975 and the exodus of refugees, Congress was compelled by 1980 to define a more coherent refugee policy. Third, after protracted debate, the government confronted its inability (and in some respects its unwillingness) to control more thoroughly the presence of undocumented aliens and enacted a sweeping amnesty program in 1986. Finally, in an effort to resolve the demands of many pressure groups, and at the same time to place an overall "cap" on admissions, Congress approved an omnibus immigration act in 1990.

Legislative Reforms: 1965–1986

The piecemeal erosion of the National Origins System since the end of World War II rendered obsolete what many Americans had come to feel was no longer necessary, namely severe restrictions on the ethnic composition of newcomers. The overhaul of that system was finally achieved by President Lyndon B. Johnson in 1965. However, the reforms were not intended to alter radically the country's foreign-born population—which had dropped from 14.7 percent of the nation's total in 1910 to merely 5.4 percent in 1960 (9.74 million persons). Indeed, congressional leaders of the bill explicitly argued that no such changes were anticipated. Still, what global events had made compelling, the Civil Rights Movement and other political realities had now made more expedient: a significant retreat from the earlier nativism—but not without compromises.

The Immigration and Nationality Act of October 1965 defined the procedures under which 15.53 million immigrants became admitted to the United States during the twenty-six fiscal years between 1966 and 1991.[1] It was then modified but not fundamentally altered by the Immigration Act of November 1990 (effective October 1, 1991), by which another 1.88 million were admitted in 1992–93. By way of contrast with a total of 17.4 million in those twenty-eight years, only 5.8 million had been admitted over the thirty-six years of the National Origins System.

The preferences were revised and made uniform for all the nations in the Eastern Hemisphere, abolishing the national origins formula and other provisions discriminating against Asians and Africans. The new ceiling of 170,000 visas contained a 20,000-per-country limit. As Figure 7.1 demonstrates, the 1965 Act now emphasized family reunification over job qualifications. In addition, it included a nonpreference option for those without family ties or needed skills and an adjustment of status option for those who entered as nonimmigrants and then applied for permanent residence—such as tourists, students, or temporary workers. With respect to immigrants from within the Western Hemisphere, the law imposed for the first time a maximum of

---

[1]Fiscal years: until 1976, July 1 to June 30, and thereafter October 1 to September 30.

| Figure 7.1 | Basic Preferences of the 1952 and 1965 Immigration Laws |

1952 (Cap: 154,657; later 156,487)	1965 (Cap: 170,000; later 290,000, in 1980, 270,000)
NONQUOTA: Spouses and minor children of citizens; inhabitants of Western Hemisphere; clergy. FIRST: Urgently needed skilled workers. 50% of quota SECOND: Parents of citizens. 30% of quota. Later, includes unmarried children of citizens. THIRD: Spouse and unmarried children of resident aliens. 20% of quota NONPREFERENCE: Siblings and older children of citizens. One-fourth of remaining visas. Later included married children of citizens and raised to 50% of remaining visas. "New Seed." Any remaining visas	NONQUOTA*: parents, spouses, minor children of citizens; clergy; and inhabitants of Western Hemisphere (the last deleted 1976) FIRST: Unmarried children of citizens and their children 20% of quota SECOND: Spouse and unmarried children of resident aliens. 20% of quota; in 1980, increased to 26%** THIRD: Members of professions and family. 10% of quota FOURTH: Married children of citizens and family. 10% of quota** FIFTH: Siblings of citizens and their families. 24% of quota** SIXTH: Needed skilled and unskilled workers and family. 10% of quota SEVENTH: Refugees. 6% of quota; deleted when the 1980 Refugee Act was passed. NONPREFERENCE: Remaining visas within the 20,000-per-country limit (scarcely available after 1976).

*Nonquota are now formally called immediate relatives and "special immigrants."

**Any unused visas from higher categories could be used by persons in the 2nd, 4th, & 5th categories.

120,000 persons. In 1978, Congress combined all the provisions into one uniform, worldwide system. Meanwhile, events following the upheavals in Cuba and Southeast Asia starkly revealed the absence of a coherent U.S. refugee policy and the presence of an ad hoc approach that had been almost entirely concerned with those fleeing Communist regimes. The Refugee Act of March 1980 incorporated the United Nations' definition of a refugee—any person unable or unwilling to return to his or her native land "because of persecution, or a well-founded fear of persecution"—and provided for a "normal" (but flexible) admission level of fifty thousand refugees per year. Also inserted into the bill was a new provision whereby each year five thousand persons already in the country could apply for political asylum.[2]

A year later, in 1981, the Select Commission on Immigration and Refugee Policy submitted to Congress a series of recommendations that included amnesty for undocumented aliens, along with sanctions against employers who knowingly hired such persons. Five years of intense debates and differing proposals pitted growers, unions, religious groups, African and Latino Americans, and anti-immigration lobbyists in varying alliances. The resulting Immigration Reform and Control Act of November 1986 (IRCA) was an extraordinary piece of compromise legislation. It provided for the legalization (amnesty) of both undocumented aliens continuously resident since January 1, 1982, and seasonal agricultural workers (Special Agricultural Workers, or SAW) employed for at least ninety days during the year preceding May 1986. All such applicants would have to take courses in English and American civics within two years before they could qualify for permanent residence. The act also provided for sanctions against employers who knowingly hired illegal aliens. Unrelated to amnesty was the introduction in the IRCA of a lottery program of five thousand visas for persons from countries "adversely affected" by the 1965 reforms—that

---

[2]Between 1981 and 1993, the yearly average of refugees and asylees admitted under this 1980 law was over 87,900.

is, nations that had been sending fewer than five thousand immigrants annually. Three million undocumented persons applied for amnesty under the IRCA; by October 1993, 88 percent had been granted permanent residence.

An Overview of Immigration, Documented and Undocumented: 1965–1995

From the perspective of nearly three decades, it is quite clear that the composition of the nation's newcomers was unexpectedly altered by the 1965 legislation, and, yet, the motives for migrating remained both somewhat new and classically traditional—and often ambivalent.

Ten-year-old Mario Lucci arrived from Italy with his mother in 1972. His father had come a few years before because, recalled Mario, "everybody said that the highways are paved with gold— that old story. Yeah, it's still going around." At about the same time, Dr. Karim Mohammed left his professorship and private practice in Cairo and brought his wife, Aziza, and children to Cleveland. After two years as an exchange professor, he decided to remain for the sake of the children: "The education is better, their future is better . . . more opportunity in the job market." In the United States "you know what will happen, you can plan for 50 years. . . . We don't know what the conditions in Egypt will be in two years. You can't plan." But Aziza then commented, "If you ask me if I'm sorry we came, I still wish I could have stayed in Egypt. . . . Yes, I do. I wish I could have been there with my family." While Rosalyn Morris had moved from Jamaica to Brooklyn at the same time the Mohammeds sold their home in Cairo, 1969, a dozen years later she declared that she would not go back. "To visit, yes, but not to live." Then, her daughter countered, "I am not an American citizen. I don't plan to become one and I'd rather go back to Jamaica where they don't have this big thing about color. I'm tired of being seen as just another black in a country where it is better to be white." Her mother dismissed the issue of prejudice because "my three children all go to college here in New York. I never dreamed of going to college."

The magnitude of the changes in American immigration since 1965 (when compared with the prior forty years) call to mind the turn of the century, when a multitude of new faces, in ever greater numbers, from ever more lands, flowed into the country, accompanied by a rather sizable outflow of those who had come as sojourners, temporary workers—"birds of passage"—and others returning who had not achieved their goals. While there are clearly some distinctive features in the immigration of the past three decades, parallels with the earlier era of mass immigration are also evident in the developments of five key factors.

First, a most outstanding indicator of the recent immigration revolution can be seen in *the broad array of countries* represented by the nation's newcomers and in *the shift in their regional origins.* In retrospect, the 1965 act had the effect of dramatically intensifying some of the changes that were already observed during the decade prior to the reform: the rising number of Asians and the increasing proportion from the Americas. As former colonies in Asia, Africa, and the Caribbean acquired independence, more and more of their citizens sought opportunities elsewhere, particularly those with more education: physicians, engineers, nurses, and other professionals. America's military presence in many nations also continued to generate immigrants who were the new spouses of U.S. military personnel. The conventional reasons for migration—political stability or civic upheavals, economic desperation or occupational ambition, and family reunification—likewise remained powerful forces exerting pressure on potential migrants. Once these processes were underway, migration networks emerged and reenforced the streams already in motion.

Table 7.1 illustrates the shifts that have taken place in the regional origins of America's immigrants since 1965. On a country level, using the most numerous nationalities for three different years, Table 7.2 readily shows how the composition changed between 1950 and 1990. In 1950, the influx of postwar refugees is apparent in the prominence of Poland, Latvia, Germany, and Lithuania. By 1970, old and new immigrants are both present as the 1965 law was first taking effect. The trends apparent by 1970

Table 7.1	Total Immigration: 1951–1965 versus 1966–1993, by Region of Birth	
	1951–65	1966–93
Total Immigration	3,965,791	17,408,177
Region		
Europe	53.1%	14.9%
Asia/Middle East	6.6	33.6
North/Central America	27.6	29.1
West Indies	6.7	13.5
South America	4.8	5.8
Africa	.7	1.4
Oceana	.6	.6

and 1980 continued in 1990, with Mexicans, Asians, and West Indians predominant, and two more refugee populations present, from Iran and the Soviet Union. Of the forty major sending countries for the whole period (1966–93) fifteen were Asian and Middle Eastern countries, nine were in the Americas, five in the West Indies, and only eleven in Europe. (See Appendix, Tables 7.2a and 7.3.)

Second, *the growth in the average yearly numbers* admitted has been dramatic, although still not at the level of the first decades of the century. On the average between 1951 and 1965, some 264,000 people entered each year. During the decade 1979–88, with the single system in place, an average of 570,000 were admitted. However, in 1990–91, because of the IRCA, more persons were admitted to permanent residence than in any other year in American history (1.54- and 1.83 million, respectively), surpassing the prior peak year of 1907.

Third, along with increasing immigration has been *persistent return (or, out-) migration*. The INS estimates that an annual average of 113,000 foreign-born persons emigrated during the 1960s, and that figure increased to approximately 133,000

Table 7.2   Leading Immigrant Groups at the Start of Each Decade, 1950, 1970, & 1990, by Country of Birth

1950		1970		1990 Non-IRCA Immigrants	
Poland	52,851 / 21.2%	Mexico	44,469 / 11.9%	Mexico	56,549 / 8.6%
Germany	31,225 / 12.5	Philippines	31,203 / 8.4	Philippines	54,907 / 8.4
Canada	18,043 / 7.2	Italy	24,973 / 6.7	Vietnam	48,662 / 7.4
Latvia	17,494 / 7.0	Greece	16,464 / 4.4	China/Taiwan	42,585 / 6.5
United Kingdom	13,437 / 5.4	Cuba	16,334 / 4.4	Dominican Republic	32,064 / 4.9
Lithuania	11,870 / 4.8	Jamaica	15,033 / 4.0	Korea	29,548 / 4.4
U.S.S.R.	10,971 / 4.4	United Kingdom	14,158 / 3.8	India	28,679 / 4.4
Italy	9,839 / 3.9	China/Taiwan	14,093 / 3.8	U.S.S.R.	25,350 / 3.9
Yugoslavia	9,154 / 3.7	Canada	13,804 / 3.7	Jamaica	18,828 / 2.9
Mexico	6,841 / 2.7	Portugal	13,195 / 3.5	Iran	18,031 / 2.7
All Others	67,462 / 27.1	All Others	169,600 / 45.4	All Others	300,908 / 45.9
TOTAL:	249,187	TOTAL	373,326	TOTAL	656,111

per year after 1980. In other words, about 3.47 million immigrants left between 1966 and 1993. That equals one-fifth of the total admitted for that period—less than during the early 1900s but still a significant proportion. This underscores the very dynamic, even circular, quality of contemporary American immigration, as was true for the period before 1924. Many more persons than most Americans would guess have continued to come with no intention of permanently settling. A great many West Indians, for example, assume that return migration is simply part of their whole migration process, and they "shuttle" between island and mainland residences.

Fourth, there has been a sizable *increase in step migration*, whereby migrants use the provision allowing nonimmigrants such as tourists, students, refugees, businesspersons, fiance(e)s, or temporary workers to apply for an adjustment of status to that of permanent resident after having entered the United States.[3] Between 1972 and 1985, to cite one period, 30 percent of "newcomers" were already present in the country, principally refugees and tourists. By the early 1990s, this group had grown to 36 percent. After deducting that percentage and those who received amnesty during those years, only one in seven had actually arrived as a new immigrant. The process of step migration has also involved those who have resided in other countries before gaining admission to the United States. It has been suggested that those who go through such "indirect migration" tend to acclimate to a new environment and begin the process of acculturation more easily than those who arrive with no prior migration experience.

Fifth, more so than previously, there have been important *shifts in terms of the cities or ports through which newcomers have entered* and where they have settled. In the decade prior to 1966, over two-fifths of all immigrants were processed in New York City, and under one-tenth at the various Pacific ports. By the

---

[3]In a comparable sense, prior to the 1920s, it was not uncommon for migrants to make several trips as sojourners before deciding to settle permanently. For decades after that time, however, this was much less the case.

early 1980s, three out of ten were being admitted in Pacific ports of entry and only about one-fifth in New York City. Although New York remains the premier portal to America for new arrivals, Los Angeles has become second. In terms of destination, a comparable shift to California has occurred. By 1982–94, one-third or more were planning to live in California and under 15 percent in New York State. High numbers of immigrants also listed an intended residence in Texas, Florida, Illinois, New Jersey, and Massachusetts. Over three-quarters of the nation's immigrants were heading to just seven states.

In 1986, a thirty-three-year-old woman from Jalisco explained why she left Mexico for Los Angeles: "My father worked a long time here in the U.S. He came here during the time of the braceros. He used to tell us children that it was beautiful here. . . . I wanted to be the one to come here, to live here, to be able to tell the family how it was here. I was 16 or 17 when I left." She came initially as a tourist and overstayed. At about the same time, thirty-five-year-old Rosa Maria Urbina described how she had made daily trips across the Rio Grande from Ciudad Juarez to El Paso, where she was a housekeeper. She had had to leave her three children in a Mexican orphanage for lack of money:

There are men who carry people across the river on their shoulders. The water is kind of rough, but that's what these men do to make a living. They charge [$1.50 to $2.50]. The water is up to their chest. . . . Suppose I am caught by the patrolmen at seven thirty in the morning. They will take me to the station and hold me for a few hours, then bus me back to Juarez. I would walk back to a crossing point and try once again. It is like a game. I think the most times I was ever caught was six times in one day. No matter how many times they catch me, I keep coming back.

A problem that appeared to have gone away in the early 1960s, the illegal alien issue reemerged as soon as the *Bracero* program was terminated in December 1964. During that fiscal year, the number of illegal aliens apprehended jumped to 111,000. Over the next twenty-eight years (1966–93), 17.4 million immigrants were legally admitted, but 25.1 million apprehensions of undocumented aliens were made (many, of course, repeated apprehensions of the same persons). During the decade 1983–92, for example, 93 percent were Mexican. For Mexicans, the channels of migration—legal, temporary, and illegal—are carved so deeply over so long a time that they have become commonplace options for millions south of the border.

Thus, it is not surprising that INS apprehension data include many repeaters. In fact, a 1990 study concluded that "all migrants who attempt undocumented entry into the United States eventually get in, and IRCA has not changed this basic fact." There are few other places in the world where a border separates two such economically disparate countries and where the pressures to migrate on one side at least equal the demands for cheap labor on the other—where a high rate of population growth, severe poverty and unemployment drive men and women north, even in the face of growing American resistance. Guadalupe, in the Mexican state of Michoachan, in 1979 illustrates the situation. In this town eight hundred miles from the border, 88 percent of 465 families had at least one member who had migrated northward. At that time, four-fifths were "in some way dependent on wages earned in the United States." A decade later, another study of two larger communities, in the state of Guanojuato, found an almost 90 percent certainty of men in their earlier twenties going north, illegally or otherwise. In early 1995, in the small town of Tlacuitapa, far to the south of the border, nearly everyone knew of the passage of California's Proposition 187 directed against illegal aliens and the stepped-up efforts of the U.S. Border Patrol (see below). Yet, three-fourths of those polled said those measures would have no effect on their plans to work in California. Devaluation of the peso, inflation, and soaring prices for food and agricultural supplies were adding to the people's sense of desperation.

The "miracle" economic growth of Mexico from the 1940s to the 1970s had already begun to falter with falling oil prices, and that growth cycle then collapsed entirely in 1981–82, followed over the next decade by hyperinflation and declining purchasing power. Although many people had initially migrated to the cities and into manufacturing, and a sizable middle class had developed, some thirty million people remained in poverty. That figure climbed to over forty-one million by 1987. Thus, in reality the "miracle" had not significantly lessened the pressures to migrate, and continuing crises in the mid-1990s intensified the desperate quest for dollars. Even natural disasters such as the 1985 earthquake in Mexico City have added to the impetus to go north. Moreover, the failing economy was also hurting the new middle class, and, during the 1980s, changes in the composition of Mexican migrants became apparent, as more urban persons, females, families, and others intending to "settle out" permanently joined the northward trek.

As one Mexican scholar put it: "More Mexicans began to migrate from a wider variety of geographic areas and a broader spectrum of social classes." A community in the state of Jalisco, studied in 1988–89, provides another case study. In Jalisco, the earlier majority that had worked in agriculture were, in contrast, "now outnumbered by those who go to Oklahoma City to work in highway and bridge construction, those who go to Las Vegas and Palm Springs to work in hotel and restaurant industries, and those who migrate to the San Francisco Bay area to work in light industry and services." In fact, a leading expert on Mexican migration observed in 1990 that "Most Mexican migrants to California today—both legal and unauthorized—are being absorbed into the urban service, construction, light manufacturing, and retail commerce sectors. In the service sector, Mexicans work primarily as janitors, dishwashers and busboys, gardeners, hotel workers, maintenance and laundry workers in hospitals and convalescent homes, car washers, house cleaners, and child-care providers." Likewise affecting the job patterns are demands by more employers for low-wage women factory workers, especially in the garment industry, and by growers who have expanded their operations to year-round.

Although the number of undocumented Mexican migrants is large and the media attention to their continuous efforts to cross the border is extensive, such illegals are not alone. The INS now reports an average of over 160 countries of birth represented among those people apprehended each year for being in

Above: Prospective immigrants lined up outside U.S. consulate in Warsaw, 1920
Right: Aerial view of Ellis Island, 1921. Foreground: hospital and other facilities; background: the great hall through which immigrants were processed

Right: Charles Petioni, seated, with his brother and sister, prior to his departure from Trinidad and Tobago for the United States, 1918. A journalist in his homeland, he became a doctor in New York City.

XV

Halahan, 1921

THE ONLY WAY TO HANDLE IT.

Above: Cartoon by Hallahan, endorsing the Emergency Quota Act of 1921
Opposite, at Ellis Island. Top: A Hungarian woman and child, January 1925. Middle:
A group of immigrants arriving, 1920s. Bottom: An interpreter assisting a newcomer,
1926.

XVII

Roy Perry, 1937

The urban environment in which many immigrants first adjusted to America. Here, Pitt and Rivington Streets in Manhattan

Above: The trial of immigrants Nicola Sacco (right) and Bartolomeo Vanzetti (center) for murder captured widespread attention in America and Europe partly because of questionable evidence and court procedures. They were executed in 1927.
Right: Al Smith, New York governor and the first Irish Catholic candidate for U.S. president

Top: Mayor Anton Cermak (seated), builder of one of Chicago's first multiethnic coalitions, was killed by an assassin's bullet intended for president-elect Franklin D. Roosevelt in early 1933. Bottom: Italian immigrant entrepreneur, Joseph Cipriani, in his grocery store in Chicago Heights, 1920s

Top: Ukrainian women displaying traditional costumes at the 1933 Chicago World's Fair. Bottom: A strike committee organized by Filipino workers during the 1930s. By this time, Filipinos had begun to increase their labor activities throughout the West (as well as in Hawaii).

Top: After Pearl Harbor, the Hollywood Association began a campaign to oust Japanese, encouraging a growing public sentiment (winter of 1941-42). Bottom: Under military guard, Japanese Americans were forced to evacuate their homes along the West Coast and relocate by train to ten concentration camps (spring 1942).

Above: One of the more than 20,000 Japanese Americans who fought during World War II, *Nisei* Nisashi Nakashima, from Hawaii, is here being greeted by his mother and wife upon his return in 1945.
Right: Sgt. William Best, who took part in the liberation of a Nazi concentration camp (Buchenwald, 1945), found and then adopted a 16-year-old orphaned survivor. Best is here greeting his son, Joseph Gottesman, now 19, who was among the first boatload of DPs, arriving on December 24, 1948.

Top: Hungarian refugees December 15, 1956, first to arrive under a new provision for temporarily "paroling" refugees into the country
Bottom: Little Italy, New York City, 1970s. Note elements of both the immigrant past (curbside push carts and Caruso's market) and present (signs of the expanding Chinese community).

Top: Cuban refugees fleeing across the Florida Straits used any means available. Here a group of men linked together three huge rubber tubes as a raft during the early 1960s.
Right: A Cuban refugee child awaits a new future in the United States, circa 1963.

Scenes from a new Ellis Island: Los Angeles International Airport, a major port of entry for nearly four decades. Procedures have changed since the 1910s and early 1920s, yet some similarities remain. Opposite top: INS officials check the documents newcomers have brought with them, 1985. Middle: Interpreters are still needed to assist immigrants arriving (see p. XVII). Bottom: Like Ellis Island newcomers decades earlier, most immigrants continue to arrive with huge tied-up bags of possessions, as has this Asian Indian couple.

Top: Since the 1950s, thousands of Korean orphans have been adopted by Americans. Here, a young Korean girl with her tiny red backpack, just arrived, awaits transfer to her new family, 1985.

East Los Angeles, 1980

New York City, 1986

Brooklyn, 1986

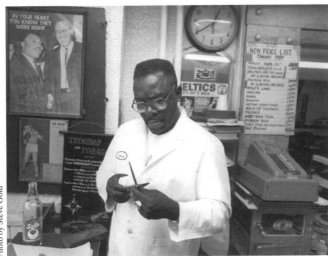

Photo by Steve Gold

Miami, 1980s

Businesses of immigrants: Opposite top: Mexican shoestore owners proudly identify their Guadalajara origins. Middle: The meticulously prepared displays of Korean green grocers have become a common sight, especially in New York City. Bottom: The arrival of many new immigrants from the West Indies has sparked the appearance of markets providing the specialty goods desired by newcomers from the Caribbean.

Top: West Indian immigrants have opened a variety of businesses catering to fellow migrants and others, as did this Trinidadian barber in Boston, 1992. Bottom: Political ties as well as business ties to homelands remain. Here, a government-in-exile sign on this building proclaims the persistent determination that many Cubans have had to pursue the overthrow of Fidel Castro.

Top: Along the Mexican border, people have employed virtually every method for illegal entry into the United States, including being tied to the undercarriage of an automobile, as was this thirteen year old, apprehended in the act ca. 1979.

Bottom: Mexican harvest workers, 1968. Mexicans have played crucial roles in American agriculture, predominantly in the Southwest but increasingly in other regions as well.

Top: Many South Vietnamese immigrants started their journey to the U.S. as refugees who began fleeing their homeland in the hundreds of thousands in 1975. Here, a family of Vietnamese boat people has arrived safely in Thailand.

Bottom: For Southeast Asians the culture gap between their former lives and that in America has been stark. Here, an older Vietnamese woman strolls in a shopping mall area near Los Angeles still dressed in her traditional Vietnamese clothing.

Thailand, late 1970s

Westminster, CA, 1980s

Top: Immigrants from the Pacific Islands have steadily increased in recent decades, with Samoans (shown here leaving church) the most numerous of them. Right, this group of American-dressed young Samoan girls shows the effects of acculturation, especially compared to the older generation (left) in traditional garments.

Bottom: The persistence of ethnicity: a young Polish American man active in an older European American community, Hamtramck, Detroit, 1981

Photo by Steve Gold

Top: Another growing ethnic group is represented here by this Arab business in Detroit, where many Palestinians and others from the Middle East have settled, 1981.

Bottom: Also from the Middle East, this group of Israeli Yemenis, Los Angeles, 1991, represents one of the many newer populations arriving since the 1960s.

Photo by Steve Gold

Top: A "pseudo-family," a household of nonrelated Vietnamese boat people (most often, men only), here share an apartment in Oakland, CA, 1983.

Bottom: A new group that has grown significantly during the past three decades, Armenians have now concentrated in Los Angeles. Here, Michael operates his Armenian deli on Hollywood Boulevard, 1987.

Hollywood, CA, 1987

Artesia, CA, 1980s

Top: Immigrants have been quick to organize to facilitate their adjustment to America and to preserve their ethnic ties. Here, a group of older Armenian boy scouts, with their leaders.

Bottom: Asian Indians are another group that has grown tremendously during the past three decades. They come from a number of different regions of India and have been unusually dispersed in the United States. In one large community, this Sikh man runs his Bombay Spices grocery shop.

Los Angeles, 1980s

New York City, 1995

Monterey Park, CA, 1980s

New York City, 1969

Opposite: The convergence of numerous ethnic groups in urban centers. Los Angeles was a key destination for Salvadoran and Guatemalan refugees from civil wars (top), and many refugees from the Soviet Union in the last two decades have settled in Los Angeles and New York (middle). Bottom: A handmade sign (English, Spanish, Chinese, and Vietnamese) inside a pharmacy in a largely Asian community in Southern California.

Above left: The political maturation of the great turn-of-the-century migration is represented here by a postelection gathering for Italian American Mario Procaccino after his attempt to become mayor of New York. Right: Having come to the political forefront in Hawaii in the 1950s, Asian Americans have also emerged as one of the newer politically active groups on the mainland during the past quarter century. Pictured here, Monterey Park's city councilwoman, Judy Chu, a psychologist, also served twice as its mayor.

Editorial cartoonist Steve Benson captured the resurgence of antiimmigrant sentiments in August 1993, which had been sparked by the seizure earlier of a freighter grounded off Long Island with over 200 illegal Chinese aboard.

See photo credits, p. 261.

the United States illegally—from Guatemalan Mayans to Pakistani Muslims. During the spring and summer of 1993, news reports focused on ships hired by Chinese gangs to smuggle in young Chinese men. In some cases, after having circled more than half-way around the globe, these freighters' crews were trying to drop their human cargoes in San Francisco, or off of Long Island, New York, and elsewhere. Some ships were apprehended, a few ran aground, and many appear to have succeeded. In September 1993, the *New York Times* reported 490,000 illegal aliens in New York State, 80 percent of them in New York City. Relatively few were Mexicans or Chinese. The largest groups were Ecuadorans, Italians, Poles, Dominicans, Colombians, Haitians, Jamaicans, and Israelis. Scenes of boatloads of illegal Chinese being smuggled into the country in 1993 raised concerns, but, actually, more illegal Italians than Chinese were present.

Public anxieties and the level of political rhetoric rose considerably by mid-1993 in reaction to both the accounts of rusting ships run aground, filled with illegal Chinese aliens, and the images of borders seemingly "out of control." Massive efforts by the Border Patrol to stem the tide in El Paso, Texas, and San Ysidro, California, and to intercept Chinese boat smugglers appear only to have forced smugglers with their cargoes of Latinos, Asians, and others into taking more circuitous routes—and usually charging higher prices for their services. The Chinese were charging their young fares twenty thousand dollars each and more, and other foreigners were willing to pay such prices, too. Meanwhile, thousands of Irish, Pakistanis, Filipinos, and many others continued to enter, overstay their visas, and begin the covert, insecure lives of illegal aliens.

In October 1992, between 3.2 and 3.8 million undocumented aliens were estimated to be in the country, with that number rising by about one-quarter million each year. Only three-tenths of those in 1992 were calculated to be Mexican; half were "overstayers"—people legally admitted (usually as tourists) from any country, who had failed to depart. The illegal alien issue is, therefore, neither entirely a Mexican one nor entirely a border problem.

Female Immigration

That the majority of immigrants since the late 1920s has been female represented a "femininization" of the nation's newcomers following the enactment of restrictive immigration laws. This has indicated, primarily, the emphasis immigrants place on creating or reuniting families and, secondarily, the willingness of more women to use migration to improve their fortunes and/or those of their families. As before the 1920s, the proportions of women immigrants reflect the culture and conditions of their homelands (that either permit or encourage migration, or actively discourage it). The greater or lesser presence of women directly affects their communities and the roles these women play in America. Besides their obvious importance in fostering family life, it is frequently the women who create the networks binding the ethnic neighborhoods, and it is their increasing economic contributions—putting in "double days" as paid workers and as wives and mothers, and thus contributing both their productive and reproductive labor—that have unavoidably compelled many immigrant men to confront the challenges to their traditional preeminence in the family. For example, Vietnamese male refugees liked to say that "In Vietnam the man of the house is king. Below him the children, then the pets of the home, and then the woman. Here [in America], the woman is the king and the man holds a position below the pets." That may not have been the exact scenario, but such speakers expressed a widespread sense that traditional homeland arrangements were not always surviving well in the new environment.

Three things have become much clearer in recent years with respect to female migration. First, there have persisted distinctive differences among many groups in terms of the proportion of females migrating. In addition to the fact that men more often initially entered as nonimmigrants (visitors, students, and temporary workers) or came from other, intermediate countries, economic and cultural preferences within particular groups have frequently resulted in greater percentages of males arriving (as among Greeks, Iranians, Egyptians, Ghanaians, and especially

Mexicans). Other groups were equally likely to have had steady majorities of females (for example, among Chinese, Koreans, Dominicans, Jamaicans, Colombians, and especially Filipinos because so many came as nurses). Others shifted toward a fairly even distribution or fluctuated in their ratio of female to male (as among Canadians, Poles, and those from the former U.S.S.R.). Second, during the past three decades, within many groups, particularly Asians, men took advantage of the new opportunities created by the legislative reforms, arrived first in great numbers, and thereafter began sponsoring their wives. Then, together, couples have been bringing over parents, many widowed. Thus, during the 1970s, 53 percent were females. It then appeared as if a "remasculinization" was taking place in the 1980s, for only 46 percent of immigrants were female between 1982 and 1992—with nine of the eleven years having more males admitted.[4] That two-thirds were males in 1991, the year of the largest number of immigrants admitted in U.S. history, provides one of the two clues to those unusual years. At the outset, many more Southeast Asian refugees were males, a pattern that began to change by the end of the 1980s. More decisively, the overwhelming numerical dominance of Mexican males largely accounted for those majorities, especially among those legalized under IRCA (1989–92). With that largely completed by 1992 and those men now permitted to petition for their immediate families, a swing occurred, with far more Mexican women entering in 1993. A similar shift had already begun with other groups, notably Indians, Iranians, and Pakistanis.

The third and rather revealing consequence of many women being admitted as wives who then find it necessary to obtain a job (along with single women who came for that purpose, Filipinas being the foremost case) is that they almost uniformly found it to be a liberating experience. They were out of the house more often, and they began to enjoy their freedom

---

[4]Incomplete INS records in the early 1980s also contributed somewhat to this overall impression.

and to insist upon a greater say over the family budget. Although frequently burdened with the dual work roles of being wife and mother as well as breadwinner, they have made renegotiation of roles and relationships commonplace. With that enhanced status, many women who had initially come temporarily became ever more reluctant to return home or to those former roles. A Hmong man, Shoua Vang, explained: "Some Hmong women would like to copy American women, who have much more social mobility and independence from their families. Back in the home country, I didn't have to do any cooking or house cleaning. Not only that—my wife had to wash my feet. But now I help do the laundry, cook and do housecleaning because my wife is working in the factory. This is a big adjustment for me, but I understand her situation."

Where their spouses resisted, more women were inclined to go it alone. Some single women saw their income as a means of insuring their sexual independence; others simply refused to get married. Deborah Padmore, from Trinidad, explained her marriage break up succinctly: "And coming here and earning my own money made me more independent than I was born. . . . But that had a *lot* to do with it, coming here. I started working for my own money, and I started making a lot of friends and seeing and observing. . . ." Some came to aid their families back home, some to escape them. Not uncommonly, homeland conditions convinced couples to migrate, as have many from the Dominican Republic, in order to preserve their middle-class status at home—even if it often meant that the woman had to do domestic work or take menial jobs, or that both spouses held jobs in the secondary labor market in the United States (manufacturing, services, hotels, restaurants, unskilled jobs). Frequently mentioned, too, is the willingness of women to suffer these jobs, and the low-wage neighborhoods that co-exist with the low-wage industrialization, in order to provide educational opportunities for their children. Networks of friends and kin have played a crucial sustaining part in the process of adaptation for such women. Large numbers of Chinese and Central American women in the west, for example, and Jamaican, Colombian, and

Portuguese women (along with Puerto Ricans) in the east, have relied upon their networks to obtain jobs in garment, toy, jewelry, electronic, and other light (or work-bench) industries. They have furnished the cheap labor that has enabled many businesses to survive although drastic declines in the manufacturing sector occurred, especially in New York City during the 1970s and 1980s. Although many Asian Indian, Filipino, and Soviet women have come with substantial education and have often sought white-collar and professional positions, at their level, networks tend to be less critical. Nevertheless, even such well-educated women have often faced the obstacles of language and lack of professional accreditation in their new country, which have forced them to accept the otherwise unacceptable. A Chinese physicist, who came to the United States in 1976 and worked as a factory seamstress, described the scene: "We are all college graduates, but working in sewing or electronics factories. . . . we are lucky to find work—any work we can do."

The Immigrant Experience

The variety of patterns involving women's migration, jobs, and family roles illustrates not only the way recent immigration has undergone continual changes but also the strains experienced by those who uproot themselves in quest of new lives—both personal strains and those between recent newcomers, older immigrants, and the American-born generations. Asian Indians, Soviet Jews, and Poles are among the many whose recent travails capture this aspect of immigration and ethnicity.

A small number of Punjabi Sikhs in California, cut off from further immigration in the 1920s, wed Mexican American women in whose names land holdings could be placed.[5] Subsequent immigrants from India responded to the Punjabi-Mexican offspring with "consternation and disbelief," regarding them as "halfbreeds." The new immigrants felt "threatened by the Punjabi-

_____

[5]Alien land laws prevented the Punjabi men from owning land, and anti-miscegenation laws prohibited them from marrying white women.

Mexican descendants and [were] anxious that their own children remain 'true to their culture.'" The Punjabi-Mexican Americans likewise felt apprehensive and viewed the "new Hindus" as resisting integration. When a new *gurdwara* (Sikh temple) was opened in Yuba City in 1970, "the Asian wives accused the Hispanic ones of poisoning the chicken curry." In a further ironic twist, near Phoenix, Arizona, Spanish-Pakistani descendants were officers of the Muslim Asians of America, but most were actually Methodists, Mormons, and Catholics!

In 1988, the United States pressured the Soviet Union to ease its emigration laws (as it had done in 1974), and, encouraged by the collapse of the Soviet Union in 1991, doubled the number of authorized refugee admissions. Between 1988 and 1993, over 259,000 Soviet refugees entered the country, compared with merely 7,200 during the prior five years. However, significant differences readily emerged between the larger Jewish American communities and the more than 86,000 foreign-born Israelis and one-quarter million Soviet Jews. Jewish Americans' organizations sponsored most Soviet Jewish refugees with a goal of integrating them rapidly into their local communities. But, it appears, they knew too little about the Soviet environment and its impact on Soviet Jews, many of whom were Jewish only to the extent that it had been so stamped on their identification papers. While the Soviet Jews have been grateful for the assistance they have received, cultural differences have led to numerous mutual misunderstandings between them and Americans. As a San Francisco Bay area activist told a Jewish American interviewer, "we are not like your grandparents, people from Sholom Aleichem. We are educated, professional people. . . . Right now, I try really to impress on American community, for us, Jewishness is non-religion." Another added that they want to be "free from all organizations, because there is no freedom in Russia this way." Israelis, though not refugees, have expressed similar attitudes of strong nationalism and a secular, nonorganizational approach to their relations with other Jews. Informal networks count most for both groups, and so the cultural chasms have persisted.

Finally, during the past half century, Polish Americans have experienced the impact of several waves of newcomers, each somewhat different than the prior ones due in considerable measure to the period during which they grew up in Poland. Earlier, there had been friction between DPs and prewar Polish Americans. Between 1953 and 1980, over 174,000 more Poles entered the country, many of whom were urban, educated under Communism. The gulf between them and the prewar generation became most apparent when, following the imposition of martial law in Poland in 1981 and the efforts to crush the Solidarity union movement there, over 67,000 additional Poles were legally admitted (1981–89).[6] These newest newcomers found themselves so at odds with those in the Polish American communities that they, too, created their own organization in 1982, *POMOST*, to express their hope for changes in Poland.

As was the case earlier, recent immigrants have significantly expanded the number of ethnic communities, from Dominicans and Jamaicans in New York City to Koreans and Mexicans in Chicago to Armenians and Iranians in Los Angeles. But it is the refugees of the past thirty-five years who have far exceeded those refugees admitted after World War II in numbers and diversity: Among them, Cubans, Haitians, and Nicaraguans in south Florida, Soviet Jews in Brooklyn and West Hollywood, Vietnamese in Seadrift (Texas) and San Jose and Westminster (California), and Iranians and Salvadorans in Los Angeles. Although they share many patterns with other immigrants, differences have emerged, particularly as a result of the horrific experiences that compelled many of them to flee.

A young Sri Lankan scholar was interviewing Cambodians regarding the escape from their homeland. She asked Look Tha, a former Buddhist monk, to recount the atrocities perpetrated by the Khmer Rouge that took the lives of an estimated one-fifth of Cambodia's seven million people (April 1975–January

---

[6]During the 1980s, Poles were also the foremost European group among those both entering and remaining illegally in the United States.

1979). He declined to do so. "When I asked him about those experiences, he replied that he could not relate them because his English was not good enough. When I asked him to tell me in Khmer, his answer was that my Khmer was not good enough." She spoke, too, with a thirty-nine-year-old Cambodian woman, whom she called Pu Ma, or friend. As they talked about her experience,

Slowly, Pu Ma took the photographs from my hand and gazed with immense tenderness at the picture of her husband, who was murdered by the Khmer Rouge. With tears welling up in her eyes, she caressed his face slowly. She uttered no sound, but the indescribable sadness that spread over her face conveyed all the pain she felt. For the first time I realized I may never understand the pain and suffering the Cambodians endured because of the holocaust; and I was humbled by the courage and humanity with which they bear it.

The Hmong of Laos, the Eritreans from Ethiopia, the Afghanis, and the Guatemalans are also among those who have fled conditions of great horror, anguish, and fear, though not on the scale of death in Cambodia. Political refugees during the past three decades from America's other Cold War enemies, most notably from Cuba, China, the former Soviet Union, Nicaragua, Vietnam, Poland, and Rumania, have had to escape their own forms of barbarities and oppression. Over nine-tenths of the three million refugees admitted (1946–94) have been those fleeing Communist regimes; the major exception were Iranians in the 1980s. Although the nation's refugees since 1960 have ranged from preliterate Guatemalan Indians and Laotians who had never seen electrical appliances and indoor plumbing to Soviet scientists and Cuban air force pilots, in many instances it has been the elites and middle classes who have most frequently escaped first. They had the resources and socioeconomic background that would facilitate their adaptation in America. So many among the first wave of Cubans had been accustomed to vacationing in Florida prior to 1960 that they were regarded as off-season tourists who were initially viewing their flight to Miami as an extended vacation. Prior to 1979, Iranians who would subsequently escape the Muslim fundamentalist takeover after the ouster of the Shah had already been transferring billions of dollars out of their country. That enabled many of these Sunnis, Zoroastrians, Christians, Baha'is, and Jews to establish a "Golden Exile," especially in California, where a majority of Iranian Americans resided in 1990. They fondly refer to their principal communities as Irangeles and Persian Hills.

Not only the refugee policy was directed at pro-Communist regimes; even the 1980 provision for 5,000 asylees each year was applied in the same manner. Permanent residence was granted to nearly 89,000 applicants (1980–93), but the bias was most glaring in the treatment of Haitians versus Cubans as well as Guatemalans and Salvadorans versus Nicaraguans: From 1984 to 1992, three-tenths of asylee visas were awarded to Nicaraguans fleeing the left-wing Sandinistas and merely 4 percent to Guatemalans and Salvadorans escaping right-wing, U.S.-backed governments. Law suits were successfully pursued to force a change in INS policy that would delay the deportation of illegal Salvadorans and Guatemalans and provide for a review of their asylum applications by late 1994. Efforts to forestall their forced departure continued into 1995.

Refugees and asylees have frequently drawn public attention because of the dramatic episodes involving their efforts to enter or remain in the United States. The incidences involving Cubans, Haitians, and Southeast Asians have been among the most riveting. In April 1980, about 10,000 Cubans stormed the Peruvian embassy in Havana seeking asylum. Castro opened Mariel port and declared that any who wished to could leave. During the next five months the spectacular "Freedom Flotilla," a vast array of boats chartered by prior Cuban exiles, brought nearly 125,000 people to Florida. Nearby, beginning in 1972, following the death of Francois "Papa Doc" Duvalier in 1971 and the succession of his young son, Jean-Claude, Haitians eager to flee their island homeland had also begun the perilous journey in small boats across six- to seven-hundred miles of open sea to Florida. Between 1977 and 1981, approximately

60,000 Haitians survived the crossing (and possibly as many did not), with a peak of nearly 25,000 landing in far more desperate conditions in 1980 than did the *marielitos* arriving at the same time. Most Cubans were immediately processed and taken in by the Cuban community, whereas by then some 45,000 Haitians had been detained on the grounds that they were economic not political refugees. Most were eventually allowed to remain, but, for these Haitian "entrants," acquiring permanent status proved to be a long struggle.

During the next seven years (1981–87), 21,000 Haitians were intercepted at sea and most were returned to Haiti. In 1991, desperately trying to flee grinding, hopeless poverty, 90 percent unemployment, and oppressive military dictatorship, possibly as many as 40,000 Haitians took to the boats again. At first detained at Guantanamo Naval Base, 23,000 were ordered repatriated by President Bush. President-elect Clinton ordered the Coast Guard to prevent refugee boats from leaving Haitian waters. In May 1994, he reversed policy and, during the early summer, Haitians took to the sea once more, desperately crowding small boats. In a period of two months, hundreds drowned, and over 21,000 were picked up by the U.S. Coast Guard and placed in detention at Guantanamo Bay. With the restoration to power of elected president Jean-Bertrand Aristide in mid-October, most of the Haitians who had not already volunteered to return were brought back to their homeland; few were given asylum.

Again, by stark comparison, over 2,500 Cuban *balseros*— "raft people"—had been taken aboard by the Coast Guard in 1992 and given immediate admission under the Cuban Refugee Adjustment Act of November 1966. In 1993, a Cuban pilot, who hijacked his own passenger plane, taking it to Miami with fifty-two on board, was also given asylum at once and not prosecuted for air piracy. Toward the end of the year, Castro's own daughter, Alina Fernandez Revuelta, and his granddaughter, Alina-Maria, were given asylum upon arrival. During the summer of 1994, again overlapping with a Haitian exodus, another mass flight from Cuba began, and some 32,000 *balseros* were picked up at sea. Forced to act by this growing number of desperate migrants, Clinton cancelled the 1966 provisions granting almost instant asylum to most arriving Cubans and ordered that the Cubans be detained at Guantanamo. Following a September accord with Cuba, the United States agreed to process 20,000 applicants annually for admission. The outflow halted; perhaps 1,000 went back; but 6,000 with relatives already in the States, elderly needing medical care, and others were quietly given asylum. By April 1995 somewhat over 23,000 remained at Guantanamo. In May, with the Cuban American community continuing its unremitting lobbying efforts, and tensions strained in the camp, an agreement was reached with Cuba to admit those in the camp but thereafter to repatriate any Cubans picked up at sea.

The Cubans' adjustment to life in America had, at the outset, been considerably eased by the skills, experience, education and even financial resources that that first wave of exiles had brought with them in the early 1960s, along with their strong ethnic bonds. They were assisted by an already existing Cuban community in Miami (over 105,000 had immigrated during the prior two decades), by VOLAGs (Voluntary Agencies), and by state and local governments. In addition, rather quickly in 1960, President Eisenhower allocated $1 million to facilitate their re-settlement, and in 1962 Congress enacted the Migration and Refugee Assistance Act, which ultimately channeled $1.4 billion by 1980 into programs for Cuban resettlement.

The parole procedure[7] and the generous financial assistance provided to Cubans served as precedents for the American response to events in Southeast Asia. In April 1975, South Vietnam fell to North Vietnam and its Viet Cong allies, and then Cambodia to the Khmer Rouge, and Laos to the Pathet Lao. All were Communist forces. By planes and boats, 130,000 Indochinese were evacuated within two weeks, nearly all of them Vietnamese. Three-fifths had had less than one day to prepare

---

[7]Begun by President Eisenhower and based on a clause in the 1952 immigration law, parole was an emergency measure to admit persons on a conditional basis until Congress authorized provisions for their permanent residence.

to leave. The Vietnamese evacuees were mostly urban, middle class, educated, and/or had been employees of their government or of the U.S. government. Four tent cities were immediately set up on military bases in the United States, and Congress moved quickly to appropriate assistance funds and, in October 1977, to permit Vietnamese, Laotians, and Cambodians to be paroled into the country and to be given permanent residence after two years (as were the Cubans).

The suddenness with which many in this first wave found themselves fleeing their homelands would prove shocking and disorienting. The extreme disparities in culture—especially for the Cambodians and Laotians—and the absence of existing ethnic communities would intensify the problems arising from their unanticipated exodus. They also arrived during one of the nation's worst recessions since the Depression. On top of that, the efforts to disperse them throughout the country—as officials had tried in vain to do with Cubans—frequently aggravated the problems of adaptation. For example, in March 1976, Shoua Vang and his family, Laotian Hmongs, arrived in Menominee, Wisconsin. He recalled:

We had no contact with other Hmong. We didn't know what happened to our relatives in the refugee camps or if they would ever join us. Being among the first of our people in this country was a very lonely experience. . . . Most Hmong men had been soldiers. It was depressing for them, after having a lot of responsibility, to enter a society where they don't speak the language and feel totally helpless. . . . For the Hmong, the freedom in this country is overwhelming.

The exodus had not ended with the first wave, for the Vietnamese government soon began a campaign against Sino-Vietnamese business families, forcing them to flee. Cambodians were starting to escape into Thailand and Malaysia from the Khmer killing fields, and Laotians, Hmong and Mien peoples were crossing over to the squalid camps in Thailand. The U.S. government found itself paroling in 7,000 refugees per month, and then 14,000 monthly in 1980 and again in 1981. Nearly 548,000 persons arrived within seven years. The plight of the "boat people" captured world media attention. Nations being asked to resettle refugees from the camps in countries of first asylum soon experienced "compassion fatigue." The United States arranged with Vietnam an Orderly Departure Program through which about 50,000 people annually came to the States directly from Vietnam (1982–87). Then, in 1987, arrangements were made between the United States and Vietnam for Amerasian children of U.S. soldiers to leave Vietnam, enabling 18,600 children to enter the States between 1988 and 1993). Overall, between 1975 and 1993, somewhat over 1 million Indochinese were received by the United States. Moreover, by the early 1980s, hopes of a quick return to their homelands had started to fade, and, as the Vietnamese became eligible for American citizenship beginning in 1981, ever larger numbers applied. More than 251,500 received American citizenship between 1981 and 1993, along with over 31,500 Laotians and 28,000 Cambodians.

By 1973, after about a dozen years, the U.S. government had spent $1 billion assisting Cuban refugees. By 1978, after merely three years, it had already spent $1 billion aiding the resettlement of Southeast Asians. No regular (nonrefugee) immigrant groups benefitted from any comparable programs or such exceptional largesse.

Ties to the Homeland

Amaury Almaguer, who fled Cuba in 1980 and is editor of *Que pasa New Orleans*, acknowledged that, if ideological conditions change in Cuba, "I will not have a valid reason for remaining here." The degree, comfort, and speed with which newcomers adapt have always depended on how well they fit in to their new environment, and that in turn has been significantly affected by the extent of their homeland ties. It may be as complicated as the interweaving of American and West Indian island politics, which has been described as a "single field of action" for some Caribbean migrants, or it may be as uncomplicated as ties to families still in the homeland. Whatever the particular bonds, the remarkably greater ease of modern-day communications and transportation has enabled more immigrants to preserve a greater social autonomy from the larger society and to engage in a form of "economic assimilation without acculturation"—a very selective adjustment to American society.

Thus, on one side there is the view of Alma Mejia Uminsky. "Honestly, I would prefer ten times to go back to Guatemala, and I know, I am fully aware that when I got back to Guatemala ..., I cannot expect to live at the same standard as I live here." Another is that of Trinidadian Deborah Padmore, who said in 1976 that "Everybody got the same thing to say—they want to go back home but there's always this but. . . . I have been away since 1960; and I always think of Trinidad as when I left it. But then you go home periodically and you see that things have changed! it's not like what you left it as, but you still have that *yearnin'* to go back home and try to fit in, although I know I can't fit in. . . . I'm too accustomed to this life in America. . . ."

Between the two extremes of an Uminsky and a Padmore fall many who have been torn, uncertain, and who say one thing and do another. In a 1994 study of Brazilians in New York City, a Brazilian resident argued that "the Brazilian is not an immigrant. The Brazilian's heart is in Brazil. He lives here but he buys a house in Brazil to die in." Many Brazilians did not participate in the 1990 U.S. census, it was found, because "they are here today, but intend to be gone tomorrow." In spite of such strong sentiments, less than a majority of those sampled actually had firm plans to return. The desire to return can affect the pace of acculturation, however, even for the Brazilian woman "who has been in New York City for fourteen years and owns a thriving business there—[and who] counted herself among the potential returnees, insisting that she, too, would go back to Brazil if the economy improved."

A prime illustration of the homeland mindset involving a much larger and more visible group is certainly that of the Cubans, for the first wave came expecting to return shortly. They fomented insurrectionary and guerrilla activities; repudiated Kennedy and the Democratic Party following the failure to support the Bay of Pigs invasion in the spring of 1961; and developed a politically powerful, coercive community consensus against all forms of negotiation with Castro. Noted one major scholar, "If from the outside the exiles' political discourse appeared as raving intolerance, from the inside it helped define who was and was not a true member of the community." As a result, the exiles were slow to develop a Cuban-American identity even as they were building a strong enclave economy. Thousands of exiles actually visited Cuba in the late 1970s yet continued to sponsor and participate in rescue operations and to support Radio Marti's anti-Castro programming beamed at Cuba. Nevertheless, by the 1980s, more and more Cubans were resigned to remaining in the United States. They applied for naturalization and began to enter local politics (electing, among others, four mayors in Dade County, including Xavier Suarez of Miami, two members of Congress, Ileana Ros-Lehtinen and Lincoln Diaz-Balart, and a dozen state legislators). By the spring of 1995, they had, in a tentative way, begun to confront the long-suppressed "splintering" of the community over future relations with Cuba and changes in U.S. refugee policies.

Of course, during the past several decades, a number of other foreign episodes have also embroiled American ethnic communities in homeland controversies. Sometimes immigrants have been swept up with a sense of obligation to offer assistance to their beleaguered compatriots in times of crisis, among them Israelis in the 1967 and 1973 wars; Greeks on behalf of Crete after Turkey's invasion in 1974; Taiwanese after American recognition of the Peoples' Republic of China in 1979; Chinese following the crackdown on dissidents in Tiananmen Square in June 1989; and Bosnians, Serbs, and Croatians of the former Yugoslavia during the wrenching civil war that so dominated the first half of the 1990s.

Finally, homeland ties of sentiment and pride were splashed across the print and television media during the World Cup soccer games held in nine stadiums across America during June and July of 1994. From immigrant faces and bodies painted with the flag designs of their homelands to immigrant spectators dressed

in traditional garb and wildly cheering their native teams—
twenty-three from Africa, Europe, Latin America, Asia, and the
Middle East—the passions demonstrated how enduring homeland ties can remain.

The arrival of over 2.5 million more Europeans after 1965
meant that a number of ethnic communities would be rejuve-
nated by the infusion of new populations with ties to the old
homelands. These ties did not necessarily connect them to all
aspects of the "traditional" (usually folk) culture. As in the two
postwar decades, 1945–65, changing compositions of new immigrant groups produced both intragroup tensions and intragroup
support: revitalization but also reformulation. Be they bearers
of new issues or founders of new organizations, the presence of
the newcomers was a reaffirmation of European American
ethnicity. It had by no means all faded before their arrival, nor is
it likely to do so in the near future.

At the same time, newer waves of groups either not here
previously or present only in small numbers—from Asia, the
Caribbean, Central and South America, Africa (particularly
Egypt and Nigeria), and even Oceana—produced a sweeping
array of immigrant communities from coast to coast, from border to border, from New York and Miami to Los Angeles and
Honolulu. The newcomers have resuscitated neighborhoods and
cities, with Miami being perhaps the most spectacular instance
of this. The impact was no less dramatic than it had been with
the earlier waves of immigrants at the turn of the century. Inseparable from this rainbow of new immigrants have been the
multiracial refugee and asylee populations that have likewise
transformed major communities throughout the country. And,
too, an inescapable part of this reality in a number of urban, and
even rural, milieus has been the steady circulation of undocumented aliens—overstayers and illegal entries—from almost as
many nations as come the legal immigrants.

The persistence of homeland ties continues to influence the
rate of acculturation, likelihood of remaining, probability (or at
least the speed) of acquiring citizenship, and long term integra-

tion. Even just the anticipation of a return has affected immigrants' adjustment experiences. Nonetheless, interest in the homeland has encouraged some groups to form active political interest groups in order to influence government policies concerning those homelands. And many people have also used personal or commercial links with the homelands to establish businesses in America that rely upon political and commercial ties between the United States and those homelands. The resumption of some such diplomatic ties with Vietnam beginning in 1994 is the latest such instance. In this manner, adaptation, acculturation, and the retention of ethnicity interweave.

In 1990, 60 percent of residents in Miami consisted of foreign-born persons, and its neighbor, Hialeah, had the highest percentage of any city in America, 70 percent. Past patterns persist: New York City, 28 percent foreign born; San Francisco, 34 percent; Los Angeles, 38 percent; and, now, Santa Ana, 50 percent. In fact, thirty-two of the forty-eight communities with one-fifth or more foreign born in 1990 were in California.[8] From Boston (20 percent) to Honolulu (21 percent), Americans faced the results of a half century of newcomers: over 22.4 million admitted between the summer of 1940 and the autumn of 1993.

---

[8]Those communities where there are 25,000 or more foreign-born persons.

CHAPTER EIGHT

Immigrant and Ethnic Adaptation in the Late Twentieth Century: Diversities within Diversity

The 1960s and early 1970s were an extraordinary time, marked by the convergence of several powerful, concurrent but also overlapping sets of events. African Americans pushed their movement for guarantees of civil rights and equality of opportunity. They sparked parallel campaigns by Latino, Asian, and Native Americans, and by women and gays and lesbians. A number of European American ethnic groups struggled to complete their own quest for incorporation into the American mainstream at the same time that they tried to cope with the impact of the civil rights struggles in their neighborhoods, schools, and work places. Then, a new wave of immigration, more racially diverse than its predecessors, placed hundreds of thousands of newcomers right in the midst of these transformative developments.

At the same time, the nation's economy was undergoing dramatic changes that would directly bear on the vitality of many ethnic communities. Manufacturing jobs declined or were transferred from long-established settings to other regions or other countries. Businesses sought job applicants with more training in finance, services, and technology, leaving in their wake great numbers of displaced workers of all races. With those demands, employment opportunities narrowed for those who had held semiskilled and skilled jobs, shrinking their hopes for the upward mobility that had been common among earlier immigrants. Aggravating these conditions was an inflation during the 1970s and 1980s that eroded the purchasing power of millions of lower- and middle-class workers.

The place of immigrants and their children in American society has been shaped by these domestic conditions as well as by a globalization of virtually all modes of contact between nations, which has enormously shrunk distances and substantially eased travel and communication between new and old homelands. Within this context of a very dynamic reshaping of domestic and international conditions, immigrant and ethnic Americans encountered a broader range of life-style choices, approaches to acculturation and adaptation, and organizational formats than were usually available before.

The changing face of the immigrant population since the 1960s includes a greater diversity of peoples along with greater diversities within those myriad ethnic groups. As before, elements of continuity have intertwined with newer ones. Traditional elements of ethnic religion, language, culture, and community have affected—and been affected by—the new immigrant groups. As earlier, too, the issues of citizenship and politics have been closely tied to those developments. In the past, there had always been a considerable plurality among the immigrants who never applied for naturalization; now, additional factors have been bearing on those decisions.

This chapter addresses several key aspects of ethnic life in post-1960 America: the white ethnic "revival" of the late 1960s and 1970s, the status of various ethnic subcultures and communities, the continuing educational and economic achievements of immigrants and their children, the context of the responses to

American citizenship and political participation, and the contrasting political efforts of Japanese and Latino Americans.

The White Ethnic "Revival"

In early 1972, Pete Hamill, a sharp-penned New York journalist, waxed euphoric: ". . . something exhilarating and wild has happened to the Irish this past year. . . . Suddenly the Irish were back in town. You saw them at big dances at Our Lady of Perpetual Help in Bay Ridge, or standing in roaring applause at Carpenter's Hall; they showed up at the Mushroom Pub on 13th Street to sing barely remembered songs. . . . One recent week, I received invitations to eleven separate Irish gatherings. . . . Two years ago, you only saw the Irish at weddings and funerals; now they seem to be everywhere."

The civil rights and antiwar movements of the 1960s and 1970s provoked various responses among many second- and third-generation ethnic Americans. Great numbers of them were inspired to reexamine their own roots; others were antagonized and felt threatened by the activists. They turned to their own ethnic communities for defense against what they perceived as assaults upon their American loyalty, their tenuous but prized material achievements, and their fairly recent political gains.

They valued neighbors and kin and the shared traditions, cultures and outlooks that reflected their social class as much as their ethnicity. Said an Italian clerk in Canarsie (Brooklyn), "We Italians and Jews are all the same, we have real good relations, but I'd be uncomfortable in a Protestant community. We all like to play mahjong in Canarsie. I don't know, I mean I really haven't met too many of them. I don't know what kind of people they're like." A Jewish housewife there put it a little differently: "It's good to meet all types of people I guess, but I'm a ghetto person. In the summer I go to a bungalow colony in the Catskills [upstate New York] where the people are just like me." And those who threatened their neighborhoods were not "just like" them.

The "white ethnic revival," which surfaced by the late 1960s and was most prominent for ten to fifteen years, was more than a reaction to the turmoil of those years. In some respects, it was the culmination of a cultural searching by second- and third-generation European Americans that coincided with their efforts to secure at last their material gains in contemporary America. They sought also to fulfill their quest for legitimacy, for an acknowledgment of their own status and respectability within the ethnic community and especially within the larger society. They had invested themselves emotionally in America's Cold War struggle against Communism and they perceived the upheavals of the 1960s and 1970s as symptomatic of the nation's corrosion. They chafed at a mass culture that treated them disdainfully—with Polish and hard hat jokes and Mafia stereotypes. They scorned the outrageous nonconformity of hippies and the countercultural movement. They retreated from that aspect of American society and culture that seemed far too much to devalue what they still cherished in their ethnic heritage—that is, America's emphasis on individualism over community and assimilation over pride in one's roots. "We did not feel this country belonged to us," intoned a well-known Slovak American writer in 1971. "We felt fierce pride in it, more loyalty than anyone could know. But we felt blocked at every turn. . . . Content with little, yes, modest in expectation. But somehow feeling cheated."

They resented what they perceived as traditional America's injunction to "Melt or get off the pot," as Monsignor Geno Baroni pithily put it. In search of some viable vestiges of their roots and identity, they reasserted what they could of their ethnic cultures in the hope of discovering a more satisfying path toward a more pluralistic integration. In other words, they did not want a solution that required their submersion in the mass society as the price of acceptance. In addition, especially in places like the south side of Boston, Brownsville and Canarsie (in Brooklyn), and Hyde Park in Chicago, they were antagonized by what they perceived as challenges by African Americans and others to their unions, schools, and neighborhoods—the hard-won homes they so dearly prized. They felt "squeezed," made to pay the price of civil rights changes by an elite that was removed and aloof. They were being made to bear the weight of compensating others for the nation's past sins. As a man in Jersey City stated, what infuriated them was that "we became the guinea pigs for the experiments of the liberals and intellectuals and politicians." In the midst of the agitation, 1970, sociologist/priest Andrew Greeley offered a summary view:

American ethnics are deeply troubled at what they consider to be "the changing of the rules". . . . *They* had to work hard to achieve the social position they presently occupy, but other groups are demanding these positions as a matter of right. *Their* children had to pass entrance exams to get into college. . . . *Their* fathers had to work long hours. . . . They fought bravely to defend America. . . . *They* lived according to the American ethic of sobriety and respectability. . . . In other words, the white ethnic is being told that the rules no longer apply.

Many were not opposed to racial equality, but, as one leader put it, "we don't want their advancement at the expense of white ethnics." Into leadership vacuums rose local leaders such as the fiery housewife, Elvira "Pixie" Palladino, on Boston's south side, the novice politicians Tony Imperiale (Newark) and Louise Day Hicks (Boston), the more right-wing extremist, Rabbi Meir Kahane, of Brooklyn, and even the more philosophical type like writer Michael Novak. And so a number of ethnic groups were galvanized and stood at the forefront of the resistance to school busing and integration of neighborhoods in Boston, Canarsie, Pontiac (Michigan), Newark, Detroit, and Chicago. Some won the struggles; many endured the changes that came; others moved on; the old ones died.

Of course, on one level, there were many third- and fourth-generation Americans who were moving more and more into the mainstream and retaining only symbolic elements of their ethnicity—especially as they acquired more education, graduated into white-collar and professional jobs, and more of them intermarried. But, about the other level—the blue-collar, white-ethnic, working-class level—the conclusion asserted by prominent observers then regarding the melting pot was that "it did not happen. At least not in New York and . . . in those parts of America which resemble[d] New York." Within this population and in those places, nationality, religion, and class significantly overlapped, for, it was argued, they were nearly synonymous—and they had not faded away.

Now, for a time, individuals on this level responded to the perceived threats to their ethnic communities by rallying around their ethnic identities as the glue for their pursuit of shared concerns. They refocused those communities into active interest groups and attempted to respond *en bloc*, as they perceived others were beginning to do. Black Power and Brown Power would be met with White Ethnic Power. Italians, Irish, Poles, Slovaks, and others searched for effective strategies. They formed new associations, put up candidates for office, lobbied for government funds, organized to resist court orders. At times, however, their quest could take bizarre turns. Fifty thousand Italian Americans of New York responded enthusiastically to a call by the Italian American Civil Rights League for an Italian American Unity Day gathering at Columbus Circle, in Manhattan, on June 29, 1970. It was in part a demonstration of their clout in the campaign against negative stereotyping. But the event was organized by Joseph Colombo, Sr., a leader of one of the city's crime families! A year later, in the midst of the second Unity Day celebration, attended by an even bigger crowd, Colombo was shot by an assassin hired by a rival leader.

Members of various white ethnic groups were also motivated by the black cultural nationalism and renaissance of the 1960s to look to their own roots and to take pride in their own ethnicity, which many had begun to neglect. For example, after visiting Poland in 1964, Edward Piszak, a successful second-generation Polish American businessman, started Project Pole to fight stereotyping and to educate Poles about their rich cultural heritage. Italians, Jews, Greeks, and others pushed for the establishment of ethnic studies programs in colleges; promoted new publications; organized festivals and parades; held language and culture classes for children and even opened up new schools; established historical associations; publicized their cuisine and other contributions to American crafts, music, and culture—and challenged media stereotypes. Some laughed at the ethnic characters on the television shows *Barney Miller* and *All in the Family*; others winced. Some fought back, particularly the Italians. Their heavy battle was successfully lobbying Paramount to omit any use of "Mafia" and "Cosa Nostra" in the film *The Godfather*. Their lighter one was threatening a boycott against Alka Seltzer for its commercial where a man laments, "Datsa soma spicy meatball!"

The reality was that, in varying degrees across the generations, ethnicity had, in fact, persisted among many groups, even among the older Irish, Dutch, Danish, and Norwegian ones. It could be seen in the private sphere of manners and mores, values and specific traditional practices, and in political attitudes, organizational activities, and frequency of voting. As Polish American Congressman Roman Pucinski put it, many white ethnic group members did not "want to be melted down to a monolith." But the white ethnic revival did not represent a rejection of America. Rather, it was a celebration of ethnicity that was meant to affirm "a sense of what is American."

A number of scholars have challenged the authenticity of the revival, ascribing it to wishful thinking and maintaining that ethnicity was rapidly becoming merely symbolic for many second- and third-generation persons of European origin. These scholars cited the decline in various measures of ethnic community and associational participation and in the increasing rates of intermarriages across nationality and even religious lines. A Census Bureau population survey in 1969 found half the respondents indicating that their ancestry was so mixed they could not readily place themselves in the original list of twelve groupings. Half to two-thirds of the men of English, German, Irish, Polish, and Russian origin said their wives were of a national origin different from their own—as did almost half of the Italians. Religious intermarriage among Catholics and Jews reached to more than one-third of new marriages among both groups by the late 1960s, and to nearly half or more among Jews in the 1980s.

The issue of authenticity is not so much an issue with respect to the immigrants or persons quite extensively integrated but for those, especially in the working and middle classes, who had surrendered much in their quest for mobility and security. Now they either had second thoughts about the costs or were sufficiently threatened by outsiders to look to the ethnic group for support. Or they were reacting to both the costs and the perceived threat. For example, a study of Irish, Italian, Polish, German, and Portuguese Catholics in an area north of San Jose, California, during the mid-1980s, found that their ethnicity was indeed in flux, often being "constructed." On the other hand, in certain respects it was quite real, commonly focused on the family, and seen as an on-going source of pleasure, of a feeling of community and belonging. This study and others suggest that assimilation might not have been occurring quite as rapidly or as inevitably as some had originally argued. Ethnic qualities do linger, and numerous groups have continued to be partly reinvigorated by new immigrants.

To sum up, despite the signs of apparent assimilation among some groups, the white ethnic "revival" was not the "Last Hurrah" of European ethnic groups in America. Nor has the decline in the proportion of Europeans among all new immigrants represented the twilight of European ethnic communities. After all, 2.5 million Europeans came to the United States between 1946 and 1965, and 2.5 million more subsequently: 5 million immigrants since the end of World War II. Whether one looks to the older European groups that have preserved some enclaves or to the ones revitalized by recent arrivals, white European ethnicity has by no means faded.

Religion, Language, Culture, and Community

In its September 1993 special issue on "The New Face of America," *Time* magazine attempted to convey an American reality. The cover portrait was a computer-generated composite of the new American woman: 15 percent "Anglo Saxon," 17.5 percent Middle Eastern, 17.5 percent African, 7.5 percent Asian, 35 percent Southern European, and 7.5 percent Hispanic. The new waves of non-Judeo-Christians and non-Europeans are a fact of American life. One need only travel through the streets of New York City, Chicago, Los Angeles, Houston, Miami, New Orleans, and even Minneapolis. One need only glance at the faces, listen to the voices, smell the foods, survey religious institutions, study the merchants, or review calendars of festive days in order to appreciate why the United States has been labelled the "first universal nation." They account for why the nation is once again struggling to define the ground on which the *Unum* in the *E Pluribus Unum* will rest.

In 1990, over 70 percent of Honolulu's population was Asian American; San Francisco's was 29 percent Asian American, Los Angeles's, 10 percent. In that year, Laredo, Texas, was 94 percent Latino, as was East Los Angeles; Miami stood at 63 percent Latino, Los Angeles two-fifths, and Chicago one-fifth. One-quarter of New Yorkers were also Latino, but almost three in ten others were black and about one-fifth of them were foreign-born. Ending the notion that this is a nation of just Protestants, Catholics and Jews, it was last reported for the late 1980s that, in addition to a vast array of Protestant denominations (with 75 million persons), nearly 55 million Catholics and 5.9 million Jews, there were well over 4 million in various Eastern Orthodox denominations, 4 million Mormons, approximately 100,000 Buddhists, quite likely well over 1 million Muslims, and perhaps 0.5 million Hindus. These figures were undoubtedly higher by the mid-1990s due to further immigration and higher birth rates among many of these groups.

Related to this myriad diversity, the 1990 census reported that 14 percent of the nation's population have or are now growing up speaking languages other than English in their homes— 31.8 million. This represents a 38 percent increase over 1980. (See Table 8.1, and see Appendix Table 8.1a for a more complete list.) Despite the census report that three-fourths of all foreign language persons indicated they spoke English "well" or "very well," the steady increase in non-English-speaking persons has alarmed those who maintain that English must be protected as the official language of the United States and who fear "dispossession" and loss in the face of such expanded pluralism.

Table 8.1	1990: Six Principal Non-English Languages "Usually Spoken at Home"
Languages	Numbers of persons
Spanish	17,340,000
French	1,700,000
German	1,550,000
Italian	1,310,000
Chinese	1,250,000 (various dialects)
Tagalog	843,300 (Filipino)

A key problem is attributed to the geographical concentration of the great numbers of recently admitted (plus undocumented) Latinos. In 1990, well over four-fifths of the 22.4 million Latinos lived in just ten states, and over half of the foreign-born had been admitted just in the 1980s. They were truly newcomers, and they have prompted claims by such groups as *U.S. English* of an imminent Spanish language onslaught, even of a Spanish Quebec.

Dade County, Florida, sparked the U.S. English movement with its 1980 English-only ordinance for all government proceedings[1]; by 1995 twenty-two states had approved referenda declaring English the official language, and a move for a U.S. Constitutional amendment to that effect has been pushed by *U.S. English.* Such efforts, reflecting public anxieties, sidestepped the considerable research showing that young immigrant children rapidly adopt English and that language difficulties are most common among older adults, those living and working largely isolated from the general society, and particularly recent refugees. The evidence also suggests that immigrants clearly recognize the value of a knowledge of English for

---

[1]By the early 1990s, six Latinos were elected as Dade County commissioners, together with four African Americans and three whites. In May 1993 they repealed that original English-only ordinance.

socioeconomic mobility—to say nothing of coping with public service agencies. In addition, the 1974 *Lau et al.* vs. *Nichols et al.* decision affirmed the right of children with "Limited English Proficiency" to receive assistance in school.[2] With respect to adults, the long waiting lists in many cities of persons seeking to enroll in English courses indicate that the problem has often been one of too few such courses, not a lack of interest or willingness to learn English.

Learning English was only one of the challenges confronting immigrants struggling to adapt to America. As newcomers, they were seeking a balance between the comforts of their traditional culture and both the appeal and indispensability of the novel American one.

The story is told about a Vietnamese family, one of many where the father had remained behind when the others escaped. The mother was troubled by her children's acculturation after only a few years. "'You're so Americanized now [the mother lamented], but you must still remain Vietnamese!' Thu preserved what she could of their native culture, speaking Vietnamese at home and preparing traditional food. But Jamie [changed from Lan] and Danielle (as Hue began calling herself) conversed together in English, and when they cooked for the family, Jamie admitted, the menu was strictly American: hamburgers or casserole. And cheese cake."

Currently, it appears that some Vietnamese and other newcomers have been accelerating the pace of acculturation—"leapfrogging" into the mainstream—thereby compressing the process of Americanization into a nearly one-generation experience. Despite strong attachments among the parents to traditional values and practices (especially surrounding obligations to family) and their oft-repeated reluctance to intermarry with outsiders, or to accept intermarriage by their children, with surprising rapidity their children have adopted American practices, foods,

---

[2]The Supreme Court declared that if the Chinese children could not speak English, they could not receive a meaningful education and that constituted discrimination.

styles of dress and grooming, slang, and other American cultural patterns—to say nothing of the music!

Armenian Americans provide a good case study of the combination of Americanization, ethnic persistence, and partial rejuvenation of the group. They had migrated earlier, mainly from Turkey and, in fewer numbers, from Lebanon, Iran, and the Soviet Union. Beginning in the late seventies and through the eighties, over sixty-one thousand more entered from Iran and the former Soviet Union.[3] They had previously had few reasons to mobilize as a group in America, yet they retained a strong identity and subscribed to traditional Armenian values—even though many were not very "willing to live by them." Thus, in the New York–New Jersey area in the 1980s, considerable intermarriage with "odars" (non-Armenians) had occurred, but such outsiders and their Armenian spouses were "shunned" by the organized Armenian community. Nonetheless, in most measures of Armenian ethnicity, there had been significant declines among younger persons (with allowances for some strong historical memories of the Armenian holocaust in Turkey in 1915). While the newcomers supported schools, businesses, neighborhood churches, even Boy Scout troops, their arrival stimulated interest and group pride among those born in America but no significant resumption of Armenian cultural forms among them. The exception was an occasional "checkbook ethnic response" to disasters and conflicts in the homeland. This illustration of a recent wave of immigrants versus the American-born represents a typical example of generational layering within an ethnic community, with each interacting at points but also pursuing their own stages of adjustment and accommodation.

As in the case of the contemporary wave of Armenians, other newer immigrants have followed prior ethnic group patterns, hastening to develop their own organizational structures, as among black West Indians, Cubans, Asian Indians, and Arabs. From churches, rotating credit associations, and mutual aid or-

---

[3]Between 1980 and 1990, there was a 45 percent increase in persons listing an Armenian ancestry.

ganizations to community development and political action groups, the process of institutional adaptation since the 1960s appears to have been quite rapid—ironically, almost as rapid as that of their children's Americanization! With it has come a quicker grasp of the role of the group in a modern democracy. To recognize this, one need only consider Cape Verdeans in Massachusetts petitioning for bilingual classes in Crioula; West Indian Carnaval organizations preparing for Mardi Gras in New York; the Hmong running the Hiawatha Valley Farm Cooperative in Wisconsin; and Iranians forming a Moslem Student Association–Persian Speaking Group in Los Angeles. From Hawaii to New England, one can find numerous other examples.

As part of the growth of group consciousness, there has also been a substantial increase since 1960 in foreign-language publications (from 698 to 960 by 1975), and many ethnic groups coast to coast have developed radio and television programs. Latinos have even created their own TV network, SIN, and, in November 1993, the first Spanish language talk radio network, Radio LABIO. Widespread, too, is the practice of importing audio and video cassettes from homeland countries. Given that India has the biggest filmmaking industry in the world, it is not surprising that Hindi film videos can be obtained in almost any Indian market!

Despite the evidence on both the individual and group levels that the new immigrants have been irresistibly drawn to American culture, there is other evidence that an ambivalence persists concerning the process. Not overtly pressed to forsake their cultures, they strive for "an accommodative pluralism": they try to preserve intrinsic features of their own cultures while adding to them selected features of American culture. (In one unsuccessful instance, Indochinese refugees had to give up hunting ducks in San Francisco's Golden Gate Park!) It is this fusion rather than replacement which has become more visible to other Americans, particularly because of the great volume of racially different immigrants, the high profile of the refugee populations, and the concentration of both in major urban areas. Thus, one can speak of the Caribbeanization of parts of New York City, as others have of the Hispanicization of Miami and Los Angeles and the "Asianification" of Honolulu and areas of San Francisco. These very visible measures of the nation's multiculturalism do not represent a refusal to acculturate but, rather, the quite varied means available to immigrants to negotiate their wedding of cultures.

The Pillars of Occupation and Education

"You name it, I've got it!" shouted Amir Mina, an Egyptian who operates a catering truck for taxi drivers at Los Angeles International Airport. "I've got Ethiopian food. I've got Turkish food. I've got food from Nigeria!" From Los Angeles to Chicago, Washington, D.C., and New York City, the taxi industry has become more than ever before a metaphor for contemporary urban America. Over one hundred different nationalities were represented among L.A. drivers in 1993, while, by 1991, 90 percent of New York's cab drivers were foreign-born. Predominant in Los Angeles are those from the former Soviet Union, Ethiopia, Mexico, and Nigeria, whereas persons from India, Pakistan, Bangladesh, Africa, the Caribbean, the former Soviet Union, and Israel dominate those jobs in New York. Be it also the Turks and Eritreans in Washington or the Nigerians in Chicago, the world of the taxi drivers reflects the great number of immigrants who, whatever their occupational background, have been willing to work at almost anything in their pursuit of the American dream.

Employment patterns form a complex immigration picture since the 1960s that includes substantial increases in the numbers of professionals, physicians, surgeons, engineers, and nurses (such as from South America, India, and the Philippines), along with considerable numbers of semiskilled and unskilled workers from Mexico, the Caribbean, and South America as well as Southeast Asia. Many of those with extensive training in their homelands have struggled to master sufficient English to pass qualifying or licensing exams; many never do and have had to seek lower-status jobs or whole new occupations. At the same time, as numerous Cubans, West Indians, and Chinese have found, this labor pool has also made it possible for businesses (often those within the various ethnic communities themselves) to exploit these new labor forces. Other immigrants and ethnics have followed an alternative model and network of fellow ethnics and opted for self-employment.

There are those who choose this course as a logical option because they have brought a strong commercial tradition with them, such as among the first wave Cubans, Armenians, and Gujarati[4] (from western India). Many others have pursued it either as the consequence of being unable to pursue their original career or because they are unwilling to work for others, especially in factories. Among the more unusual instances of carving out a niche through self-employment are the Afghanis who opened fast-food chicken outlets in New York City and the Cambodians who now operate 80 percent of the donut shops in southern California. Koreans, Greeks, and Iranians have been particularly good examples of those who have sought to make the best of their opportunities in America by concentrating their efforts in their own businesses. In 1990, foreign-born Korean, Iranian, and Greek men and women were far more frequently self-employed than among all others, quite commonly in retail and wholesale businesses. In a number of cities, the effect has been to spur a substantial revitalization of central city business districts. (See Appendix, Table 8.2.)

Cha Ok Kim had earned a degree in Korea but went to New York for an MBA. Needing money but hampered by poor English, he began peddling imported black Korean wigs door to door in Harlem and then in other African American communities throughout the Northeast. Soon, he was so successful that his fellow Korean students ("medical doctors, pharmacists, engineers," noted Kim) began working for him, and he gradually expanded to include a dozen salesmen in what had become a multimillion dollar import business. In numerous other instances among Koreans, a large percentage brought financial resources with them, usually from having sold their homes in Korea, or (as a family) rapidly accumulating savings through multiple incomes.

---

[4]Their concentration in the motel business and in the operation of newsstands has already become almost legendary.

At times, they even supplemented that with assistance from a *kae* (or *kye*), a rotating credit association. Like Kim, they then began their own businesses, notably importing from and/or exporting to Korea, or operating fresh fruit and vegetable stands, grocery and liquor stores, or other retail outlets, both within their own and frequently within other minority communities. In many cases, family members would subsequently sell the business to other kin who wished to migrate, and the first family would go on to another venture. Koreans, of course, were not the only ones doing this. A case study of the pizza business among Greek relatives in Connecticut is shown in Figure 8.1.

Miami's Cubans provide an especially valuable illustration of the interplay of cultural, situational, and political factors in the development of a contemporary ethnic business community in a central city. Partly, the Cuban enclave economy evolved as a response to the initial exclusion of Cubans from many existing businesses and unions. They pooled their own resources through a "collective entrepreneurialism" as well as benefitted from enormous federal assistance. They employed household strategies where more wives worked, more family members were employed in their businesses, fewer children were born, and couples relied more on grandparents or other kin for child care. Rather rapidly, Cubans built a business infrastructure that transformed Miami and much of south Florida, making it a commercial and financial hub for many points in Latin America and invaluable in assisting the absorption of later waves of refugees. Even though most Cuban immigrants there continue to work outside the ethnic community—in construction, hotels, restaurants, garment factories, and government offices—the vitality of this community has played an important role in their lives.

One result is that the umbrella of ethnic businesses is so extensive that, it is said, "in Miami one can proceed from birth to death Cuban style." Elsewhere, too, newcomers have labored to construct enclave economies, as did the Vietnamese in San Jose and Westminster (California) and the Soviet Jews in Los Angeles and Brighton Beach (Brooklyn). The following description of the latter's West Hollywood community would be as true for

Figure 8.1

**A Case Study Illustrating Ethnic Self-Employment:
Connecticut Greeks in the Pizza Business**

Rough Chronology

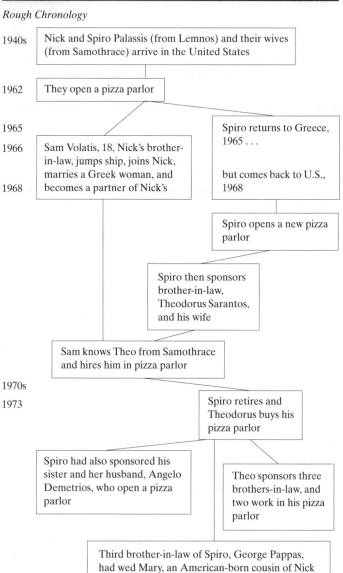

1940s	Nick and Spiro Palassis (from Lemnos) and their wives (from Samothrace) arrive in the United States
1962	They open a pizza parlor

1965

1966 — Sam Volatis, 18, Nick's brother-in-law, jumps ship, joins Nick, marries a Greek woman, and 1968 — becomes a partner of Nick's

Spiro returns to Greece, 1965 . . .

but comes back to U.S., 1968

Spiro opens a new pizza parlor

Spiro then sponsors brother-in-law, Theodorus Sarantos, and his wife

Sam knows Theo from Samothrace and hires him in pizza parlor

1970s

1973

Spiro retires and Theodorus buys his pizza parlor

Spiro had also sponsored his sister and her husband, Angelo Demetrios, who open a pizza parlor

Theo sponsors three brothers-in-law, and two work in his pizza parlor

Third brother-in-law of Spiro, George Pappas, had wed Mary, an American-born cousin of Nick and Spiro. George quits factory job and buys luncheonette with his and Mary's savings, then learns pizza business and adds it to luncheonette

Vietnamese as for Cubans in Miami and Mexicans in East Los Angeles—and as it was for many earlier immigrants: "Soviet Jews can socialize with neighbors, shop for food, clothes, real estate, securities, or appliances; see a doctor or dentist; attend religious services; take in a floor show, read a newspaper, watch cable TV, visit a local park to play dominoes; and interact with numerous acquaintances, all without speaking a word of English."

In the case of those from the Soviet Union or Korea, for example, who quite commonly brought few business skills with them, and/or a limited knowledge of English, their business opportunities were necessarily to be found within their own ethnic communities (or as middlemen in others), gradually branching out to the more general markets as the newcomers become more experienced, more proficient in English, and (quite often) as the younger, more acculturated children join them. In contrast, many Asian Indians have expanded their prior business experiences and knowledge of English in a greater variety of American enterprises, some of which serve their ethnic communities but very many the broader one as well (including motels, newsstands, groceries, travel agencies, real estate firms, and retail electronics and appliance stores). The considerable number of Asian Indians who have gone into computer hardware and software design and production represent another important illustration of successful transfers of skills, business acumen, and language ability. Of course, they are not alone in doing that, and it is not something only men venture to do. Among the numerous instances from other groups two will make the point: Nancy Marinovic, of Bolivia, opened an architecture and engineering company in New Orleans in 1980, and Soffy Botero, a Colombian opthamalogist, together with her physician husband, opened the Botero Eye Clinic in that same city.

Because of the large-scale transformations in the American economy since the 1970s, the educational background of recent immigrants has certainly played a far more important role in their occupational patterns than was the situation among most immigrant groups earlier in this century. And incomes have likewise reflected the broader occupational array of contemporary immigrant workers. In 1990 (see Appendix, Table 8.3), one-quarter of foreign-born men had eight or fewer years of education, whereas over three-tenths had earned some college degree (two or more years of college education, from associate degrees to doctorates). Only among Laotians, Cambodians, and Mexicans did a large majority of the men and women possess an eighth-grade education or less. In contrast, merely 2 to 3 percent of Africans[5] had so little. Indeed, at the other end of the scale, three-fifths to three-quarters of Indian and Taiwanese men and women had some college or university degree.[6]

Tied to educational achievements were the trends visible in the occupations listed upon admission. Beginning in the late 1960s, the percentage of foreign-born workers citing white-collar jobs rose, reaching 50 percent by the 1980s. Over 70 percent of Asian workers admitted in the late 1960s and early 1970s had been so employed, with especially high numbers of Filipinos and Koreans. Even among Mexicans one could see a change, for a decade later serious disruptions in the Mexican economy prompted many more of that nation's white-collar workers to emigrate northward. In fact, there was nearly a five-fold increase in their numbers in 1988–92, compared with the early 1980s. Going beyond the broad category of white-collar workers, between 1966 and 1988, from one-fifth to one-quarter of all immigrants who included an occupation on their applications were professionals, versus just one-sixth in the late 1950s (particularly, physicians, nurses, engineers, and scientists).

In fact, the emphasis on attracting immigrants with more training and skills during the past several decades has encouraged what is now a quite common pattern: Individuals first arrive as nonimmigrants, secure a job offer, and then apply for a

---

[5]Little data for individual African groups are published. The five principal foreign-born African peoples in 1990 were Egyptians, Nigerians, Ethiopians, South Africans, and Ghanaians.

[6]Twenty percent of non-Latino whites had college degrees, as did 40 percent of Asians but only 9 percent of Latinos.

visa—shortening the process significantly. The "new arrivals," therefore, were and are quite often already present—and working—in the country. The cumulative effect of the admission of many persons with advanced training was that, by the early 1990s, 9 percent of the nation's nurses, 12 percent of its engineers and natural scientists, 15 percent of high school teachers, and 20 percent of its physicians were foreign-born. (See Appendix, Table 8.4.)

Although many in the initial waves of recent immigrants were rather highly skilled, white-collar workers, many were not. Family reunification and the admission of refugees frequently altered the occupation picture quite dramatically. Consider the example of Cubans again. While half of working immigrant Cubans before the revolution held white-collar jobs (20 percent were professionals) and over three-fifths of the first wave of refugees after the revolution cited white-collar occupations, by the late sixties that percentage was already dropping. It reached one-quarter by the early 1990s.

That many Cubans were compelled to settle for lower-skilled jobs serves as a reminder not only that many immigrants have had to lower their initial expectations but also that most working immigrants have held blue-collar jobs, one-fifth of them in manufacturing in 1990 (as with Cubans). Moreover, as with the professionals, managers, and self-employed business persons, one finds pronounced ethnic variations in blue-collar employment. For example, whereas limited skills and networks led one-quarter to one-half of Dominicans and Southeast Asian refugees into factories, similar networking guided Guyanans, Haitians, and particularly Jamaicans into the health services, especially in the hospitals of New York City. And last, one-sixth of working Mexicans in 1990 continued to be engaged in agriculture, compared to merely 1.4 percent of all other foreign-born persons.

Not surprisingly, income has often corresponded with education and occupation. That the group with the highest per capita income among those surveyed in 1989 were Asian Indians and the second highest those from the United Kingdom indicates that among both traditional and newer groups there are those who have achieved significant economic success in America. On the other hand, the reality that among the lowest were three refugee peoples likewise underscores the major challenges that face many newcomers in acclimating to life in a new land. (See Appendix, Table 8.5.)

Brain Drain or Reciprocal Gain?

Speaking about a decade ago, Ari Amichai, a chemist who came from Israel in 1964, may have put his finger on the key problem facing many with advanced degrees and living in homelands unable to employ them. "I had educated myself out of my country. Israel—and quite a few developing countries—doesn't have substantial industry to maintain research at high levels. So if one wishes a high level of specialization in certain fields, you find that while it is very easy to obtain a job in an industrialized country like the States or Germany or England, you can't . . . in Israel or India or Taiwan. . . ." Another case in point is that of Argentinian emigration. A sociologist observed during the 1970s that it was precisely the imbalance between the ability of that nation to produce such large numbers of highly trained personnel and its capacity to absorb them which played a major role in pushing such persons out. In fact, some countries were said to have "pent up stocks of potential migrants," due to an overly rapid modernization that led to an exodus of scientists, engineers, physicians, surgeons, and nurses.

One question, long debated, concerns how much "brain drain" has been generated by America's immigration laws (and those of other immigrant receiving nations) as a consequence of the number of foreign-born students who have been permitted to continue their education in the United States. Their numbers have increased markedly since the early 1980s. Between 1972 and 1985, 2.45 million students came to study, over two-fifths of whom were from Asia and the Middle East. In merely the next seven years, over 2 million students came. Japanese, Chinese,

Korean, Malaysian, and British men and women have been especially visible, as well as over 116,000 Mexicans in the decade after 1981. Great numbers of these students then applied for permanent residence: Between 1982 and 1992, for example, 236,400 were granted permanent visas. Has this represented brain drain from less developed countries, notably from India, the Philippines, and parts of Latin America? Perhaps, in part. By way of contrast, in the case of Canada, so many Americans have gone northward as Canadians were migrating southward that one scholar referred to it as an "exchange of brains." Principally, skilled and professional persons have emigrated because their native countries trained more individuals than their economies could absorb, or their economies had deteriorated, shrinking opportunities, as in Mexico. While undoubtedly some countries such as Bangladesh and Lebanon have experienced actual losses, there have been counterbalancing factors. A June 1994 report indicated that such emigration has been found to decrease unemployment among the educated who do remain, in effect, providing a double benefit—a safety valve for relatively highly skilled persons with greater expectations for social mobility, for those who depart as well as for those who remain. Much of the Dominican migration has been ascribed to just those motives.

In addition, the "losses"—to the extent they have occurred—have been strikingly offset by the enormous remittances which immigrants of all occupations have been sending home to families: For example, at a level equal to one-third of the total exports of the Dominican Republic and the Philippines. Not only do such moneys in turn stimulate various segments of the local economies but such foreign employment also results in "ethnic tourism"—emigrants and their descendants who return for visits to the old homelands—providing still more sizable sums of income for several countries. Moreover, among a number of groups such as the Koreans and Asian Indians, educated immigrants have embarked on business ventures that have involved considerable economic ties with the home countries, thereby stimulating trade and employment in both that homeland and the United States—as was the case with Cha Ok Kim and his imported wigs from Korea.

To a significant extent, therefore, the migration of professionals and other highly trained persons has formed an important part of the global exchanges of labor, capital, and resources. Less skilled and temporary workers also provide important labor pools for many segments of the economy, often keeping them competitive with foreign businesses. As more of the world's nearly 190 nations hook up with the "global village," these human factors of migration form intrinsic strengths in the linkages upon which nations have come more and more to depend. And last, the emigration of Arab professionals from the Middle East due to invasion, civil war, and severe political crises (and, most recently, as a consequence of clashes with Muslim fundamentalists) are reminders that professionals in many countries have also been among the great masses fleeing domestic crises. "Brain drain" has not always been a consequence of the search for better employment.

Citizenship and Politics: To Do or Not To Do

About acquiring American citizenship, Irishwoman Mary Curran simply said: "I feel very temporary here. Haven't become a citizen so I can't vote." Trinidadian Deborah Padmore was more emphatic: "I don't want citizenship. You still want to know where your roots are." Mexican Graciela Liceaga, mother of four U.S.-born children and now herself a legalized alien (through IRCA), also refuses to apply for citizenship: "I don't want to grow old here. Here, one can be so alone." The Korean Cha Ok Kim felt he had a very practical reason for eschewing American citizenship: "I haven't become a U.S. citizen. Someday, if I want to be a candidate for Congress in Korea, I don't want people criticizing me, 'You're a U.S. citizen. Why did you come back?'" Mexican American César Caballero described how the issue could divide families: "After we were living in El Paso for five years, my father and then the kids who were born in Mexico became U.S.

citizens. My mother has never become a citizen. She is a die-hard Mexican." Obviously, people of the same nationality do differ on this. Cambodian Bun Thab reflected, "Sometimes I think of becoming an American citizen, but I love my country too. I miss everything I had in Cambodia. . . . I would love to go back and become a farmer again. . . ." And yet, Celia Noup, also Cambodian, recognized that citizenship actually did not require an all-or-nothing cultural choice: "When I became an American citizen a few months ago, it was very emotional for me. I was happy to be part of my new country. I do feel loyalty to the United States. I think of myself as both Cambodian and an American citizen." Finally, such attitudes have neither been all-or-nothing nor the-same-forever. Consider the changing perspective of Armando Espinosa, of Ecuador. "I am Ecuadoran in my blood and gut. I do not even like apple pie." Nonetheless, as his children began growing up in America, he became more interested in public affairs. Unable to vote either in Ecuador or the United States, he felt nationless and then angry about the political weakness of Latinos in New York. "If people like me retain our allegiance to home and refuse to participate in electoral politics here, the lot of our race will never improve."

Ethnic groups have learned to use their ethnicity, mobilizing their members for specific, shared interests such as patronage jobs, positions on a party ticket, and government funds for community projects. To do so, they have had to promote citizenship in order to strengthen their vote. Yet, not only has this strategy been comparable to that of earlier groups but so have been the ambivalent/mixed responses to acquiring citizenship. As we have seen, immigrants weigh their attachment to America, their remigration plans, employment needs or requirements, concerns about family reunification, retention of property rights in their homelands, the political and economic climate in America and in their homeland, their perceptions about the naturalization process itself (usually intimidating) and even about the meaning, value, and need for changing citizenships. Many Caribbean immigrants in New York City, for example, emphasize that they no longer see citizenship as the test of their loyalty to America but they do perceive their dual political activities (in the islands and in New York City) as mutually reinforcing. Given the "revolution" in immigration, how much of one has taken place among the nation's new citizens? A comparison of three equal time periods of a dozen years each sheds much light on how dramatically altered the portrait of new citizens has become. In Table 8.6, the first set of years, 1957–68, reflects the immigration/refugee policies of the 1950s and early 1960s. Two-thirds of those naturalized were Europeans. German, Hungarian, Polish, and Dutch refugees were prominent. So, too, were the Asian spouses and adoptees of U.S. citizens. During the second period, 1969–80, there was a 20 percent increase in new citizens. A surge of southern and eastern Europeans entered the country after 1965 and tended to apply for naturalization rather quickly. Greeks, Yugoslavs, and Portuguese stand out. Meanwhile, the European refugee movements were waning, many families were already reunited, and widespread prosperity in Europe dampened the economic drive of Europeans to emigrate. At the same time, "new seed" immigrants—those entering based on job skills or with nonpreference visas—were usually quite

Table 8.6	A Comparison of Changing Naturalization Patterns, by Region of Origin, 1957–1968, 1969–1980, and 1981–1992		
Region of Last Allegiance	Total Naturalized 1957–68	Total Naturalized 1969–80	Total Naturalized 1981–92
All Persons	1,392,437	1,673,880	2,762,575
Europe	944,913	561,750	444,556
Asia	150,574	506,944	1,320,036
North America	242,066	462,818	696,075
South America	22,017	88,023	184,159
Oceana	4,883	6,839	17,475
Africa	6,186	23,809	74,079

eager for citizenship. There was, for example, well over a 200 percent jump in numbers of Africans and Asians naturalized. (See also Appendix, Tables 8.6a and 8.6b.) After initial years of uncertainty, the new wave of refugees, Cubans especially, was also responsive to the appeal of American citizenship.

The third period (1981–92), marked by nearly a two-thirds leap in the number of new citizens, begins with the first year during which a large number of Vietnamese refugees received American citizenship. American involvement in Southeast Asia was now visible in the names and faces of the new citizens. Southeast Asians were soon being joined by increasing numbers of Russian, Polish, Iranian, Haitian, and Salvadoran refugees. Finally, the extension of immigration restrictions to the Americas had prompted double the number of South Americans to apply for citizenship, notably Colombians. For the entire period during which most of those arriving from 1965 on became eligible for naturalization, 1968–93, ten groups contributed at least 3 percent to the 4.85 million total.[7] Five were Asian, three Latino or West Indian, and two European. (See Table 8.7 and, in Appendix, Table 8.7a.)

How have the trends in citizenship—as well as the maturation of the American-born generation—been manifested in the political sphere? The death in 1976 of Mayor Richard Daley, head of the Chicago Democratic political machine, represented the passing of an era: a century of largely Irish-dominated urban machines providing generations of newcomers to the cities with their introduction to American-style politics—principally through the Democratic Party. By 1980, crucial segments of the older first and second generations who had relocated to suburbia were now also moving out of the Roosevelt Democratic coalition and gradually into the political camp first of Richard Nixon and then of Ronald Reagan and George Bush. In 1992, Democrat Bill

---

[7]The figures, of course, include persons who entered prior to 1965 but do not include a major proportion of those admitted after 1987 because they would either not yet have been eligible by the end of 1993, or they would not have been fully processed.

Table 8.7	Naturalization, by Region and Ten Leading Groups, 1968–1993	
Region/Country of Last Allegiance	Total Number Naturalized	Percent of Total Naturalized
ALL PERSONS	4,853,862*	
Asia/Middle East	1,987,270	40.9%
North America**	1,269,811	26.2
Europe	1,106,735	22.8
South America	301,727	6.2
Africa	110,086	2.3
Oceana	18,683	.4
Philippines	490,162	10.1
Mexico	364,202	7.5
Cuba	357,203	7.4
China/Taiwan	295,102	6.1
Vietnam	264,378	5.4
Korea	252,840	5.2
United Kingdom	223,544	4.6
India	173,381	3.6
Italy	148,339	3.1
Jamaica	145,478	3.0

*Includes 59,550 unknown or other categories not listed.
**Includes the Caribbean and Central America.

Clinton's carefully planned, nonracially oriented emphasis on economic issues drew enough white ethnic voters back to give him the presidency, but the Republican congressional sweep in 1994 indicated that a realignment was on-going and political allegiances were by no means fixed.

Still, the decline of machine politics in most cities did not mean the sudden death of ethnic politics, only its further readjustment. For example, Abraham Beame, the first Jew to win the Democratic nomination for mayor of New York City in 1965, lost to a very WASPish John V. Lindsay. A key issue in that year and for the next quarter century was how Jews and Italians would vote. Many among both groups had supported Lindsay, and did so again in 1969. Then, four years later, Beame became the first Jewish mayor and was followed by three-term mayor Edward Koch, also Jewish. However, by the mid-1980s, Jewish/Catholic political battles were being overshadowed by the ever-increasing racial polarization, stirred by Jesse Jackson's impressive run for the presidency in 1984 and by his 45 percent victory in the 1988 primary in New York City—with nine-tenths of the black vote and three-fifths of the Latinos. Manhattan Borough president David Dinkins, also an African American, moved to capitalize on Jackson's success. In the 1989 mayoral contest, he won with a coalition of blacks, Latinos, West Indians, and liberal whites, but then in 1993 was defeated by Italian American Rudolf Giuliani (with a Puerto Rican and a Jew running on his ticket).[8]

In Los Angeles, African American mayor Tom Bradley was succeeded by white Richard Riordan, who outcampaigned Councilman Michael Woo (a Chinese American) in a city with only a 36 percent white population. In Miami, in 1993, a former county commissioner, Steve Clark, was elected to succeed Cuban American Xavier Suarez—in a city whose population included only 10 percent non-Latino whites; his Cuban American opponent was considered too extremist even for many fellow Cuban exiles. On the other hand, the first sizable mainland city with an Asian majority, Monterey Park, California (the "Chinese Beverly Hills"), saw Chinese-born Lily Chen become its mayor in 1983 and American-born Judy Chu in 1989 and 1994. In the early 1990s, the California communities of Carson and Daly elected their first Filipino councilmen, and Tony Lam became the first elected Vietnamese, to the city council in Westminster, in southern California. Finally, coming full circle, Richard J. Daley, Jr., won reelection as mayor of Chicago in

---

[8]Critical political, economic, and racial issues, many quite divisive, underlay these various political outcomes.

1995, building on a carefully constructed, multiracial coalition that included blacks and Latinos.

Most Asian Americans on the mainland traditionally have been reluctant to enter political frays (compared with their prominence in Hawaiian politics since the mid-1950s). They continue to prefer playing more indirect roles, lobbying officials and providing financial contributions to sympathetic candidates. But, as two more signs of the gradual changes, in 1984, Shien Biau Woo was elected lieutenant governor of Delaware and, in 1992, Hawaii's senators Daniel Inouye and Daniel Akaka and congresswoman Pat Takemoto Mink and California congressmen Norman Mineta and Robert Matsui were joined by the first Korean congressman, Californian Jay Kim.

Contrasting Studies of Ethnic Activism: Japanese Americans and Chicanos and Other Latinos

Among the fastest to seek citizenship, Asians have been among the slowest to develop interest-group politics. One of the major exceptions to the pattern was the long campaign by Japanese Americans, largely beginning in 1970, to obtain adequate compensation for their losses in World War II and an acknowledgment that their internment had been unwarranted and unconstitutional. The Japanese American Citizens' League established a National Committee for Redress and brought the matter to public attention in 1978, recommending $25,000 for each survivor. They lobbied Congress, relying on the efforts of senators Inouye and Spark Matsunaga, congressmen Mineta and Matsui, and a growing number of other congressional supporters. In July 1980, Congress established the Commission on Wartime Relocation and Internment of Citizens (CWRIC). The Commission's report in June 1983 was the culmination of eighteen months of research. During this period, political scientist Peter Irons and a team of Asian American legal researchers also discovered important evidence of a government cover-up during the war, which lead to the setting aside of the earlier Supreme Court decisions on the evacuation and curfew. The CWRIC's final report sharply rebuked the government for its wartime actions and recommended $20,000 compensation for survivors. Five more years of lobbying and negotiations followed before President Reagan signed the Civil Liberties Act in August 1988, which contained an apology for the internment and awarded the $20,000 to each living survivor, beginning in 1990. By spring 1995, a total of $1.59 billion had been dispersed to nearly eighty thousand persons, over 70 percent of whom were living in California.

In the convergence between the civil rights movement and the new immigration laws, one group's experience, that of the Mexican Americans, uniquely bridges both, for their roots extend back nearly four hundred years and they now are more than three-fifths of all Latinos in the nation. Between 1965 and 1993, almost 3.8 million were granted permanent residence and over 364,000 were naturalized (1968-93).[9] However, Mexicans have also had one of the lowest naturalization rates this century, affecting their political influence. The most visible (if not most vocal) effort of Mexican Americans to enter recent American ethnic politics was the Chicano movement of the 1960s and early 1970s. It represented a quest for identity, self-determination, and political power. Although decidedly not a political movement, the unionizing campaigns by Cesar Chavez and the United Farm Workers—energized by Luis Valdez's brilliant innovation, *El Teatro Campesino*—indirectly gave great visibility to the Chicano struggle for recognition, a movement that largely involved the native born (in contrast to the farmworkers). Highlighting it were the efforts of Reyes López Tijerina in New Mexico, Corky Gonzalez in Denver, and José Angel Gutiérrez in Starr County (Crystal City), Texas, and those by such activist groups as the Brown Berets, MECHA (*Movimiento Estudiantil Chicano de Aztlan*), *La Raza Unida Party*, and the Chicano Moratorium

---

[9]Because of minimum residence requirements, beginning in 1965, few who came could have received citizenship before 1968.

Committee (antiwar), led by Rosalio Muñoz. It was the latter's peaceful marches in the late summer of 1970 that sparked un-provoked police attacks and three bloody riots within six months.

In the final analysis, the Chicano movement attracted few *mexicanos* (the foreign born) and relatively small numbers of Mexican Americans overall. Together with the continuing large-scale immigration and low naturalization rates, the Mexican Americans' lower socioeconomic levels have contributed to lower percentages of voter registration and voter turn out, further slow-ing the emergence of the ethnic community as a more viable political force. In New Mexico, however, where a long-present ethnic group, the Hispanos, made up 38 percent of the popula-tion, the elite (*los ricos*) have had an on-going political voice. Elsewhere in the Southwest, a variety of factors—not the least of them economic and political vulnerability and a sometimes violent reception by Anglos—had long discouraged much overt political participation by Latinos before the 1950s, except where they constituted a considerable proportion of the population, as in southern Texas.

Having largely failed to mobilize Mexican Americans po-litically, or to draw them from their attachment to the Demo-cratic Party, Chicano activists recognized that working within the political system rather than confronting it would be the only prac-tical strategy. The National Council of La Raza and, subsequently, the Southwest Voter Registration Project began campaigns to promote citizenship and voting. The Mexican American Legal Defense and Education Fund (MALDEF) was organized in the early 1970s to fight for Latino civil rights. The National Associa-tion of Latino Appointed and Elected Officials (NALEO) ap-peared in 1975, and the Congressional Hispanic Caucus in 1976. In several parts of the country Latinos began to make political gains. Raul Castro was elected governor of Arizona and Jerry Apodaca governor of New Mexico in 1974. Eight years later, Tony Anaya was elected governor of New Mexico, and a few years afterwards Bob Martinez reached the Governor's seat in Florida. The election of four more Latinos to Congress in 1982 raised the total to eleven; a decade later it was seventeen, including the first Cuban American, Ileana Ros-Lehtinen,[10] The growing political role of Latinos can also be seen in their election to state legislatures, state supreme courts, city councils, county boards (notably Herman Badillo in New York [a Puerto Rican elected to several posts] and, in 1991, Gloria Molina's victory for the post of county supervisor in Los Angeles). They have been mayors of major cities, such as Maurice Ferre (Miami) in 1977, Henry Cisneros (San Antonio) in 1981, Xavier Suarez (Miami) in 1985, and Federico Peña (Denver) in 1987. (Both Cisneros and Peña were subsequently selected as cabinet members by President Clinton). Between 1974 and 1988, the number of Latino elected officials doubled to over three thousand. Nevertheless, the class, cultural, and political divisions among and between the various Latino populations are substantial and likely to continue.

In urban areas the political environment confronting the great majority of contemporary ethnic groups has been most complex, for they have often had to compete with one another and with the older and more established groups. While few achieved the relative solidarity and prominence of the Irish, Italians, Jews, and Cubans, the continuing change in the ethnic composition of the major cities, as was the case at the turn of the century, suggests that more ethnic succession in American politics is forthcoming. And as before, even without political machines, the longer-resident groups have been providing role models for those most likely to take their place.

Several aspects of present-day immigrant communities reveal that the networks among them and between them and their homelands have produced multipolar ethnic groups. Communications and media as well as commercial arrangements and cir-

---

[10]The total of seventeen Latinos and six Asians in Congress did not change in the 1994 election, although Norman Mineta resigned in October 1995. There are also one nonvoting Latino and two nonvoting Pacific Islanders.

cular migration by individuals and families have created links far more effectively than was the case with their predecessors. Thus, while American culture is, in some instances, quickly replacing much of the immigrant cultures, in more and more cases it is being quite deliberately fused to them. Of course, immigrants have all along negotiated the process of cultural overlay, producing by the second generation a more ethnic than immigrant one. It appears, however, that the process has been accelerating since the 1920s and currently may well be more telescoped in time—even for recent refugees—with some, it is said, "leapfrogging" into the mainstream. An exception would be where a group such as the Hasidic Jews is determined to maintain with active deliberation its social and cultural boundaries, or where certain refugee groups, as some among the Cambodians and Hmong, had to flee quickly and brought with them sharply different cultures that they have been most reluctant to foresake.

In numerous cases, new groups have replicated old patterns of organizing, while many individuals have found sufficient reasons to acquire American citizenship as part of their integration. In fact, 7.6 million persons had done so between the end of World War II and 1993. Along with the practical economic and family reunification motives, and concerns about discrimination against noncitizens, becoming naturalized has been part of the immigrants' strategy for advancing their political participation.

The intriguing complexity of American immigration and ethnicity has been the continuing co-existence of new immigrant generations beginning these processes of adaptation and incorporation along with second, third, and even later generations whose status in society spans from substantial acculturation to nearly complete assimilation. The profound changes during the 1960s caught many second-generation Americans in the midst of their own struggles to cement their material achievements and to affirm a pluralistic identity as ethnic Americans. In response to black and Latino activism, a variety of white ethnic groups' members began to recognize their communities as interest groups—political blocs—that might be mobilized. In the process, they reasserted a sense of ethnicity which they hoped would both strengthen their identities and provide a bond that could unify them in pursuit of shared objectives. Although the revival became for many who were American-born an effort to cope with their own feelings of marginality, enough of those truly ethnic cultures, values, and identities had survived—often reenforced by new immigrants. The variety of impulses to action confirm that the revival was actually part revival, part accommodation, and part a quest for affirmation from (and incorporation into) the larger society. What they were struggling to achieve (as were contemporary generations of Chinese and Japanese) the newer, even more racially mixed, immigrants have also begun to pursue. What the final outcome of all this welter of immigrant and ethnic experiences will be depends in no small measure on how Americans come to terms with the racial and religious diversity of today's immigrants—and with the diversities within the diversity, as well.

CHAPTER NINE

The 1990s: New Directions or Full Circle?

By 1995, three decades had elapsed since the reforms of 1965 and over seven since the nation first substantially shut its doors. During those years immigrants continued to make their way through the stages of adaptation and integration. Some assimilated, shedding much of their pasts in exchange for full membership in American society. Meanwhile, America itself was changing dramatically. Achieving the heights of world economic, technological, military, and diplomatic leadership transformed many aspects of American life. Then, what the extraordinary material gains made possible for many, the civil rights achievements began to open up for many more. What the quota system of the 1920s closed off to many who wished to migrate, the reforms after World War II made available to the next generations of aspiring immigrants and anxious refugees. America reopened its door further, and still they came. But by the 1960s they did not come principally from Europe, and they did not, in large numbers, enter legally. As their racial, religious, and cultural diversity increased, and as the volume of undocumented aliens increased, Americans became steadily more uneasy. The old ambivalence about strangers in the land resurfaced. The nation continued to struggle with it for three decades of war and refugees and peoples of all hues and faiths.

In numerous ways, the nation relished the cultural enrichment from its newcomers, benefitted from their labor and entrepreneurialism, and marveled at the revitalization they wrought in various urban centers around the country. But not without problems: the massive volume of illegal aliens; the clashes between newcomers and older generations of Americans, African Americans and white ethnic Americans in particular; the crowded schools and novel language requirements imposed by court decisions; and the compounding effects of inflation, huge losses of industrial jobs, the decline in strength of many unions, and the immense dislocations precipitated by the shift to a postindustrial economy and the post-Cold War economic "downsizing." There were also more outspoken challenges to immigration voiced by various environmental- and population-focused citizens groups. And, finally, one saw again the emergence of politicians eager to capitalize on such public discontent. Immigrants were portrayed as part of the problem, not part of any solution. Had the nation reached the point where it needed an immigration hiatus—or a scapegoat—again?

1990: A New Census and New Immigration Reforms

The 1990 census confirms just how profound have been the consequences of the new immigration. Between 1960 and 1990, the U.S. population rose by 39 percent; the foreign-born population more than doubled (to 19.77 million). The proportion of foreign-born went from 4.7 percent in 1970 to 7.9 percent in 1990, and well over two-fifths had been admitted to permanent residence after 1979.[1] Of the twenty-six leading groups (see Table 9.1), eight

---

[1] A late (August) 1995 census report found that the foreign-born population had reached 8.7 percent in 1994, 22.6 million people, one-fifth of whom had been admitted between 1989 and 1994. That 8.7 percent nearly equaled the 8.8

Table 9.1	U.S. Foreign-born Population, 1990: Rank Order, Top Twenty-six Countries of Birth		
1. Mexico	4,298,014	14. Dominican Republic	347,858
2. Philippines	912,674	15. Jamaica	334,140
3. China & Taiwan	773,939*	16. U.S.S.R.	333,725
4. Canada	744,830	17. Japan	290,128
5. Cuba	736,971	18. Colombia	286,124
6. Germany	711,929	19. Guatemala	225,739
7. United Kingdom	640,145	20. Haiti	225,393
8. Italy	580,592	21. Iran	210,941
9. Korea	568,397	22. Portugal	210,122
10. Vietnam	543,262	23. Greece	177,398
11. El Salvador	465,433	24. Laos	171,577
12. India	450,406	25. Republic of Ireland	169,827
13. Poland	388,328	26. Nicaragua	168,659

*With Hong Kong, total would be 921,070.

were from Asia, eight from Europe, and ten from the Americas. Six were refugee populations.

Although Mexicans and the eight Asian peoples are among the ten largest foreign-born populations, it is the recent ancestry data which still demonstrate that the origins of the nation's population will remain firmly "traditional" for some time, that is European and African American as well as Native American. (See Appendix, Table 9.2.) The published report provides the first and second ethnic ancestries Americans listed on the census forms in 1990, the second by those with mixed ancestry, of course.[2]

---

percent of 1940. The 1994 survey found that two-thirds of the foreign born were white, one-fifth Asian or Pacific Islander, one out of every fourteen black, and 46 percent Latino.

[2]The 1970 census was the last to include second-generation data: 23.96 million persons. A recent estimate places that figure at 24.1 million in 1990. The 1980 census introduced the ancestry category.

Besides those claiming African American, Native American, or Puerto Rican background, twenty-two other nationalities had over 1 million persons each. Of the twenty-two, eighteen were European (or Canadian) in origin. Nearly 146.6 million Americans in 1990 gave a first ancestry that included one of these eighteen. Add in all other European answers and over two-thirds of all the responses were European (or Canadian). In terms of either relative recency of arrival or substantial recent growth, only three ethnic groups really stand out: the Chinese, Filipinos, and Mexicans.

"Revolution" is not a word to be used lightly, but the scale and rapidity of global changes and the corresponding volume and new diversity of the nation's immigrants justify use of that word in describing recent demographic changes. While the census data do confirm that two-thirds of Americans still trace their principal ancestries to Europe, the white European immigrant and ethnic experience, rather than being the dominant one today, is rapidly becoming one of several prominent ones in American ethnicity. Some view these developments with alarm. They fear the impact of this diversity on American culture and American unity, fear the consequences of the immigrants' numbers on the nation's resources and environment, fear that the rapid growth of "nontraditional" peoples will threaten the nation with unassimilating, unabsorbable persons, creating, in effect, an American Latino Quebec (see p. 185). Such anxieties have been expressed before, particularly during the 1910s and early 1920s.

Whether or not the environmental and demographic arguments are subterfuges for cultural and racial concerns, or legitimate ones in their own right, the heightened preoccupation with the immigrants' impact on American society and political life once more underestimates the factors of time and process: For the most part, immigrants, and especially their children, have acculturated, have incorporated basic elements of the American core culture and values. Where permitted, most of the immigrants' descendants have integrated into the larger American society. Although misgivings had been expressed especially since the mid-1970s, they intensified in 1993. However, in the midst of that growing debate, sufficient confidence in the merits of immigration prompted Congress to enact one more round of reforms. In fact, Raul Yzaquirre, president of the National Council of La Raza, observed that, with the 1990 law, "Congress was clearly more liberal than the public." Congress sought a balance between its optimism regarding the nation's ability to absorb and benefit from more immigration and a more cautious approach that included periodic reviews of the numbers admitted and the concept of a "cap" on total immigration. Several concerns influenced the decision to enact the 1990 reforms, including: a) the desire to better protect American workers while also encouraging more professional and skilled persons to immigrate; b) the growing backlog of visa applicants (2.4 million in January 1990); and c) the pressure from certain European groups (notably the Irish) to continue the lottery for supplementary visas outside the existing preferences.

A two-year battle pitched distinctive Senate and House bills against one another and saw anti-immigration groups such as the Federation of Americans for Immigration Reform (FAIR) at loggerheads with the Irish Immigration Reform Movement, the Japanese American Citizens' League, the National Council of La Raza, and other Latino and Asian organizations. The final measure, signed in November 1990 and effective October 1, 1991, was once again a series of compromises. While it reaffirmed the principles of family reunification, it also provided for a Commission on Immigration Reform, subsequently chaired by former congresswoman Barbara Jordan, to review the effectiveness of the legislation and to report back to Congress in 1994 and again in late 1997.

Figure 9.1 presents the key provisions of the 1990 Immigration Act, comparing them to the 1965 Act. Four additional provisions ought to be noted. First, the per country limit for quota immigrants was raised from 20,000 to 25,620. Second, to assist families divided by the Immigrant Reform and Control Act, special visas over a three-year period were allocated for spouses and children of legalized aliens. Third, the law doubled the number of asylum visas and granted Salvadorans "temporary protected status" for eighteen months beyond their initial visas, thereby creating a new category akin to the earlier parole.[3] Fourth, changes were made in naturalization procedures in order to make applying less complex and intimidating. The law also offered a bit of delayed justice by granting long-promised citizenship to Filipino veterans of World War II who had fought with American forces (9,800 were naturalized in F.Y. 1992–93).

The 1990 Immigration Act overwhelmingly preserved the nation's commitment to family reunification, while expanding the opportunities for employment-based applications and making permanent a lottery system for underrepresented nationalities. Although Congress established the 700,000 "cap,"[4] in reality refugees, asylees, and IRCA legalizations, among some others, are not counted under it. And since there remains no actual limit on the number of "immediate relatives" and "special immigrants" (nonquota persons), the so-called cap will likely be "pierced" by them, as well.

What impact the flexible cap and the various special provisions will have, notably those concerning job-skill requirements, diversity visas, asylum, and temporary protected status, is difficult to determine at this time. But the fact that there were significant unintended consequences to the 1965, 1980, and 1986 reforms would certainly suggest that unpredictable effects are likely again. Whether the Commission's initial recommendations, including a 30 percent cut in immigration—which President Clinton endorsed—and mounting public unease will convince Congress to enact restrictive legislation already pending in the fall of 1995 remains to be seen.

The "Costs" of Immigration—Legal and Undocumented

Atul Vaidya wrote an essay for an Asian Indian newspaper in southern California, warning that "a resentful electorate is a dangerous electorate." The events of the early 1990s bore him out

---

[3]For example, in 1991, President Bush conferred that status on fifty thousand persons from the Middle East.

[4]Reduced to 675,000 in F.Y. 1995.

| Figure 9.1 | Preference Categories of the 1965 and 1990 Immigration Laws |

1965 (Cap: 170,000; later 290,000; in 1980, 270,000)	1990 (Cap: 700,000 for 3 yrs; then 675,000)

NONQUOTA*: Parents, spouses, minor children of citizens; clergy and inhabitants of Western Hemisphere (the last deleted in 1976)

FIRST: Unmarried children of citizens and their children. 20% of quota

SECOND: Spouse and unmarried children of resident aliens. 20% of quota. In 1980 increased to 26% of quota***

THIRD: Members of professions and family. 10% of quota

FOURTH: Married children of citizens and family. 10% of quota***

FIFTH: Siblings of citizens and their families. 24% of quota***

SIXTH: Needed skilled and unskilled workers and family. 10% of quota

SEVENTH: Refugees. 6% of quota. Removed in 1980

NONPREFERENCE: Remaining visas within the 20,000-per-country limit (scarcely available after 1976).

I. FAMILY BASED (Cap: 465,000; then 480,000)
NONQUOTA*: Parents, spouses and minor children of U.S. citizens
FAMILY SPONSORED (minimum "floor" of 226,000)**
FIRST: Same as before 10.4%: 23,400 visas
SECOND: Same as before 50.5%: 114,200 visas
THIRD: Same as old Fourth 10.4%: 23,400 visas
FOURTH: Same as old Fifth 28.8%: 65,000 visas

II. EMPLOYMENT BASED (140,000)
FIRST: High priority workers; no certification 28.6%: 40,000 visas
SECOND: Exceptional professionals with advanced degrees; certification required. 28.6%: 40,000 visas
THIRD: Skilled workers, other professionals, and needed unskilled workers —with job certification 28.6%: 40,000 visas (one-fourth for unskilled)
FOURTH: Special immigrants, including clergy 7.1%: 10,000 visas
FIFTH: Substantial investors creating jobs in the United States. 7.1%: 10,000 visas

Figure 9.1	*Continued*

1965	1990
(Cap: 170,000; later 290,000; in 1980, 270,000)	(Cap: 700,000 for 3 yrs; then 675,000)

| | III. DIVERSITY VISAS: 40,000 for 3 years, then 55,000 nonquota and by lottery |
| | IV. OUTSIDE THE ACT: Refugees and asylees, IRCA legalizations, Amerasians, etc. |

*Nonquota now formally called "immediate relatives" and "special immigrants"

**Unused family visas spilldown to other family categories and surplus Fourth could be used by First category

***Any unused visas from higher categories could be used by persons in the 2nd, 4th, and 5th categories.

fully. In the spring of 1994 it appeared that the governors of Florida, California, New York, Texas, and Arizona would sue the federal government for millions of dollars. They claimed that the moneys were owed as promised reimbursements for costs connected with the legalization of IRCA applicants and for the reputed costs of illegal aliens as a result of their states providing health services, welfare benefits, prison incarceration, and children's education for such persons. The cases failed, but they reflected the rising levels of public frustration and anger, and Republican congressional leaders in late 1995 proposed federal aid for the states most affected. One particular target was the Supreme Court's decision in *Plyler* vs. *Doe* (1982). Critics of the current levels of immigration—and especially of the federal government's handling of the illegal alien issue—have been trying to set up a challenge in hopes that a now more conservative Supreme Court would overturn *Plyler* vs. *Doe*. In that decision, the Court denied states (in this case, Texas) the right to deprive children of illegal aliens of an education on the grounds that it would be shortsighted to make them pay for the actions of their parents. In this continuing public debate, legal and undocumented migration have often been merged.

The more alarmist view was expressed by Republican presidential hopeful Pat Buchanan. There is an anticipation, he wrote, that southern California will soon be "almost exclusively Latino," possibly demanding a "Quebec-like status." Furthermore, "Ethnic militancy and solidarity are on the rise . . . ; the old institutions of assimilation are not doing their work as they once did; the melting pot is in need of repair. . . . If America is to survive as 'one nation, one people,' we need to call a time out on immigration, to assimilate the tens of millions who have lately arrived. . . ." A more moderate view, echoing the concerns of a variety of organizations, came from John Martin, of the Center for Migration Studies, in Washington, D.C.: "We are coping with urban crowding, highway gridlock, poverty, income disparity, population pressures on wetlands and other environmental concerns. Since these issues are exacerbated by the level and composition of immigration, it is prudent to include immigration reform on the national agenda. Our history has shown that we have incorporated newcomers best during periods of moderate immigration and least well when the level was high, as it is today." The laws need to be modified, he concluded, to "relate more closely to our absorptive capacity and workplace needs."

Emotions and anxieties have been escalating on both sides, particularly as a result, in November 1994, of the passage of Proposition 187 in California and the Republican congressional victories, giving them a majority in both houses for the first time in forty years. Approved by 59 percent of the voters, Proposition 187 made illegal aliens ineligible for most nonemergency public social, health, and educational services and required such agencies to report those persons to the INS. Overwhelmingly, the motive given for supporting Prop. 187 was to send a message to Washington. As one Los Angeles woman put it in a Letter to the Editor, "People who are here illegally are breaking the law; I don't think we should pick and choose which laws we should abide by." One common response to that view, this one by the manager of a car wash, pinpointed a major dilemma facing employers: "What am I going to do, hire a bunch of white guys? I tried that before and none of them were willing to work for what I could pay them."

Nonetheless, rather quickly in fifteen other states moves were made to introduce similar legislation. Although the courts suspended implementation of Proposition 187 pending determination of its constitutionality, the widespread calls for action to regain "control of our borders" received an enormous boost from the conservative thrust of the voters in November. Within the first month after convening of the 104th Congress, more than ten bills had been introduced to curb legal as well as illegal immigration. Commentators repeatedly referred to the "seething," "huge anger" of the public and the renewed mentality of "Fortress North America."

While several local studies have tried to assess the "costs" of immigration, Professor Donald Huddle conducted a national study for the Carrying Capacity Network, an anti-immigration, nonprofit group. He concluded that the overall annual cost to government on all levels was $42.5 billion. Most such studies have seriously underestimated the taxes immigrants actually pay, directly and indirectly, and significantly overestimated the service costs of immigrants. The Urban Institute of Washington, D.C., reported in mid-1994 that Huddle had, in fact, overestimated the costs by $71.2 billion by, among other things, underestimating the taxes paid by $50 billion. Such studies critical of immigration's impact have also usually omitted the contributions of immigrant-owned businesses (1.3 million immigrants were self-employed in 1990—and the percentage increases with their length of time in America). They have likewise ignored the extent to which immigrants stimulate other, related sectors of the economy both as entrepreneurs and as consumers. Other flaws in these studies surface, too, but part of the problem is that precise figures on illegal aliens are so difficult to determine accurately. Undocumented and legal aliens are sometimes lumped together. A February 1995 RAND Corporation study concluded that the various state and local studies are inconclusive because they are so inconsistent and so varied in how they categorize immigrants, service costs, and revenues. That illegals contributed less in revenues than other aliens was due more to "differences in average income . . . rather than immigration status."

What also appeared to be a valid case was that, while nationally immigrants were not a net burden, on the state level the picture was more complex because one-half to two-thirds of tax revenues from immigrants went to the federal government. Because a far smaller percentage went to local agencies (perhaps 10 to 15 percent)—agencies that were bearing more of the service burdens—there did appear to be a real inequity on that local level and especially for those areas with greater concentrations of both legal and undocumented aliens. And, too, part of the problem had been the failure of the federal government to reimburse states some $4 billion in IRCA-related expenses, as pledged by Congress in 1986.

In terms of the impact of immigrants on the job market, the most recent studies indicated that competition with native-born workers has occurred in some places, but, overall, there was no adverse impact on jobs or wages, except for low-skilled workers living in areas to which many immigrants come (such as Miami and south Texas). It was also somewhat more evident in locations where the economy had been stagnant. In these circumstances, those likely (or more frequently) to be adversely affected were actually other immigrants who had preceded the later newcomers. Initially, these persons have been disproportionately concentrated in lower paying, nonunion manufacturing, construction, and service-related jobs, which the newest arrivals commonly seek out, as well.[5] On the other hand, concluded the Urban Institute, immigrants "create more jobs than they themselves fill and recent immigrants from abroad create as much employment growth as internal migrants from other areas of the United States," especially in a place like Los Angeles.

Illegal aliens, it is generally acknowledged, continued to come because people were still willing to hire them. The public re-

---

[5]This, obviously, is not describing those professionals and other skilled workers who are usually meeting unfilled labor demands.

sented the perceived "costs" and alleged job losses but remained deeply divided over such potential remedies as more effective employer sanctions and uniform, noncounterfeitable employee identification cards (together with a computerized verification system), both of which the Commission on Immigration Reform recommended to Congress in the fall of 1994. (The verification system is now being tested in several states.)

Finally, it was often overlooked that undocumented aliens were consumers and taxpayers, people who buy groceries, clothes, cars, appliances (often to take back home), pay for utilities, and use automobiles. Be they Mexican, Chinese, Jamaican, Dominican, or Irish, they did often fill the semiskilled and unskilled jobs—usually deadend jobs—that studies have found native-born Americans unwilling to take. It was also undocumented aliens who had, in some measure, partially underwritten another important aspect of American life: lower prices or costs for fruits, vegetables, and many other products and services, especially in the garment, hotel, and restaurant industries. It is they who have enabled marginal businesses and those facing stiff foreign competition to keep from failing or leaving the country.

Former New York governor Mario Cuomo, son of Italian immigrants, expressed the liberal view in this regard in 1993:

It is hard to imagine how New York's health system could function without the immigrant doctors, nurses, technicians, and food services staff. In fact, our newest newcomers have saved several key industries in New York—like garment manufacturing, which would have left the city had immigrants not provided a new source of labor. Immigrant entrepreneurs also start new businesses; in New York, today, they own over 40,000 firms, firms that add jobs and $3.5 billion to our economy every year.

In even more passionate terms, Los Angeles reporter Robert Scheer wrote in exasperation prior to the passage of Proposition 187: "How dare we deny education to the children of women who clean our homes and raise our children? . . . How dare we deny medical care to those who harvest our crops, clip our lawns and golf courses, bus our dishes, wash our cars and every night leave spotless the very office towers whose top executives support . . . this mean proposal."

With crises periodically flaring up in the nation's inner cities that involve immigrants and undocumented aliens, the anxieties among broad segments of the American public about the capacity of the nation to absorb so many newcomers, legal or not, have intensified. Following four major riots in Miami since 1980, a prime example in this decade was the Los Angeles riot of late April 1992, one of the nation's first multiethnic riots. About 45 percent of those arrested were Latino and some 41 percent were African American. Approximately twelve hundred of those Latinos arrested—over one-third—were determined to be undocumented aliens and were turned over to the INS; half were deported. In the light of such events, the difficulty which the public found in appreciating the benefits derived from the employment of such workers—as argued by Cuomo and Scheer—versus their costs, which are real in some places, in part explains why politicians have been able to exploit this as a political issue. At a March 1995 news conference, the chair of a bipartisan Congressional task force on illegal immigration, Elton Gallegly (California), delivered its message to illegal immigrants—present and future: "If you are thinking of coming to this country illegally, forget about it, and if you're here already, pack your bags."

The Challenge and the Toll of Immigration

Nineteen-year-old Korean Lee Ki Chuck, who had come to America in 1973, recalled two years later that, "If I come to America, I thought that America was really heaven country. I saw so many movie. I saw cars, everyone drives car. If I go to America, I can drive. I can watch TV, everything. I thought I was really heading to heaven. But that's wrong. You have to try to make heaven." Josef Patyna, an activist in the Polish Solidarity movement, fled to America in 1983 with his wife, Krystyna. She was stunned: "Sometimes the people where women work [in Poland] will let them leave an hour or two early to stand in line to shop. When we came to West Germany and Rhode Island, it was unbelievable to walk into a supermarket and see so much food. And no long lines!"

But the changes could take a toll, and the impact personally could be devastating. A young Taiwanese woman recalled the effect of migration on her father, who had left Taiwan because he feared the consequences of United States recognition of Communist China. There, he had been well-known; here, he had become a janitor. "His pride was shot. He had been the head editor of a newspaper.... He had a lot of influence ... in Taiwan. All of a sudden he was this janitor who didn't *know* the language and a lot of people perceived [him] as *stupid*.... I remember this man just *disappearing*.... There was no more life left in him." Monica Dickens provides a completely opposite example, for she had come from England and admired America and cherished her experience: "I like the fact that people here can get anywhere. You can be born with very little and come from a fairly poor family, and you can make it if you're intelligent and hard working. In England that is still difficult...."

Even when not devastating, the process was obviously not always smooth, and newcomers often brought hostilities with them (Vietnamese versus Cambodian most recently; Irish versus English earlier) or they experienced the strains of being thrust among strangers. A Greek living in Astoria, Queens (New York), put it tersely: "We have no tensions with other groups. We just don't associate with them." Inevitably, of course, most do, and do so with the larger society in myriad ways. However, such encounters today, one historian has observed, are "much more complex and unpredictable." Immigrants are more and more seen practicing selective adaptation while negotiating new identities. On one level, the grandchildren and great grandchildren of the pre-1930 European immigrants may have exchanged much of their traditional immigrant roots for American ones, retaining a few parts of their culture, choosing to emphasize aspects of their identity when convenient and useful, and dwelling on group interests when practical. Still, some retain enough feelings for the past to respond to current crises affecting the old homelands.

On another level, the diversity of contemporary immigrants ranges from fair-skinned English and Irish to soft brown Tongans and Samoans to very dark West Africans and West Indians. They will attempt the same processes of adjustment, accommodation, and integration as their forerunners—and some will find the path of adaptation easy—but for those of color, who constitute a majority of the contemporary immigrants, their ethnic identity will remain far less a matter of choice in a society that continues to be very clearly racially self-conscious.

Perhaps America is in the process of becoming the first "universal nation," but it is not a colorblind one and it never has been. Nonetheless, the legitimization of this diversity has created novel challenges. Many Americans daily confront the reality of groups with different degrees of social advantage and disadvantage (due to class and color) and differing legal statuses, and this has been labelled a "new and different multiethnic spectrum." One result of the racial variety is that the immigrants have been caught up in the escalating debate in the mid-1990s over affirmative action: over group rights versus individual rights, over meritocracy versus economic need, and over questions of just how level "the playing field" really is and precisely which minorities ought to be eligible for special programs. Notwithstanding these conflicts—and even the urban explosions—many peoples of the world remain anxious and eager to migrate to the United States. In January 1994, over 3.6 million applicants for visas were awaiting openings, and 96 percent of these were waiting for family reunification.

One question now before the nation is whether it is about to come full circle: Are Americans again experiencing "ethnic overload"—are they ready to insist on more breathing space, an immigration hiatus? Or, are they responding to the disruptions and perceived dangers from extensive worldwide social and economic (and post–Cold War) changes by seeking scapegoats and stability—"fixed points" on which to anchor their need for security? The racial climate may prove to be critical in this regard, for some believe that the growing public resistance reveals the underlying misgivings of the middle and working classes, an unwillingness to accept the more multiracial society that has taken form over the past three decades. Certainly, the escalation of hate crimes against racial minorities, dramatized in 1982 by the brutal murder of twenty-seven-year-old Vincent Chin by two automobile assembly workers, was unsettling evidence of the tensions that periodically surface and of the inseparability of the racial climate from the state of the economy—and from attitudes toward immigrants.

The changed political and economic climate includes a number of weaker labor unions, a relatively conservative Supreme Court, and a Congress still in the process of shrinking and readjusting the immense defense industries. In 1995, it was also debating legislation designed to cut government programs to noncitizens and shift responsibility for social services more to the states—measures that would reduce benefits to an estimated 2.2 million legal immigrants. Numerous proposals to cut legal immigration were likewise introduced. Resident immigrants had not waited to take some form of action in response, especially those legalized under IRCA and now eligible for American citizenship. While many leaders were condemning the new proposals and the hostile climate, there was, between October 1994 and January 1995, an 80 percent leap in applications for American citizenship—over 300 percent in Los Angeles; 120 percent in the West.[6] As Cuban-American congressman Lincoln Diaz-Balart (Florida) put it, "There has been an alert sent out. We are being targeted. It's risky to be a legal immigrant." For Yoon Kyun Hur, of Korea, the decision was easy: "I'm going to live here the rest of my life, so I think it makes sense that I become a citizen." For Mexican immigrant Teofilo Avad, father of eight children, the decision to become a citizen in April 1995 had taken twenty-five years. It took the unsettled climate to convince him: "I'm very happy here, and I don't want any problems." Fiscal Year 1994–95 was expected to surpass 1944 in the number naturalized.

Notwithstanding the role of politicians in framing public issues, public attitudes do remain complex. The sight of rusting freighters grounded off the shores of America in mid-1993, filled with illegal Chinese aliens being smuggled into the country, brought directly home for many the overall immigration issue,

---

[6]In the fiscal year ending September 30, 1992, 240,252 persons had been naturalized. In the fiscal year ending September 30, 1994, 406,223 had received American citizenship.

because Americans at times do lump all migrants together—legal and illegal. Thus, back in June 1965 a Gallup poll found that one-third of Americans wished for immigration to be decreased; that figure reached 49 percent on the eve of the IRCA (1986), and, in June 1993, stood at 61 percent. A *Newsweek* poll the following month reported that three-fifths of those polled saw contemporary immigration as a "bad thing"—but past immigration was a "good thing"! In September, a *Time* magazine poll suggested that 64 percent believed that most immigrants arrive illegally and 73 percent favored strict limits on immigration. Finally, a spring 1994 California poll reported 49 percent endorsed the view that the amnesty program of IRCA had been "a bad thing."

Perhaps some optimism regarding the way American opinions do evolve over the long term with respect to the waves of newcomers can be seen in a 1982 Gallup poll. It was conducted two years after the floodtide of Cuban and Haitian refugees during the summer of 1980. Respondents were asked if the groups listed "have been a good thing or a bad thing for this country." Eleven years later, in 1993, a Gallup poll tried a slightly different question: Had particular immigrants "generally benefitted the country or generally created problems?" As Table 9.4 indicates, American attitudes toward groups regarded with distaste and fear earlier in the century had considerably changed; it was now the newest groups that were of greater concern, or represented the greater unknown. Indeed, the negative perceptions of Mexicans, Vietnamese, Cubans, and Haitians had increased by 1993, and the one new group, Iranians, were now, along with Cubans and Haitians, held in the lowest esteem.

Can Americans, as one immigrant woman wrote in 1992, "engage our diversity to yield a nation greater than the sum of its parts"? Charles Keely, a leading demographer, put the whole issue quite poignantly: "Without the *pluribus* and without an environment that allows plurality to flourish, there is no *unum* in America. America cannot be united unless we are free to be different. Nothing will destroy the unity of America as completely as uniformity imposed by some of us on all of us."

Table 9.4	Perceptions of Immigrants in Gallup Polls, 1982 and 1993*			
Listed Ethnic Groups	Good for Country 1982	Benefitted Country 1993	Bad for Country 1982	Created Problems 1993
English	66%	n/a	6%	n/a
Irish	62	75%	7	11%
Jews	59	n/a	9	n/a
Germans	57	n/a	11	n/a
Italians	56	n/a	10	n/a
Poles	53	65%	12	15%
Japanese	47	n/a	18	n/a
Blacks	46	n/a	16	n/a
Chinese	44	59%	19	31%
Mexicans	25	29	34	59
Koreans	24	53	30	33
Vietnamese	20	41	38	46%
Puerto Ricans	17	n/a	43	n/a
Haitians	10	19%	39	65%
Cubans	9	24	59	64
Iranians	n/a	20	n/a	68

*1982: "On balance, have they been a good thing or a bad thing for the country?" 1993: "Have the listed groups 'generally benefitted the country or generally created problems?'"

In 1983, following a dinner at a friend's home in Pune, India, an American historian departed with another guest, a young Indian executive. He had a fine job in Bombay, a high salary, a precious condominium, and a chauffered car. While riding in the three-wheeled taxi with the American, he asked how he could enter the United States. Astonished, the American pointed out that, by Indian standards, he had it all; he had already "made it." Why would he wish to leave? "Because," the Indian replied, "I hear it's better in America." So he believed, and so have millions of others. In fact, in June 1994, in a country where the average industrial worker earned $37 per month and a farm laborer less, six million Bangladeshis applied for thirty-eight hundred diversity visas available to their country under the 1990 U.S. legislation. Said a thirty-five-year-old farmer, "I am applying for [the visa] even if it costs me the last piece of my land. Why should I rot in Bangladesh and starve almost every day if I [can] have a place in America?"

Consider: the former chairman of the U.S. Joint Chiefs of Staff, son of a Jamaican immigrant, Colin Powell, and his successor in the fall of 1993, Gen. John Shalikashvili, a Polish immigrant born in Warsaw in 1936. Consider: the irony of the Vietnam Memorial in Washington, D.C., designed by a young Asian American, Maya Ying Lin. And, finally, consider the experience of Oleg Jankovic, a Ukrainian born in a DP camp who came to America at the age of seven with his mother. He rose to become a commander in the U.S. Navy, and, in 1987, was appointed assistant for policy to the secretary of the Navy in the Pentagon. After his mother died, Jankovic visited his old sponsor in Massachusetts, who apologized for not having done more for him and his mother. Jankovic replied, "What more could you have done? You gave us everything there was to be given. You gave us a chance."

And, so, they still come.

APPENDIX
Additional Tables

(See Contents, p. X, for complete list of Tables and Figures)

Table 2.1	Immigration to the United States: 1901–1920 versus 1921–1930 (percent of each total period)				
Principal Region or Country	1901–1910	1911–1920	1921–1930 Total	1921–1924	1925–1930
TOTAL	8,795,386	5,735,811	4,107,209	2,344,599	1,762,610
Avg/Year	(879,539)	(573,581)	(410,721)	(586,400)	(293,768)
Northern/ Western Europe	1,910,035 21.7%	997,438 17.4%	1,284,023 31.3%	577,763 24.6%	706,260 40.1%
Southern/ Eastern Europe	6,225,981 70.8%	3,379,126 58.9%	1,913,830 29.0%	963,245 41.1%	230,585 13.1%
Asia	243,567 2.8%	192,559 3.4%	97,400 2.4%	75,067 3.2%	22,333 1.3%
Canada	179,226 2.0%	742,185 12.9%	924,515 22.5%	436,828 18.6%	487,687 27.7%
Mexico	49,642 .6%	219,004 3.8%	459,287 11.2%	203,413 8.7%	255,874 14.5%
West Indies	107,548 1.2%	123,424 2.2%	74,899 1.8%	51,963 2.2%	22,936 1.3%

Table 2.2	U.S. Foreign-born Population: 1930 versus 1920	
Country of Origin	1930	1920
ALL FOREIGN-BORN	14,204,149	13,920,692
Austria	370,914	575,627
Belgium	64,194	62,687
Czechoslovakia	491,638	362,438
Denmark & Iceland	182,238	189,154
Finland	142,478	149,824
France	135,592	152,072
Germany	1,608,814	1,686,108
Greece	174,526	175,976
Hungary	274,450	397,283
Ireland	744,810	[U.K.]
Italy	1,790,429	1,610,113
Lithuania	193,606	135,068
Netherlands	133,133	131,726
Norway	347,852	363,863
Poland	1,268,583	1,139,979
Portugal & Azores	108,775	103,976
Rumania	146,393	102,823
Russia	1,153,628	1,400,495*
Spain	59,362	49,535
Sweden	595,250	625,585
Switzerland	113,010	118,659
Turkey	48,911	16,303
United Kingdom	1,402,923	2,172,723**
Yugoslavia	211,416	169,439
Other Europe	43,516	34,571
Armenia	32,166	36,628
China	46,129	43,560
Japan	70,993	81,502
India	5,850	4,901
Syria	57,227	51,901
Other Asia	10,509	5,236
Canada/Newfoundland	1,310,369	1,138,174
Mexico	641,462	486,418
West Indies	106,241	78,962
Central America	10,514	4,912
South America	33,623	18,551
Africa	8,859	5,781
Oceana & Australia	17,343	14,626

*Included Latvia and Estonia, which in 1930 counted 20,673 and 3,550, respectively.

**Includes all Ireland, which counted separately at 744,810 in 1930.

Table 2.3	Naturalization of Principal Foreign-born Groups, 1925–1930	
Country of Last Allegiance	Number Naturalized	Percent of Total
ALL PERSONS	**1,125,852**	
All Europeans	1,044,038	92.7%
Austria	20,767	1.8
Czechoslovakia	48,432	4.3
Germany	64,171	5.7
Greece	39,307	3.5
Hungary	28,541	2.5
Italy	228,320	20.3
Norway	15,582	1.4
Poland	177,740	15.8
Rumania	28,073	2.5
Sweden	27,387	2.4
U.S.S.R.	94,786	8.4
United Kingdom	143,877	12.8
Yugoslavia	31,897	2.8
Canada	40,829	3.6
Mexico	745	—

Table 6.1	Immigration and Emigration, 1931–1965		
Immigrants to U.S.		Emigrants from U.S.	
1931-40:	528,431	1931–45:	502,434
1941-45:	170,952	1946–57:	294,680
1946-65:	4,829,878	1958–65:	260,000 (est.)
Total:	5,529,261	Total:	1,057,114 (est.)

Table 6.2	1960: Median Years of Education Completed by Foreign-born and Second-generation Men and Women			

	Foreign-born		Second-generation	
Country of Origin	Males	Females	Males	Females
ALL PERSONS*	8.4	8.5	10.9	11.1
Austria	8.3	8.2	11.6	11.6
Czechoslovakia	8.3	8.1	10.5	10.4
Finland	7.9	8.0	10.7	12.0
Germany	9.0	8.9	8.9	9.0
Ireland	8.6	8.6	11.3	11.7
Italy	6.2	5.5	10.9	10.9
Lithuania	6.8	4.6	12.1	12.0
Norway	8.6	8.6	9.9	11.6
Poland	7.6	6.3	10.9	10.6
Sweden	8.5	8.6	11.1	12.0
United Kingdom	10.0	10.1	11.5	12.0
Yugoslavia	7.3	7.0	11.7	11.9
Canada	9.8	10.5	11.1	11.7
Mexico	4.7	5.0	8.6	8.5

*TOTAL U.S. NATIVES   10.6 Males   11.1 Females
*TOTAL U.S. WHITE NATIVES   10.9 Males   11.6 Females
(Natives: Third and later generations)

Table 6.3	1960: White-collar Employment Among Foreign-born and Second-generation Men and Women (percent of those employed)*			

	Foreign-born		Second-generation	
Country of Origin	Males	Females	Males	Females
ALL PERSONS**	33.2%	41.9%	41.4%	61.7%
Austria	43.4	46.0	46.6	63.8
Czechoslovakia	30.3	32.6	31.4	55.3
Germany	35.6	44.2	36.4	59.5
Ireland	27.0	38.9	48.0	75.0
Italy	21.5	21.3	37.2	54.5
Poland	35.4	34.9	36.6	52.2
U.S.S.R.	50.1	51.1	66.3	78.3
United Kingdom	44.1	57.5	48.1	71.6
Canada	38.1	59.0	40.6	60.8
Mexico	10.2	21.2	17.0	38.1

*White-collar here includes professional and technical; manager, and proprietor; clerical, and sales workers

**TOTAL U.S. NATIVES   33.2 Males   53.4 Females
**TOTAL U.S. WHITE NATIVES   36.1 Males   60.0 Females
(Natives: Third and later generations)

Table 6.4	Selected Naturalized Groups and Regions, 1957–1968		
Region/Country of Last Allegiance	Total Naturalized 1957–68	Region/Country of Last Allegiance	Total Naturalized 1957–68
ALL PERSONS	1,392,437		
Africa	6,183	North America	242,066
Asia	150,574	Oceana	4,883
Europe	944,913	South America	242,066
France	15,042	Netherlands	30,488
Germany	203,024	Poland	81,421
Greece	46,826	Portugal	17,206
Hungary	42,438	U.S.S.R.	31,194
Ireland	41,238	United Kingdom	124,529
Italy	142,139	Yugoslavia	30,640
China/Taiwan	34,414	Japan	37,115
India	2,088	Korea ('58–68)	11,407
Iran ('59–92)	2,541	Philippines	26,538
Israel	21,347	Vietnam ('60–68)	406
Canada	112,541	El Salvador ('60–68)	1,179
Colombia	4,265	Haiti ('60–68)	1,744
Cuba	30,264	Jamaica ('63–68)	2,437
Dominican Rep. ('60–68)	2,733	Mexico	70,686

Table 7.2a	Leading Immigrant Groups at the Start of Each Decade, 1950–1990, by Country of Birth

	1950			1960	
1. Poland	52,851 / 21.2%		1. Mexico	32,684 /	12.3%
2. Germany	31,225 / 12.5		2. Germany	31,768 /	12.0
3. Canada	18,043 / 7.2		3. Canada	30,990 /	11.7
4. Latvia	17,494 / 7.0		4. United Kingdom	24,643 /	9.3
5. United Kingdom	13,437 / 5.4		5. Italy	14,933 /	5.6
6. Lithuania	11,870 / 4.8		6. Cuba	8,283 /	3.1
7. U.S.S.R.	10,971 / 4.4		7. Poland	7,949 /	3.0
8. Italy	9,839 / 3.9		8. Ireland	7,687 /	2.9
9. Yugoslavia	9,154 / 3.7		9. Hungary	7,257 /	2.7
10. Mexico	6,841 / 2.7		10. Portugal	6,968 /	2.6
11. All Others	67,462 / 27.1		11. All Others	92,236 /	34.8
TOTAL:	249,187		**TOTAL:**	265,398	

	1970			1980	
1. Mexico	44,469 / 11.9%		1. Mexico	56,680 /	10.7%
2. Philippines	31,203 / 8.4		2. Vietnam	43,483 /	8.1
3. Italy	24,973 / 6.7		3. Philippines	42,316 /	8.0
4. Greece	16,464 / 4.4		4. Korea	32,320 /	6.1
5. Cuba	16,334 / 4.4		5. China/Taiwan	27,651 /	5.2
6. Jamaica	15,033 / 4.0		6. India	22,607 /	4.3
7. United Kingdom	14,158 / 3.8		7. Jamaica	19,714 /	3.7
8. China/Taiwan	14,093 / 3.8		8. Dominican Rep.	17,519 /	2.3
9. Canada	13,804 / 3.7		9. United Kingdom	15,485 /	2.9
10. Portugal	13,195 / 3.5		10. Cuba	15,054 /	2.8
11. All Others	169,600 / 45.4		11. All Others	237,810 /	44.8
TOTAL:	373,326		**TOTAL:**	530,639	

1990
Non-IRCA Immigrants

1. Mexico	56,549 /	8.6%
2. Philippines	54,907 /	8.4
3. Vietnam	48,662 /	7.4
4. China/Taiwan	42,585 /	6.5
5. Dominican Republic	32,064 /	4.9
6. Korea	29,548 /	4.4
7. India	28,679 /	4.4
8. U.S.S.R.	25,350 /	3.9
9. Jamaica	18,828 /	2.9
10. Iran	18,031 /	2.7
11. All Others	300,908 /	45.9
TOTAL:	656,111	

Table 7.3	Total Immigration: Forty Leading Groups Admitted, 1966–1993, by Country of Birth
TOTAL	17,408,177
1. Mexico	3,797,128
2. Philippines	1,127,927
3. China/Taiwan/Hong Kong	1,011,694
4. Vietnam	777,930
5. Korea	700,349
6. India	588,388
7. Dominican Republic	587,357
8. Cuba	552,212
9. Jamaica	478,460
10. United Kingdom	422,492
11. Canada	363,790
12. El Salvador	356,846
13. Haiti	295,139
14. Italy	294,626
15. Colombia	283,029
16. Former U.S.S.R.*	297,878
17. Iran	254,148
18. Poland	242,523
19. Germany	227,416
20. Portugal	218,442
21. Greece	199,098
22. Laos**	196,187
23. Guyana	175,397
24. Guatemala	171,073
25. Ecuador	150,744
26. Trinidad	150,405
27. Peru	136,690
28. Pakistan	136,152
29. Thailand**	132,709
30. Cambodia**	132,439
31. Japan	127,986
32. Former Yugoslavia	119,055
33. Nicaragua	96,468
34. Lebanon	96,320
35. Republic of Ireland	89,956
36. Romania	86,161
37. Jordan	85,772
38. Israel	85,169
39. Egypt	82,101
40. Spain	69,121

*Breakdowns for the former Soviet Union and former Yugoslavia were first provided with the 1993 data.

**Cambodia and Laos, 1972–93 only; Thailand, 1969–93 only.

Table 8.1a	1990: Principal Non-English Languages "Usually Spoken at Home"
Language	Numbers of persons
Spanish	17,340,000
French	1,700,000
German	1,550,000
Italian	1,310,000
Chinese*	1,250,000
Tagalog**	843,300
Polish	723,500
Korean	626,500
Vietnamese	507,100
Portuguese	429,100
Japanese	427,700
Greek	388,300
Arabic	355,200
Hindu, Urdu+	331,500
Russian	241,800
Yiddish	213,100
Thai	206,300
Persian	201,900
Armenian	149,700
Hebrew	144,300
Dutch	142,700
Mon-Khmer++	127,400

*various dialects
**Filipino
+and other Indian dialects
++Cambodian

Table 8.2	Percent of Self-Employment Among Selected Groups of Foreign-born Men and Women in 1990*	
Country of Birth	Men	Women
ALL U.S. NATIVE-BORN	8.6%	5.1%
ALL FOREIGN-BORN	7.6	5.7
All Europe	11.1	7.2
Germany	11.0	7.7
Greece	17.3	9.3
Italy	12.6	5.7
United Kingdom	9.3	7.3
Soviet Union	12.8	6.6
All Asia/Middle East	9.0	6.3
Cambodia	5.6	4.7
China	8.9	6.3
India	6.9	5.3
Iran	13.5	8.4
Korea	21.5	14.6
Laos	2.3	2.0
Philippines	3.8	2.8
Taiwan	8.1	6.8
Vietnam	5.6	6.0
Canada	11.7	7.4
Cuba	9.8	4.0
Dominican Republic	6.5	3.3
Jamaica	5.1	3.0
Mexico	4.6	4.4
El Salvador	3.8	5.9
Colombia	7.2	5.9
All Africa	7.9	5.3

*All employed, 16 and older.

Table 8.3	Educational Attainment of Selected Foreign-born Groups of Men and Women in 1990, 25 Years and Older			
	Eighth Grade or Less		Two Year College Degree or More	
Country of Birth	Men	Women	Men	Women
ALL U.S. NATIVE-BORN	8.8%	8.6%	29.0%	24.3%
ALL FOREIGN-BORN	25.4	27.2	29.9	22.9%
Greece	28.0	39.9	23.3	13.4
Ireland	13.9	19.0	31.4	16.6
Italy	38.8	49.7	14.8	7.9
U.S.S.R.	18.7	24.2	38.7	28.7
United Kingdom	4.1	6.3	45.0	22.4
Cambodia	37.7	59.7	15.7	6.1
China	21.3	31.9	43.2	29.8
India	3.0	9.7	76.7	60.4
Iran	3.8	10.3	67.5	42.8
Korea	5.0	13.9	60.4	32.2
Laos	37.8	62.0	13.8	6.0
Philippines	9.9	12.1	39.7	49.8
Taiwan	2.7	6.6	79.7	63.5
Vietnam	16.5	28.6	31.8	19.2
Cuba	26.5	29.5	23.0	20.4
Dominican Republic	32.9	39.3	12.4	9.9
Mexico	57.5	58.8	6.1	5.9
Colombia	12.8	17.2	24.9	20.6

Table 8.4	Employment of Selected Foreign-born Groups of Men and Women in 1990: Professional and Managerial Positions				
	Professionals		Managers/Proprietors		All Professionals & Managers
Country of Birth	Males	Females	Males	Females	
ALL U.S. NATIVE-BORN	12.1%	16.8%	13.4%	11.5%	26.8%
ALL FOREIGN-BORN	11.7	13.0	10.6	8.9	22.0
Europe	15.8	15.0	17.2	11.7	30.0
Greece	10.8	10.9	21.4	10.0	28.6
Italy	8.2	8.8	13.6	8.6	20.3
United Kingdom	23.7	17.6	23.4	14.9	39.9
U.S.S.R.	21.1	18.7	11.9	9.5	30.9
Asia	20.4	17.1	14.3	10.4	31.5
China	20.1	12.8	13.1	10.5	28.9
India	37.1	28.2	16.5	10.4	48.3
Iran	25.6	20.5	19.8	13.1	41.9
Korea	15.7	10.8	15.0	9.4	25.5
Philippines	13.2	21.6	11.3	9.6	28.3
Taiwan	36.2	20.0	18.5	18.9	47.4
Canada	19.7	22.4	19.3	14.2	37.9
Caribbean	5.0	8.8	6.5	5.9	13.0
Cuba	9.7	12.6	12.7	10.7	22.8
Mexico	1.9	4.1	3.0	3.6	5.8
Central America	3.7	5.6	5.2	4.8	9.5

Table 8.5	Income of Selected Foreign-born Groups, 1989, Ranked by Per Capita Income	
Country of Birth	Median Family Income	Per Capita Income
India*	$52,908	$25,275
United Kingdom	45,681	23,008
Canada	39,995	21,904
Iran	40,273	21,371
Germany	41,757	21,628
Europe	40,428	20,904
Greece	39,024	20,727
Africa	36,783	20,117
Italy	37,673	18,712
Taiwan	45,325	18,551
Philippines	47,794	17,740
Asia	39,395	16,661
Cuba	32,007	16,482
Caribbean	29,464	14,225
ALL FOREIGN-BORN	31,785	15,033
U.S.S.R.	28,799	15,012
ALL U.S. NATIVE-BORN	35,508	14,367
Colombia	30,342	13,733
Vietnam	30,496	11,012
Central America	23,587	9,446
Dominican Republic	19,694	9,358
Mexico	21,585	8,483
El Salvador	21,818	8,405
Cambodia	19,043	7,354
Laos	19,615	6,724

*Among those Asian Indians who had been admitted before 1980, the median income was $65,500, per capita was $39,542, and average family income was $87,887!

Table 8.6a	A Comparison of Changing Naturalization Patterns: Selected Nationalities, 1957–1968, 1969–1980, and 1981–1992		
Region/Country of Last Allegiance	Total Naturalized 1957–68	Total Naturalized 1969–80	Total Naturalized 1981–92
ALL PERSONS	1,392,437	1,673,880	2,762,575
Europe	944,913	561,750	444,556
Asia	150,574	506,944	1,320,036
North America	242,066	462,818	696,075
South America	22,017	88,023	184,159
Oceana	4,883	6,839	17,475
Africa	6,186	23,809	74,079
Germany	203,024	79,534	31,711
Greece	46,826	59,351	34,573
Hungary	42,438	15,764	8,821
Ireland	41,238	18,841	9,403
Italy	142,139	98,921	36,544
Netherlands	30,488	12,921	5,902
Poland	81,421	36,941	42,717
Portugal	17,206	35,867	35,396
U.S.S.R.	31,194	8,415	54,071
United Kingdom	124,529	99,073	105,847
Yugoslavia	30,640	54,679	19,732
Cambodia ('70–92)	—	226	24,916
China/Taiwan	34,414	104,700	162,981
India	2,088	37,206	119,366
Iran ('59–92)	2,541	9,117	52,343
Israel	21,347	19,179	24,088
Japan	37,115	20,135	11,434
Laos ('70–92)	—	178	27,655
Korea ('58–92)	11,409	83,408	158,043
Philippines	26,538	150,365	303,126
Vietnam ('60–92)	406	12,678	229,138
Canada	112,541	53,570	40,225
Mexico	70,686	120,338	214,100
Cuba	30,264	208,916	126,394
Dominican Republic ('60–92)	2,733	19,908	70,028
Haiti ('60–92)	1,744	17,666	35,403
Jamaica ('63–92)	2,437	37,111	103,362
El Salvador ('60–92)	1,179	5,280	24,098
Colombia	4,265	21,496	53,406

Table 8.6b	A Comparison of Percentage Changes in Naturalization Patterns: Selected Nationalities, 1957–1968, 1969–1980, and 1981–1992		
Region/Country of Last Allegiance	Percent Change 1969–80 vs. 1957–68	Percent Change 1981–92 vs. 1969–80	Percent Change 1981–92 vs. 1957–68
ALL PERSONS	+ 20.2%	+ 65.0%	+ 98.4
Europe	– 40.6	– 20.9	– 53.0
Asia	+236.7	+160.3	+776.7
North America	+ 91.2	+ 50.4	+187.6
South America	+300.0	+109.2	+736.4
Oceana	+ 40.1	+ 48.8	+108.4
Africa	+284.9	+211.1	+1,097.5
Germany	– 60.8	– 60.1	– 84.4
Greece	+ 26.7	– 41.7	– 26.2
Hungary	– 62.9	– 56.0	– 79.2
Ireland	– 54.3	– 50.1	– 77.2
Italy	– 30.4	– 63.1	– 74.3
Netherlands	– 57.6	– 54.3	– 80.6
Poland	– 54.6	+ 15.6	– 47.5
Portugal	+108.5	– 1.3	+105.7
U.S.S.R.	– 73.0	+542.6	+ 73.3
United Kingdom	– 20.4	+ 6.8	– 15.0
Yugoslavia	+ 78.5	– 63.9	– 35.6
Cambodia ('70–92)	—	+109.2	—
China/Taiwan	+204.2	+ 55.7	+373.6
India	+1,681.9	+220.8	+5,616.8
Iran ('59–92)	+258.8	+474.1	+1,960.0
Israel	–10.2	+ 25.6	+ 12.8
Japan	– 45.7	– 43.2	– 69.2
Laos ('70–92)	—	+1,544.0	—
Korea ('58–92)	+631.1	+ 89.5	+1,285.2
Philippines	+466.6	+101.6	+1,042.2
Vietnam ('60–92)	+3,022.7	+1,707.4	+56,337.9
Canada	– 52.4	– 24.9	– 64.3
Mexico	+ 70.2	+ 77.9	+202.9
Cuba	+590.3	–39.5	+317.6
Dominican Republic ('60–92)	+628.4	+251.8	+2,462.3
Haiti ('60–92)	+913.0	+100.4	+1,930.0
Jamaica ('63–92)	+1,422.8	+178.5	+4,141.4
El Salvador ('60–92)	+347.8	+356.4	+1,943.9
Colombia	+404.0	+148.4	+1,152.2

Table 8.7a	Naturalizations, by Region and 22 Leading Groups, 1968–1993		
Region/Country of Last Allegiance		Total Number Naturalized	Percent of Total Naturalized
ALL PERSONS*		4,853,862	
Asia/Middle East		1,987,270	40.9%
North America**		1,269,811	26.2
Europe		1,106,735	22.8
South America		301,727	6.2
Africa		110,086	2.3
Oceana		18,683	.4
Philippines		490,162	10.1
Mexico		364,202	7.5
Cuba		357,203	7.4
China/Taiwan		295,102	6.1
Vietnam		264,378	5.4
Korea		252,840	5.2
United Kingdom		223,544	4.6
India		173,381	3.6
Italy		148,339	3.1
Jamaica		145,478	3.0
Germany		126,491	2.6
Canada		107,441	2.2
Dominican Republic		102,573	2.1
Greece		99,315	2.0
Poland		89,102	1.8
Colombia		85,465	1.8
Former Yugoslavia		78,676	1.6
Portugal		76,935	1.6
Iran		68,823	1.4
Former U.S.S.R.		66,136	1.4
Haiti		58,574	1.2
Israel		48,147	1.0

*Includes 59,550 unknown or other categories not listed.
**Includes the Caribbean and Central America.

Table 9.2	1990 Census Totals for First and Second Ethnic Ancestries (in thousands)*

TOTAL U.S. Responses: 298,560

1. German	57,717	14. Canadian	2,723
2. British	46,820	15. Puerto Rican	1,955
3. Irish	38,736	16. Slovak	1,883
4. African American	23,777	17. Chinese	1,729
5. Italian	14,718	18. Danish	1,635
6. Mexican	11,587	19. Hungarian	1,582
7. French	10,321	20. Filipino	1,451
8. Polish	9,336	21. Czech	1,296
9. Native American	8,777	22. Portuguese	1,153
10. Dutch	6,227	23. Greek	1,110
11. Swedish	4,681	24. Swiss	1,045
12. Norwegian	3,869	25. Japanese	1,005
13. Russian	2,957		

*List omits such mixed or nonethnic categories as Spanish, Asian, white, and American. Several related categories have been combined for this table, such as Italian and Sicilian and Russian and Belorussian. Because of the mixed ancestry responses, the overall total is 50 million above the actual population.

Table 9.3	Ethnic Intermarriage for Selected Groups: Rank Order by Percentage of Second Ancestries in 1990*

Ancestry Group 1990 Census	Percent of Group Total Where A Second Ancestry was Reported
Welsh	48.9%
Dutch	44.2
Irish**	41.4
Czech	40.6
Swedish	38.4
Canadian	35.5
Norwegian	34.9
English	33.1
Ukrainian	30.6
Australian	30.4
Polish	30.1
UNITED STATES TOTAL	29.7
Syrian	26.6
Italian	23.3
New Zealander	22.5
French Canadian	21.6
German	21.4
Greek	17.0
Israeli	15.5
Argentinian	14.0
Armenian	13.0
Colombian	11.9
Samoan	10.7
Japanese	9.6
Filipino	8.1
Dominican	7.3
Chinese	6.7
Iranian	6.3
Cuban	6.3
Jamaican	5.5
Nigerian	5.2
Korean	4.6
Asian Indian	3.6
Mexican	3.6
Salvadoran	3.3
Vietnamese	3.1
Haitian	3.0
Cambodian***	2.1
Khmer***	0

*Of the 248.7 million in the 1990 census, 90.4% gave an ancestry response. Almost one-third (73.77 million) reported a second, or multiple, one—proportionally more in the Midwest and least in the South.

**Excludes Northern Irish and Celtic responses.

***Those who identified as Cambodian revealed some intermarriage, whereas the 2,979 who listed themselves as Khmer reported none.

A Note on Sources Used in the Tables and Figures

The tables and figures presented in this volume were developed by the author from a variety of U.S. government publications, which are discussed in the second section of the Bibliographical Essay. The three principal sources are, first, the decennial census reports and their separate subject reports (depending on the year) on foreign-born persons, national origins and language, persons of Spanish/Hispanic origin/Spanish language usage, those of Asian and Pacific Islander origin, and population by ancestry. While the latter two were available beginning in 1970 and 1980, respectively, various reports on foreign-born persons and foreign-language usage have been available since before the beginning years of this study (and on Spanish and Hispanic origin/language since at least 1930). Second, the annual reports of the Bureaus of Immigration and Naturalization (restructured as the Immigration and Naturalization Service in 1940) have been the chief source of annual data on newcomers and new citizens. Third, unpublished data covering most of this century were made available to the author by the INS, including data derived from his own computer analyses of INS immigration and naturalization records for the years since 1972, when computerized record keeping began. Thus, for example, in this Appendix, Tables 2.2, 6.2, 6.3, 8.1, 8.1a, 8.2, 8.3, 8.4, 8.5, 9.2, and 9.3 are derived from census data, while 2.1, 2.3, 6.1, 6.4, 7.2, 7.2a, 7.3, 8.6, 8.6a, 8.6b, and 8.7, 8.7a were developed from published as well as unpublished INS reports and data files. Finally, the U.S. Census Bureau introduced for 1990 a series of eleven short pamphlets, summarizing (and presenting graphically) key findings from the 1990 census. Among the various subjects, which almost all contain titles beginning *We the American . . .* , are *Blacks, Hispanics, Asians,* and *Pacific Islanders,* and *We the First Americans.*

BIBLIOGRAPHICAL ESSAY

Basic Collections, Studies, and Bibliographies

Many historians, archivists, compilers of immigrant letters, and novelists have concentrated much of their research and writing energy on the great era of open immigration, roughly between 1880 and 1930. From that enormous pool of materials have come many splendid works that have set the tone—if not the standards—for subsequent volumes. Oscar Handlin's Pulitzer prize-winning *The Uprooted: The Epic Story of the Great Migrations that Made the American People*, 2nd ed. (Boston, 1973) excelled in its style and powerful portrayal of "the classic" experience and inspired (if not provoked) a generation of scholars to examine the validity of his all-encompassing work, beginning especially with Rudolph Vecoli's essay, "*Contadini* in Chicago: A Critique of *The Uprooted*," *Journal of American History* 51 (December 1964): 404–17. Alan M. Kraut's volume for this Harlan Davidson series, *The Huddled Masses: The Immigrant in American Society, 1880–1921* (Wheeling, IL, 1982) reflected much of the newer research. That more recent body of works was then superbly synthesized and refocused by John Bodnar in *The Transplanted: A History of Immigrants in Urban America* (Bloomington, IN, 1985), which also concentrates on the old "new" immigration that ended in the 1920s.

Vecoli has written several invaluable, comprehensive reviews of the literature on immigration and ethnicity that include works that go beyond 1930. Among his most recent essays are "Return to the Melting Pot: Ethnicity in the United States in the Eighties," *Journal of American Ethnic History* 5.1 (Fall 1985): 7–20; "Immigration, Naturalization and the Constitution," *News for Teachers of Political Science* (American Political Science Association), 50 (Summer 1986): 9–15; "From *The Uprooted* to *The Transplanted*: The Writing of American Immigration History, 1951–1989," pp. 25–54 in *From 'Melting Pot' to Multiculturalism: The Evolution of Ethnic Relations in the United States and Canada*, edited by Valeria Gennaro Lerda (Rome, 1990); and "An Inter-Ethnic Perspective on American Immigration History," pp. 16–23 in *Swedes in America: Intercultural and interethnic perspectives on contemporary research*, edited by Ulf Beijbom (Växjö, Sweden, 1993).

Two other outstanding literature reviews that also include more works on the post-1930 decades are Ewa Morawska, "The Sociology and Historiography of Immigration," pp. 187–238 in *Immigration Reconsidered: History, Sociology, and Politics*, edited by Virginia Yans-McLaughlin (New York, 1990), and John J. Bukowczyk and Nora Faires, "Immigration History to the United States, 1965–1990: A Selective Critical Appraisal," *Canadian Ethnic Studies* 33.2 (1991): 1–23. Not as comprehensive and somewhat uneven in the time periods covered but useful for its separate review/bibliographic essays on more than ten groups is *Multiculturalism in the United States: A Comparative Guide to Acculturation and Ethnicity*, edited by John D. Buenker and Lorman A. Ratner (Westport, CT, 1992). Although mostly regional in its focus, one other extensive list is the very up-to-date *Europeans in the American West Since 1800: A Bibliography*, compiled by Florence R. J. Goulesque (Albuquerque, 1995). Another compilation of materials that addresses older as well as more contemporary migrations is the bibliography by Francesco Cordasco that includes pre-1965, post-1965, and illegal immigrants as well as an Appendix with the 1981 Executive Summary of the Select Commission on Immigration and Refugee Policy, in *The New American Immigration* (New York, 1987). Finally, a useful but different type of source is A. William Hoglund's compilation, *Immigrants and Their Children in the United States: A Bibliography of Doctoral Dissertations, 1885–1982* (New York, 1986). Although marred by the uneven quality of the reproductions, an invaluable aid is the twenty-volume collection of articles, edited by George E. Pozzetta, *American Immigration and Ethnicity* (New York, 1990–91). The volumes are thematic, and most essays concern the 1880s–1930s (or earlier), with the last, on "Contemporary Immigration and American Society," containing essays on post-1965 newcomers. The first volume, *Themes in Immigration History*, has a number of outstanding general essays. For other relevant articles, see volume 3, *Ethnic Communities*; 8, *Politics and the Immigrant*; 11, *Immigrant Family Patterns*; 12, *Ethnicity and Gender*; especially 13, *Assimilation, Acculturation, and Social Mobility*; 14, *Americanization, Social Control, and Philanthropy*; 16, *Ethnicity, Ethnic Identity, and Language Maintenance*; 17, *Law, Crime, and Justice: Naturalization and Citizenship*; and 19, *The Immigrant Religious Experience*.

Again, although the overwhelming focus of the essays is on the two centuries prior to 1930, an indispensable point of departure is the *Harvard Encyclopedia of American Ethnic Groups*, edited by Stephan Thernstrom, with Ann Orlov and Oscar Handlin (Cambridge, MA, 1980). The thematic and group-focused essays (on some one hundred groups) by many leading scholars make this a premier source for scholarship up to the 1960s and early 1970s. A related collection of important studies can be found in Joshua Fishman, Vladimir C. Nahirny, John E. Hoffman, et al., *Language Loyalty in the United States: The Maintenance and Persistence of Non-English Mother Tongues by American Ethnic and Religious Groups* (The Hague and New York, 1966). Roy S. Bryce-LaPorte also edited an impressive collection of essays addressing the newest wave of migration, in *The Sourcebook on the New Immigration: Implications for the*

United States and the International Community (New Brunswick, NJ, 1980).

Government and Institutional Publications

Two key factors have affected the types of materials available for this study covering specifically 1920 to the 1990s. First, works on immigration tended to be briefer on the post-1930 (but especially post-1965) years or to concentrate on the American-born generations after 1920, and historical studies of ethnicity coming up to the present have been scarce. Second, besides a host of government-sponsored works, extensive materials started to appear from sociologists, demographers, geographers, political scientists, economists, anthropologists, and specialized research institutes.

Five types of publications from the U.S. government are valuable sources of information: First, there are those from the Government Printing Office, such as: the U.S. Bureau of Naturalization, Department of Labor, *Historical Sketch of Naturalization in the United States* (Washington, DC, 1926); *History of the Immigration and Naturalization Service*, U.S. Senate, Committee on the Judiciary, 96th Congress, 2nd Session (Washington, DC, 1980); *U.S. Immigration Policy and the National Interest* [The Final Report of the Select Commission on Immigration and Refugee Policy], Joint Committee of House and Senate, 97th Congress, 1st Session (Washington, DC, 1981); *U.S. Immigration Law and Policy, 1952–1986*, U.S. Senate Subcommittee on Immigration and Refugee Affairs, Committee on the Judiciary, 100th Congress, 1st Session (Washington, DC, 1988); and *Immigration and Nationality Act (As Amended Through January 1, 1989)*, 8th edition, *Ibid.* (Washington, DC, 1989). Second are the reports to Congressional committees from the U.S. General Accounting Office, for example, *Vietnamese Amerasian Resettlement: Education, Employment, and Family Outcomes in the United States*, GAO/PEMD-94-15 (Washington, DC, March 1994), and *Welfare Reform: Implications of Proposals on Legal Immigrants' Benefits*, GAO/HEHS-95-58 (Washington, DC,

1995). Third is the Immigration and Naturalization Service, which publishes its annual reports on immigration matters. Prior to 1979 they were entitled, for example, *1970 Annual Report: Immigration and Naturalization Service*, and, since 1979, *1993 Statistical Yearbook of the Immigration and Naturalization Service*, etc. (prior to the 1940s the titles were different). Its monthly *I & N Reporter* has been a good source of articles. Fourth, the decennial reports of the U.S. Bureau of the Census have been a principal source of statistical information on foreigners and their children ("the foreign stock") and, for 1980 and 1990—in lieu of second- generation data—on ancestry groups. They have also included specific Subject Reports on the foreign born, mother-tongue usage, Latinos (the titles have varied during the past six decades, from Spanish Language and Spanish Surname, to Persons of Hispanic Origin), and on Asians (at first, just Chinese and Japanese, then additionally Filipinos, and now Asians and Pacific Islanders) as well as on African Americans, Puerto Ricans, and Native Americans. Finally, special agencies of the federal government have published works related to immigration, such as that by the 1981 Select Commission on Immigration and Refugee Policy and, most recently, the U.S. Commission on Immigration Reform's *U.S. Immigration Policy: Restoring Credibility*, its interim report to Congress (Washington, DC, 1994).

Three nongovernmental organizations have been prominent in providing reports on immigration and related issues. First, the Population Reference Bureau, under its *Population Bulletin*, has prepared such pamphlets as Leon F. Bouvier and Robert W. Gardner, "Immigration to the U.S.: The Unfinished Story," 41.4 (November 1986); William P. O'Hare, "America's Minorities—The Demographics of Diversity," 47.4 (December 1992); and Philip Martin and Elizabeth Midgley, "Immigration to the United States: Journey to an Uncertain Destination," 49.2 (September 1994). Under its *Population Trends and Public Policy* listings, it has offered Rafael Valdivieso and Cary Davis, "U.S. Hispanics: Challenging Issues for the 1990s," no. 17 (December 1988); William P. O'Hare and Judy C. Felt, "Asian Americans: America's Fastest Growing Minority Group," no. 19 (February 1991); and a work by Warren and Kraly, on emigration, cited below. Second, the Urban Institute has provided important studies, among them, Thomas Muller and Thomas J. Espenshade, *The Fourth Wave: California's Newest Immigrants* (Washington, DC, 1985), and Michael Fix and Jeffrey Passel, *Immigration and Immigrants: Setting the Record Straight* (Washington, DC, 1994). Third, the RAND Corporation has produced numerous studies analyzing immigration issues, many with the Urban Institute, such as *Immigration and International Relations* (on the effects of IRCA), edited by Georges Vernez (Santa Monica, CA, 1990), and Michael Fix and Paul T. Hill, *Enforcing Employer Sanctions* (Santa Monica, CA, 1990). Included in the many publications of its Center for Research on Immigration Policy are Beth J. Asch, *Emigration and Its Effects on the Sending Country* (Santa Monica, CA, 1994); Julie DaVanzo, Jennifer Hawes-Dawson, R. Burciaga Valdez, and Georges Vernez, *Surveying Immigrant Communities: Policy Imperatives and Technical Challenges,* on Salvadorans and Filipinos (Santa Monica, CA, 1994); and Vernez and Kevin McCarthy, "The Fiscal Costs of Immigration: Analytical and Policy Issues," (Santa Monica, CA, 1995). Finally, the Washington, D.C., Manhattan Institute has published John J. Miller, *Strangers at Our Gate: Immigration in the 1990s* (1994).

Journals

Space does not permit a detailed enumeration of many of the articles (besides those included by Pozzetta in his twenty volumes) that pertain to this period. However, the most seminal journals ought to be noted. The foremost in terms of scope and coverage of contemporary issues and policy by social scientists of various stripes is surely the *International Migration Review*. Its cumulative index for volumes 1–23 (1964–1989) details the journal's emphasis on refugees, illegal aliens, women, ethnicity, adaptation, assimilation, various economic dimensions of migration, and the evolution of immigration policies. Most recently, for example, one of its special issues, edited by Alejandro Portes, is entirely devoted to "The New Second Generation," 28 (Winter 1994). Second in importance, and more broadly historical in its thrust, is the *Journal of American Ethnic History*, which has been published since 1981. Although focused mostly on European groups, it has published a number of essays on Asian, Latino, and Caribbean migration as well as essays on women, ethnicity, and assimilation theory. In its Winter 1995 issue, for example, is an essay that has influenced the approach in this study, a forum beginning with "Race, Religion, and Nationality in American Society: A Model of Ethnicity—From Contact to Assimilation," by Elliott Barkan, 14.2: 38–75. Published in the same journal and very highly regarded is the essay by John Higham, "Current Trends in the Study of Ethnicity in the United States," *JAEH*, 2 (Fall 1982). *The Annals of the American Academy of Political and Social Science* has occasionally published several outstanding volumes on topics related to ethnicity and migration, including *America as a Multicultural Society*, edited by Milton M. Gordon, 454 (March 1981); *Immigration and American Public Policy*, edited by Rita J. Simon, 487 (September 1986); *Interminority Affairs in the U.S.: Pluralism at the Crossroads*, edited by Peter Rose, 530 (November 1993); and *Strategies for Immigration Control: An International Comparison*, edited by Mark J. Miller, 534 (July 1994). Among other useful journals are *Amerasia Journal, Ethnic Forum, Demography, Journal of Ethnic Studies, Ethnic and Racial Studies, Aztlan, Ethnicity, Phylon,* and *Asian and Pacific Migration Journal.*

Surveys of Immigration History and Policy

There have been a number of surveys of American immigration and ethnic history, although their emphases have usually been on the pre-1930 periods. One superb interdisciplinary tool, however, is that by James Paul Allen and Eugene James Turner, *We The People: An Atlas of America's Ethnic Diversity* (New York, 1988), which contains outstanding multicolored, computer-generated U.S. maps based on the 1980 census and a text that provides backgrounds on over sixty different groups, along with comparative information and accompanying maps based on the

1920 census. Lawrence H. Fuchs has provided one of the most comprehensive analyses of American ethnicity, emphasizing the expansion of civic rights, the extent of integration, and the progress in intergroup relations during the past four decades in *American Kaleidoscope: Race, Ethnicity, and the Civic Culture* (Hanover, NH, 1990). Philip Gleason's collection of his essays provides excellent introductions to the scholarly treatment in this century of a number of key issues related to minorities, ethnicity, assimilation, the status of ethnic groups, and the Catholic Church in *Speaking of Diversity: Language and Ethnicity in the Twentieth Century* (Baltimore, 1992).

One of the better known, though rather conventional, surveys covering up to 1960, with a chapter added in 1992 broadly reviewing the intervening years, is Maldwyn Allen Jones, *American Immigration* (Chicago, 1992). In 1979, James Stuart Olson provided one of the earliest contemporary efforts presenting American ethnic history, including that of African and Native Americans. The revised edition of *The Ethnic Dimension in American History* (New York, 1994) has three updated chapters on the period since 1945, on Latinos, Asians, and other "Newest Arrivals." Olson also did a more focused study, *Catholic Immigrants in America* (Chicago, 1987). Jay P. Dolan's *The American Catholic Experience: A History from Colonial Times to the Present* (Notre Dame, IN, 1992), although emphasizing the 1820–1920 century, does contain three chapters on the period after 1920. Leonard Dinnerstein and David M. Reimers put together two very readable surveys of the American ethnic experience, *Ethnic Americans: A History of Immigration and Assimilation*, 3rd ed. (New York, 1990), and (with Roger Nichols) *Natives and Strangers: Blacks, Indians, and Immigrants in America*, 2nd ed. (New York, 1990). A more detailed, statistical, and analytical study was done by Thomas J. Archdeacon, *Becoming American: An Ethnic History* (New York, 1983), which better than most attempted to weave the different stories together rather than consign them to different chapters. Maxine Schwartz Seller offered a somewhat different approach, with more emphasis on women and cultural history and more integration of the various experiences and reactions of white ethnics and native Americans in the 1970s and early 1980s, in *To Seek America: A History of Ethnic Life in the United States*, rev. ed. (Englewood Cliffs, NJ, 1988). Roger Daniels' contribution contains useful details not found elsewhere, but its organization by groups over large time periods makes it somewhat harder to integrate the different experiences, in *Coming to America: A History of Immigration and Ethnicity in American Life* (New York, 1990). A new survey of immigration history for the period since 1945 is Reed Ueda's *Postwar Immigrant America: A Social History* (Boston, 1994). Finally, emigration during the more recent period (the government ceased keeping records in 1957) can be found in a few works, particularly Robert Warren and Jennifer M. Peck's, "Foreign-Born Emigrants from the United States, 1960–1970," *Demography* 17 (1980): 71–84, and Warren and Ellen P. Kraly's, *The Elusive Exodus: Emigration from the United States* (Washington, DC, 1985).

Focusing on the story of Asians in particular, Ronald Takaki has written one of the most engaging and readable works on American ethnic history, *Strangers From a Different Shore: A History of Asian Americans* (Boston, 1989), which not only provides exceptional vignettes but chapters on the Hawaiian experience. Unfortunately, he is also strongest on the pre-1965 experiences. This is apparent, too, in his more recent survey, likewise quite readable but covering largely up through World War II, with separate chapters for the various groups, *A Different Mirror: A History of Multicultural America* (Boston, 1993). Sucheng Chan offers a more traditional history of Asian Americans but a very substantive one, in *Asian Americans: An Interpretive History* (Boston, 1991). One other survey that is very accessible, albeit divided up by ethnic groups, too, is Tricia Knoll's *Becoming Americans: Asian Sojourners, Immigrants, and Refugees* (Portland, OR, 1982).

Since Ellis Island's central role in immigration history is altered and then ended during the years covered here, its history ought to be briefly noted, beginning with the outstanding *Ellis Island: An Illustrated History of the Immigrant Experience*, by

Ivan Chermayeff, Fred Wasserman, and Mary J. Shapiro (New York, 1991), which utilizes many of the materials presented at the new museum on the island. Thomas M. Pitkin, *Keepers of the Gate: A History of Ellis Island* (New York, 1975), presents a very thorough account. August C. Bolino, in *The Ellis Island Source Book* (Washington, DC, 1985) traces the last years and the efforts of many to restore the island. Containing much anecdotal information is Mary J. Shapiro, *Gateway to Liberty: The Story of the Statue of Liberty and Ellis Island* (New York, 1986), as well as David M. Brownstone, Irene M. Franck, and Douglass L. Brownstone, *Island of Hope, Island of Tears* (New York, 1979). Alan Kraut's investigation of medical issues also carries the story forward in time, in *Silent Travelers: Germs, Genes, and the "Immigrant Menace"* (New York, 1994), while M. Mark Stolarik's edited collection of essays, *Forgotten Doors: The Other Ports of Entry to the United States* (Philadelphia, 1988), is a reminder that Ellis Island was not the only gateway to America. The essays by Raymond Mohl on Miami and Elliott Barkan on Los Angeles particularly cover the years after 1920. The more recent place of New York City is recounted by David Reimers and Elliott Barkan in two essays in *Immigration to New York*, edited by William Pencak, Selma Berrol, and Randall M. Miller (Philadelphia, 1991).

A number of works that focus on the pre-1920 years partially overlap the later period, with some useful materials for the interwar years. A collection of fine essays, beginning with Frank Thistlewaite's classic piece on European migration and then studies on a variety of specific European migrations, can be found in *A Century of European Migrations, 1830–1930*, edited by Rudolph J. Vecoli and Suzanne M. Sinke (Urbana, IL, 1991). Philip Taylor's *Distant Magnet: European Emigration to the U.S.A.* (New York, 1971) chiefly covers the earlier epoch but discusses assimilation thereafter. Sucheng Chan edited essays concentrating on the early Chinese, though her essay on Chinese women goes up to 1943, in *Entry Denied: Exclusion and the Chinese Community in America, 1882–1943* (Philadelphia, 1991). Mark Wyman's recent study of return migration also included some materials from the post-1920 years in his *Roundtrip to America: The Immigrants Return to Europe, 1880–1930* (Ithaca, NY, 1993). Moving beyond the 1920s, the issues of policies and the European refugee dilemma are treated in a number of books that warrant close comparison. Parts nine and ten of Ronald Sanders' *Shores of Refuge: A Hundred Years of Jewish Emigration* (New York, 1988) offers a fairly straightforward account of the 1930s and 1940s. Henry L. Feingold presents an extraordinary history of Jews during this era and the parts they played—and failed to play—in the formation of public policy in his *A Time for Searching: Entering the Mainstream, 1920–1945*, vol. 4 of the five-volume *The Jewish People of America* (Baltimore, 1992), edited by Feingold. David S. Wyman, in an unrelenting examination of the period, indicts many policymakers for their inaction in his *The Abandonment of the Jews: America and the Holocaust, 1941–1945* (New York, 1984), while Alan Kraut and Richard Breitman present an alternative view in *American Refugee Policy and European Jewry, 1933–1945* (Bloomington, IN, 1988).

Lauri Fermi wrote an account of some of those who fled Europe, *Illustrious Immigrants: The Intellectual Migration from Europe, 1930–1941*, 2nd ed. (Chicago, 1971), a topic also treated in Donald Fleming and Bernard Bailyn, eds., "The Intellectual Migration: Europe and America, 1930–1960," *Perspectives in American History* 2 (1969). Two related essays, among several others covering later topics, are in Wolfang Hölbling and Reinhold Wagnleitner's *The European Emigrant Experience in the U.S.A.* (Tübingen, Ger., 1992). Mark Wyman provides a dramatic account of migration after World War II, in *DP: Europe's Displaced Persons, 1945–1951* (Philadelphia, 1989), and Leonard Dinnerstein carefully unravels the formation of policies enabling survivors to gain entry in *America and Survivors of the Holocaust* (New York, 1982). Gil Loescher and John A. Scanlan examine America's long-term refugee policy and its anti-Communist bias, in *Calculated Kindness: Refugees and America's Half-Open Door* (New York, 1986), and Norman L. and Naomi F. Zucker present a sharp critique of that policy in *The Guarded Gate: The Reality of American Refugee Policy* (San Diego, 1987).

A number of works have now been published on the contemporary waves of immigration and their more global nature. Very good for its international perspective is *International Migration Today*, vol. 1, *Trends and Prospects*, edited by Reginald Appleyard (Paris and Nedlands, Western Australia, 1988). An engaging combination of anecdote and analysis is Thomas Kessner and Betty Boyd Caroli's *Today's Immigrants: Their Stories* (New York, 1981). A very useful exploration of the new trends is in Pastora Cafferty, Barry Chiswick, and Andrew Greeley, *The Dilemma of American Immigration* (New Brunswick, NJ, 1983). In the midst of the fierce debate leading up to IRCA, a series of essays expressing various concerns about the nation's immigration laws and the impact of the new immigration were collected in *Clamor at the Gates: The New American Immigration*, edited by Nathan Glazer (San Francisco, 1985). A brilliant set of essays on migration from Asia and the Pacific were edited by James T. Fawcett and Benjamin Cariño, *Pacific Bridges: The New Immigration from Asia and the Pacific Islands* (Staten Island, NY, 1987). Luciano Mangiafico's volume, which overlaps theirs but is somewhat marred by errors, is *Contemporary American Immigrants: Patterns of Filipino, Korean, and Chinese Settlement in the United States* (New York, 1988). Heavy on theory but offering much of the current research (especially on Latinos, their specialty) is Alejandro Portes and Rubén G. Rumbaut's *Immigrant America: A Portrait* (Berkeley, 1990). Densely statistical and theoretical but extremely useful for understanding contemporary immigration and naturalization patterns is Guillermo Jasso and Mark R. Rosenzweig, *The New Chosen: Immigrants in the United States* (New York, 1990). Offering an updated set of propositions on migration and a global model of contemporary migration strategies, based on the individual INS records for 1972-1985, is Elliott Barkan's *Asian and Pacific Islander Migration to the United States: A Model of New Global Patterns* (Westport, CT: 1992). Finally, beginning with World War II, Ellis Cose builds up to an analysis of the legislative debates of the 1980s and the anxieties over the racial diversity of contemporary immigration in *A Nation of Strangers: Prejudice, Politics, and the Populating of America* (New York, 1992).

Several other works provide almost encyclopedic amounts of information on immigration policy, notably Edward P. Hutchinson's *Legislative History of American Immigration Policy, 1798–1965* (Philadelphia, 1981). The first half covers each Congress separately and the second half a whole array of thematic issues on policy formation and its impact. Another standard work on a most undertreated period has been Robert A. Divine's *American Immigration Policy, 1924–1952* (New Haven, CT, 1957). Although marred by some factual errors, an overall readable survey of the history of immigration policy up to 1986 is Michael C. LeMay's *From Open Door to Dutch Door: An Analysis of U.S. Immigration Policy Since 1820* (New York, 1987) and his substantial followup study that concentrates on the issues and policies of the 1980s and 1990s, *Anatomy of a Public Policy: The Reform of Contemporary American Immigration Law* (New York, 1994). Clearly regarded as one of the best studies of the evolution of American policy since World War II is David M. Reimers' *Still the Golden Door: The Third World Comes to America*, 2nd ed. (New York, 1992), ending with the 1990 reforms. It is Reimers who has argued most persuasively about the unintended consequences of our various pieces of reform legislation since 1965. Finally, a new collection of essays which addresses the current concerns about handling the influx of immigrants, legal and illegal, from an international perspective is *Controlling Immigration: A Global Perspective*, edited by Wayne A. Cornelius, Philip L. Martin, and James F. Hollifield (Stanford, 1995).

Women and Immigration

The study of women has virtually exploded during the past quarter century. A number of useful articles are in Pozzetta, *American Immigration and Ethnicity: Ethnicity and Gender* (vol. 12). Maxine Schwartz Seller edited a collection of first-person accounts, some of which extend beyond 1920, in *Immigrant Women* (Philadelphia, 1981). Among a number of valuable journal articles are four that warrant mention: Seller, "Beyond the Stereotype: A New Look at the Immigrant Woman, 1880–1924," *Journal of Ethnic Studies* 3 (Spring 1975): 59–70; Marion Houston et al., "Female Predominance of Immigration to the United States Since 1930: A First Look," *International Migration Review* 18 (Winter 1984): 908–65; Donna Gabaccia, "Immigrant Women: Nowhere at Home?" *Journal of American Ethnic History* 10 (Summer 1991): 61–87; and, leading off a forum on this topic, Sidney Stahl Weinberg, "The Treatment of Women in Immigration History," *JAEH*, 11 (Summer 1992): 25–46. Donna Gabaccia assembled an extensive, interdisciplinary bibliography in *Immigrant Women in the United States: A Selective Annotated Multidisciplinary Bibliography* (Westport, CT, 1989) and a stimulating collection of essays on women and immigration in *Seeking Common Ground: Multidisciplinary Studies of Immigrant Women in the United States* (Westport, CT, 1992). She followed that with a challenging, thematic survey of immigrant women's experiences, *From the Other Side: Women, Gender, and Immigrant Life in the U.S., 1820–1990* (Bloomington, IN, 1995). Sucheng Chan edited a collection of essays examining a variety of aspects of the lives of (principally) women of color, *Social and Gender Boundaries in the United States* (Lewiston, NY, 1989).

Deborah Dash Moore, Sydney Stahl Weinberg, and Neil M. and Ruth S. Cowan looked at Jewish women in, respectively, *At Home in America: Second Generation New York Jews* (New York, 1981); *The World of Our Mothers: Lives of Jewish Immigrant Women* (Chapel Hill, NC, 1988); and *Our Parents' Lives: The Americanization of Eastern European Jews* (New York, 1989). Virginia Yans-McLaughlin and Miriam Cohen explored the adjustment of Italian and Italian American women in, respectively, *Family and Community: Italian Immigrants in Buffalo, 1880–1939* (Ithaca, NY, 1977) and *Workshop to Office: Two Generations of Italian Women in New York City, 1900–1950* (Ithaca, NY, 1993). Among those works on the experiences and perspectives of Asian women are: Judy Yung, *Chinese Women in America: A Pictorial History* (Seattle, 1986); Akemi Kikumura, *Through Harsh Winters* (Novato, CA, 1981), the fascinating story of her mother's life in America, to which she later added views from and regarding her father's perspective, in *The Life of an Issei Man* (Novato, CA, 1991); Mary Paik Lee, *Quiet Odyssey: A Pioneer Korean Woman in America*, edited by Sucheng Chan (Seattle, 1990), the autobiography by a Korean woman who arrived as a child in 1905; and Mei Nakano, *Japanese American Women: Three Generations, 1890–1990* (Berkeley, 1990). Asian Women United of California put together an interesting and diverse set of materials in *Making Waves: An Anthology of Writings By and About Asian American Women* (Boston, 1989). Most recently, Nancy D. Donnelly investigated the impact of migration on the *Changing Lives of Refugee Hmong Women* (Seattle, 1994).

With respect to Mexican American women, an early perspective was provided by Margarita B. Melville in her collection of essays, *Twice a Minority: The Mexican American Woman* (St. Louis, 1980). Sarah Deutsch wrote a most interesting analysis of the evolution of gender roles in the Southwest, although one that focuses mostly on Hispano rather than immigrant Mexican or Mexican American women, *No Separate Refuge: Class, Culture, and Gender on an Anglo Hispanic Frontier in the American Southwest, 1880–1940* (New York, 1987). Vicki Ruiz examined Mexican women at work in *Cannery Women/Cannery Lives: Mexican Women, Unionization, and the California Food Processing Industry, 1930–1950* (Albuquerque, 1987), and then assembled, with Ellen DuBois, an extensive collection of essays on a wide variety of topics concerning women of color, *Unequal Sisters: A Multicultural Reader in U.S. Women's History* (New York, 1990, 1994). A somewhat comparable composite of women's experiences, but with a more academic, comparative focus on Latinas and Asians versus blacks and whites is the collection edited by Maxine Baca Zinn and Bonnie Thornton Dill, *Women of Color in U.S. Society* (Philadelphia, 1994). Also containing a number of articles on women's experiences within a variety of American ethnic groups is the collection edited by Rita J. Simon and Caroline B. Brettell, *International Migration: The Female Experience* (Totowa, NJ, 1986). One other work that provides a fascinating look at a wide range of women's recollections is Elfrieda

B. Shukert and Barbara S. Scibetta's *War Brides of World War II* (New York, 1988).

Immigration and Economic Issues

Many studies address economic issues related to immigration and the impact of immigrants on the American economy, society, culture, and immigration policy. Two outstanding studies on the earlier decades are Lizabeth Cohen's *Making a New Deal: Industrial Workers in Chicago, 1919–1939* (New York, 1990) and Gary Gerstle's *Working Class Americanism: Politics and Labor in a Textile City, 1914–1960* (New York, 1989), both of which, in exceptional fashion, look at the interweaving of union, labor, ethnic, and larger cultural issues. Lucie Cheng and Edna Bonacich edited an excellent set of essays on a variety of economic enterprises on the mainland and in Hawaii, *Labor Migration Under Capitalism: Asian Workers in the United States Before World War II* (Berkeley, 1984). Ivan Light's pathbreaking analysis of ethnic values and business patterns compared Chinese, Japanese, and blacks, in *Ethnic Enterprise in America* (Berkeley, 1972). Roger D. Waldinger's examination of the impact of immigrants in a specific industry has also shed considerable light on the place of immigrants in a changing economy, *Through the Eye of the Needle: Immigrants and Enterprise in New York's Garment Trades* (New York, 1986). His forthcoming study will expand his exploration of such issues in *Still the Promised City? New Immigrants and African Americans in New York, 1940–1990* (Cambridge, MA, in press). An ethnographic look at immigrants in various work settings in Kansas City, Miami, and Philadelphia is that by Louise Lamphere, Alex Stepick, and Guillermo Grenier, *Newcomers in the Workplace: Immigrants and the Restructuring of the U.S. Economy* (Philadelphia, 1994). Ivan Light and Parminder Bhachu edited some of the essays from a 1990 conference that compared the American experiences of immigrant businesses with those in several other countries, *Immigration and Entrepreneurship: Culture, Capital, and Ethnic Networks* (New Brunswick, NJ, 1993). Another work offering a comparative perspective on immigration, labor, and business is *Unsettled Relationship: Labor Migration and Economic Development*, edited by Demetrios Papademetriou and Philip L. Martin (Westport, CT, 1991). Highly valued for its analysis of migration and the impact of immigrants on the job market and immigration policy is Michael Piore's *Birds of Passage: Migrant Labor and Industrial Societies* (London and New York, 1979). In the debate over this issue, two other works have provided critical evaluations: Vernon M. Briggs, Jr., *Immigration Policy and the American Labor Force* (Baltimore, 1984), and George Borjas, *Friends or Strangers: The Impact of Immigrants on the U.S. Economy* (New York, 1990), both of which express concern for the consequences of the changing profile of immigrants. Finally, presenting analyses of immigrants in a particular industry so dependent upon them, and placing that within a regional context—a situation becoming a reality for more and more industries—is *Global Production: The Apparel Industry in the Pacific Rim*, edited by Edna Bonacich, Lucie Cheng, Norma Chinchilla, Nora Hamilton, and Paul Ong (Philadelphia, 1994).

American Hostility to Immigration

A number of studies provide important perspectives on racism, nativism, and anti-Semitism, especially during the interwar years. The classic study remains John Higham's *Strangers in the Land: Problems of American Nativism, 1860–1925*, with an Afterword some thirty years later (New Brunswick, NJ, 1955, 1988). Leonard Dinnerstein provides a comprehensive overview across the nation's history of *Antisemitism in America* (New York, 1994). While Kenneth T. Jackson presented a broad view of *The Ku Klux Klan in the Cities, 1915–1930* (New York, 1967), two rather revisionist portraits are in Kathleen M. Blee's *Women of the Klan: Racism and Gender in the 1920s* (Berkeley, 1991), and *The Invisible Empire in the West: Toward a New Appraisal of the Ku Klux Klan of the 1920s*, edited by Shawn Lay (Urbana, IL, 1992). John V. Baiamonte, Jr., gives a disturbing portrayal of injustice against Italians in *Spirit of Vengeance: Nativism and Louisiana Justice*,

1921–1924 (Baton Rouge, 1986), while William G. Ross examines responses in the Midwest and West in *Forging New Freedoms: Nativism, Education, and the Constitution, 1917–1927* (Lincoln, NE, 1994). Paul Avrich presents his latest findings on one of the most spectacular cases of the century in *Sacco and Vanzetti: The Anarchist Background* (Princeton, 1991). Since nativism and racism involve widespread public sentiments, two works that assess public opinion via the media and opinion polls are presented by Rita J. Simon in *Public Opinion and the Immigrant Print Media Coverage, 1880–1980* (Lexington, MA, 1985) and Simon and Susan H. Alexander, *The Ambivalent Welcome: Print Media, Public Opinion, and Immigration* (Westport, CT, 1993).

Urbanization and Immigrants

Given the concentration of twentieth-century immigration in urban centers, a number of works on the convergence of groups there are important to the general story. Containing an overview in this Harlan Davidson series is Carl Abbott's *Urban America in the Modern Age: 1920 to the Present* (Wheeling, IL, 1987). Exploring issues of accommodation, group conflict, anti-Semitism, and the need for a revised concept of pluralism—"pluralistic integration"—John Higham once more provided a provocative perspective in *Send These Unto Me: Immigrants in Urban America*, rev. ed. (Baltimore, 1984). Distinctive for their focus on the Midwest, with a number of very informative essays on a wide variety of ethnic groups, are Peter d'A. Jones and Melvin G. Holli, editors, *Ethnic Chicago*, 4th ed. (Grand Rapids, 1995), and Holli and Jones, editors, *The Ethnic Frontier: Essays in the History of Group Survival in Chicago and the Midwest* (Grand Rapids, 1977). Well regarded for its comparison of several different ethnic groups during the interwar years is Ronald Bayor's *Neighbors in Conflict: The Irish, Germans, Jews and Italians of New York City, 1929–1941* (Baltimore, 1978). Examinations of two other cities are John Bodnar, Roger Simon, and Michael Weber, *Lives of Their Own: Blacks, Italians, and*

Poles in Pittsburgh, 1900–1960 (Urbana, IL, 1982), and Edward R. Kantowicz, *Polish American Politics in Chicago, 1888–1940* (Chicago, 1975). A major analysis at that time of immigrants and their American-born children is W. Lloyd Warner and Leo Srole's *The Social Systems of American Ethnic Groups* (New Haven, CT, 1945). Arnold Hirsch explored interethnic conflict during and after World War II in *Making the Second Ghetto: Race and Housing in Chicago, 1940 to 1960* (Cambridge, MA, 1983); and Donald Capeci did the same for Detroit, in *Race Relations in Wartime Detroit: The Sojourner Truth Housing Controversy, 1937–1942* (Philadelphia, 1984).

Undoubtedly, one of the most formidable and influential urban studies of multiple ethnic urban groups has been Nathan Glazer and Daniel P. Moynihan's *Beyond the Melting Pot: The Negroes, Puerto Ricans, Jews, Italians, and Irish of New York City* (Cambridge, MA, 1963, 1970), and especially the introductions to both editions. Jonathan Rieder added very important perspectives from his in-depth exploration of one community, *Canarsie: The Jews and Italians of Brooklyn Against Liberalism* (Cambridge, MA, 1985). Ronald P. Formisano has written a fascinating study of one of the most highly divisive issues of the last three decades, in *Boston Against Busing: Race, Class and Ethnicity in the 1960s and 1970s* (Chapel Hill, NC, 1991). The Cubans were then altering the entire nature of Miami and, in addition to essays by Raymond Mohl noted elsewhere in this essay, three books especially examine the multiethnic nature of that city since 1960: Guillermo J. Grenier and Alex Stepick, editors, *Miami Now! Immigration, Ethnicity, and Social Change* (Gainesville, FL, 1991), Alejandro Portes and Stepick, *City on the Edge: The Transformation of Miami* (Berkeley, 1993), and David Rieff's more journalistic approach in *The Exile: Cuba in the Heart of Miami* (New York, 1993). Rieff has done a similarly interesting study, *Los Angeles: Capital of the Third World* (New York, 1991). A different perspective comes from investigations of one of the nation's first multiethnic riots that occurred in 1992 in Los Angeles: *Reading Rodney King, Reading Urban Uprising*, edited by

Robert Gooding-Williams (New York, 1993), and *The Los Angeles Riots: Lessons for the Urban Future*, edited by Mark Baldassare (Boulder, CO, 1994).

Because of the continuing dynamism of the New York scene, a number of other works have detailed the continuing impact of newcomers there besides Kessner and Caroli. In addition to the essays by Reimers and Barkan, noted above, Michel S. Laguerre began examining a group that had just then grown enormously, in *American Odyssey: Haitians in New York City* (Ithaca, NY, 1984). Nancy Foner edited a fine collection of interdisciplinary essays on the quite varied *New Immigrants in New York* (New York, 1987). An equally exciting companion collection from that same year was edited by Constance R. Sutton and Elsa M. Chaney, *Caribbean Life in New York City: Sociocultural Dimensions* (Staten Island, NY, 1987). At the same time, Barry B. Levine contributed a collection of essays on *The Caribbean Exodus* (Westport, CT, 1987), which included Central Americans and migrant destinations inside as well as outside North America. Philip Kasinitz added an excellent study of the evolution of West Indian community in New York—from a community that was part of the blacks' to one with West Indians' own distinctive combination of styles and agendas—in *Caribbean New York: Black Immigrants and the Politics of Race* (Ithaca, NY, 1992). Most recently, Andres Torres provided another multiracial perspective with *Between the Melting Pot and Mosaic: African Americans and Puerto Ricans in the New York Economy* (Philadelphia, 1995), which does include discussions of West Indians, Chinese, and larger issues of race. Two of the many other books on New York's contemporary ethnic groups and its politics are Jim Sleeper, *The Closest of Strangers: Liberalism and the Politics of Race in New York* (New York, 1990), and Chris McNickle, *To Be Mayor of New York: Ethnic Politics in the City* (New York, 1993), the latter an overview of the past century.

Thomas Muller has recently written a most interesting study of the overall issues related to the impact of immigrants on the nation's cities. He focuses on such things as environmental concerns, the deterioration and revitalization of inner cities, and the impact of immigrants' range of skills in *Immigrants and the American City* (New York, 1993). Several other works address related facets of this theme of ethnic groups in today's cities: *Urban Ethnicity in the United States: New Immigrants and Old Minorities*, edited by Lionel Maldonado and Joan Moore, vol. 29, *Urban Affairs Annual Reviews* (Beverly Hills, 1985); *Race and Ethnic Conflict: Contending Views on Prejudice, Discrimination, and Ethnoviolence*, edited by Fred L. Pincus and Howard J. Ehrlich (Boulder, CO, 1994); *Blacks, Latinos, and Asians in Urban America: Status and Prospects for Politics and Activism*, edited by James Jennings (Westport, CT, 1994); and *In the Barrios: Latinos and the Underclass Debate*, edited by Moore and Raquel Pinderhughes (New York, 1993), the latter containing essays on a variety of Latino groups around the country.

The Ethnic Press

A few works have detailed the ethnic press during these decades, particularly Sally Miller, ed., *The Ethnic Press in the United States: A Historical Analysis and Handbook* (Westport, CT, 1987); *Ethnic Periodicals in Contemporary America: An Annotated Guide*, compiled by Sandra Jones Ireland (Westport, CT, 1990); and *The Immigrant Labor Press in North America, 1840s–1970s: An Annotated Bibliography*, edited by Dirk Hoerder and assisted by Christiane Harzig, vol. 1: *Migrants from Northern Europe*, vol. 2: *Migrants from Eastern and Southeastern Europe*, and vol. 3: *Migrants from Southern and Western Europe* (Westport, CT, 1987).

First-person Accounts

Especially vital in the narrative here have been the many works providing first-person accounts of their immigrant or second- and sometimes third-generation experiences in adjusting to America. Three most noteworthy collections, each with a rich variety of voices, are Joan Morrison and Charlotte Fox Zabusky, *American Mosaic: The Immigrant Experience in the Words of Those*

Who Lived It (New York, 1980); Al Santoli, *New Americans, An Oral History: Immigrants and Refugees in the U.S. Today* (New York, 1988); and June Namias, *First Generation: In the Words of Twentieth-Century American Immigrants*, rev. ed. (Urbana, IL, 1992). Thomas C. Wheeler offered some very engaging stories—both immigrant and migrant (black and Puerto Rican)—in *The Immigrant Experience: The Anguish of Becoming American* (New York, 1971). Two decades later, two other anthologies provided many insights, *Writing Our Lives: Autobiographies of American Jews, 1890–1990*, edited by Steve J. Rubin (Philadelphia, 1991), and especially Joann Faung Jean Lee's *Asian Americans: Oral Histories of First to Fourth Generation Americans from China, the Philippines, Japan, India, the Pacific Islands, Vietnam, and Cambodia* (New York, 1991). More literary approaches can be found edited by Oscar Handlin in *Children of the Uprooted* (New York, 1966) and in Edward Ifkovic's *American Letter: Immigrant and Ethnic Writing* (Englewood Cliffs, NJ, 1975). A most novel and interesting intergenerational approach was taken by Corinne A. Krause in *Grandmothers, Mothers, and Daughters: Oral Histories of Three Generations of Ethnic American Women* [Italian, Jewish, and Slavic] (Boston, 1991). Dale R. Steiner mixes narrative and immigrant story, conveying the experiences of selected group figures very effectively, in *Of Thee We Sing: Immigrants and American History*, (San Diego, 1987). Although most collections of letters are weighted toward the earlier years, two do contain some useful items: *News from the Land of Freedom: German Immigrants Write Home*, edited by Walter D. Kamphoefner, Wolfgang Helbich, and Ulrike Sommer, translated by Susan Carter Vogel (Ithaca, NY, 1991), and *In Their Own Words: Letters from Norwegian Immigrants*, edited and translated by Solveig Zempel (Minneapolis, 1991).

An interesting investigation of a community that yielded valuable recollections and insider views is *Longtime Californ': A Documentary Study of an American Chinatown* (San Francisco), by Victor G. and Brett de Bary Nee (Stanford, 1986), which can be compared with Thomas W. Chinn's *Bridging the*

Pacific: San Francisco Chinatown and Its People (San Francisco, 1989). Besides those works on the Japanese American Internment experience (see below), it has been with the Southeast Asian refugees that scholars have particularly applied the oral history technique extensively. Three focus on the Vietnamese: James M. Freeman, *Hearts of Sorrow: Vietnamese-American Lives* (Stanford, 1989); John Tenhula, *Voices from Southeast Asia: The Refugee Experience in the United States* (New York, 1991); and Nazli Kibria, *Family Tightrope: The Changing Lives of Vietnamese Americans* (Princeton, 1993). Usha Welaratna did a masterful job of conveying the anguish of the Cambodian experience, in *Beyond the Killing Fields: Voices of Nine Cambodian Survivors in America* (Stanford, 1993). Sucheng Chan, who edited Mary Paik Lee's autobiography, cited earlier, also edited a series of stories done by her Hmong students and their families in the Santa Barbara area, in *Hmong Means Free: Life in Laos and America* (Philadelphia, 1994). Although not presented as extensively as others have, Maxine L. Margolis has given voice to a group rarely heard in America, in *Little Brazil: An Ethnography of Brazilian Immigrants in New York City* (Princeton, 1994), and Jacqueline Maria Hagan has done an impressive job relating the decisions of members of another newer group to seek amnesty in *Decision to be Legal: A Maya Community in Houston* (Philadelphia, 1995).

In telling new aspects of the story of Mexican Americans, two young scholars have also relied on interviews used in their studies, Zaragosa Vargas, *Proletarians of the North: A History of Mexican Industrial Workers in Detroit and the Midwest, 1917–1933* (Berkeley, 1993), and especially George J. Sánchez, *Becoming Mexican American: Ethnicity, Culture, and Identity in Chicano Los Angeles, 1900–1945* (New York, 1993). While many other such voices could be mentioned, for example in fiction, note two of another genre, autobiography, Angelo Pellegrini, *American Dream: An Immigrant's Quest* (San Francisco, 1986) and Mario T. García, *Memories of Chicano History: The Life and Narrative of Bert Corona* (Berkeley, 1994).

Other Works on Specific Periods

In addition to the many works cited, a number of others, on diverse but more general topics, proved quite useful for their particular eras (others on specific groups will be noted below): John P. Gavit, *Americans By Choice* (New York, 1922), a major study of immigrants and citizenship; Niles Carpenter, *Immigrants and Their Children, 1920* (Washington, DC, 1927), for valuable statistical data from the 1920 census; Edmund deS. Brunner, *Immigrant Farmers and Their Children* (Garden City, NY, 1929), presenting research and census data on agricultural areas in the northern states for the first quarter of the century; Edward P. Hutchinson, *Immigrants and Their Children, 1850–1950* (New York, 1956); April R. Schultz, *Ethnicity on Parade: Inventing the Norwegian American Through Celebration* (Amherst, 1995), a very readable study of Norwegian Americans during the 1910s and 1920s, culminating with their Centennial in 1925 and their efforts to preserve elements of their ethnicity; William Preston, Jr., *Aliens and Dissenters: Federal Suppression of Radicals, 1903–1933*, 2nd ed. (Urbana, IL, 1994), a disturbing study of government practices during those years; Thomas Lee Philpott, *The Slum and the Ghetto: Immigrants, Blacks, and Reformers in Chicago, 1880–1930* (Belmont, CA, 1991), regarded as a classic sociological analysis of the period and city; *Swedish-American Life in Chicago: Cultural and Urban Aspects of an Immigrant People, 1850–1930*, edited by Philip J. Anderson and Dag Blanck (Urbana, IL, 1992), with some good essays on the early twentieth century; Ewa Morawska, *For Bread and Butter: Life Worlds of East Central Europeans in Johnstown, Pennsylvania, 1890–1940* (New York, 1985), a major study of the mechanisms of survival and adaptation in this industrial center; Mary Anne Thatcher, *Immigrants and the 1930s: Ethnicity and Alienage in Depression and On-Coming War* (New York, 1990), a dissertation with a considerable amount of very useful information; *American Education and the European Immigrant, 1840–1940*, edited by Bernard J. Weiss (Urbana, IL, 1982), especially the essay by Nicholas Montralto; Lewis R. Marcuson, *The Stage Immigrant: The Irish,*

Italians, and Jews in American Drama, 1920–1960 (New York, 1990), also a dissertation with insightful summaries and excerpts from a wide variety of plays; Alfred Fried, *The Rise and Fall of the Jewish Gangster in America*, rev. ed. (New York, 1993) and Francis A. J. Ianni, *A Family Business: Kinship and Social Control in Organized Crime* (New York, 1972), just two of the works on a notorious aspect of the prewar decades and after; Richard Polenberg, *One Nation Divisible: Class, Race, and Ethnicity in the United States Since 1938* (New York, 1980), a most readable survey of those four succeeding decades; Will Herberg, *Protestant—Catholic—Jew: An Essay in American Religious Sociology* (Garden City, 1955; rev. ed., 1960), a work that reflected and significantly influenced the 1950s; and Samuel Lubell, *The Future of American Politics*, 3rd ed. (Garden City, NY, 1965).

Other Works on European Ethnic Groups

A number of works concentrate on specific European American ethnic groups during this period, with several arguing for or against the white ethnic revival of the 1960s and 1970s: Kenneth Lines, *British and Canadian Immigration to the United States Since 1920* (San Francisco, 1978), which uses surveys and interviews to cover an often forgotten group. John Bukowczyk provides an important overview of Poles in *And My Children Did Not Know Me: A History of Polish Americans* (Bloomington, IN, 1987), and Helena Znaniecka Lopata, in *Polish Americans: Status Competition in an Ethnic Community*, rev. ed. (New Brunswick, NJ, 1994), gives a sociological analysis, with the last chapter being a welcome update. Juliana Puska, ed., *Overseas Migration from East-Central and Southeastern Europe, 1880–1940* (Budapest, 1990), has a few essays on the interwar years. Joseph J. Barton, *Peasants and Strangers: Italians, Rumanians, and Slovaks in an American City, 1890–1950* (Cambridge, MA, 1975), is an outstanding comparative and intergenerational study of these ethnic groups in Cleveland. Myron B. Kuropas, *The Ukrainian Americans: Roots and Aspirations, 1884–1954* (Toronto, 1991), is an expansion of his earlier work, such as in Holli and Jones on Chicago, a useful study of a sizable group also frequently overlooked. Several of Andrew M. Greeley's numerous works have made important arguments about ethnicity, including *That Most Distressful Nation: The Taming of the American Irish* (New York, 1972), on the assimilation of the Irish and yet their surviving differences from others, and *Why Can't They Be Like Us?* (New York, 1971), a brief exploration of white ethnic groups and the persistence of ethnic differences, which he considerably expanded upon in *Ethnicity in the United States: A Preliminary Reconnaissance* (New York, 1974), a major sociological study in which he argues for the enduring signs of white ethnicity. Michael Novak wrote one of the most significant books expressing the sentiments of the white ethnic revival, *The Rise of the Unmeltable Ethnics: Politics and Culture in the Seventies* (New York, 1972). Several interesting excerpts from the period can be found in *Viewpoints: The Majority Minority*, edited by Drew McCord Stroud (Minneapolis, 1973). The literature on the debate about the white ethnic revival is extensive and two essays especially merit attention: Charles Hirschman's "American Melting Pot Reconsidered," *Annual Review of Sociology* 9 (1983): 397–423, and, noted at the outset, Rudolph Vecoli, "Return to the Melting Pot: Ethnicity in the United States in the Eighties." Peter Kivisto edited a fine collection of essays, reexamining issues related to ethnic integration and persistence among several groups, in *The Ethnic Enigma: The Salience of Ethnicity for European-Origin Groups* (Philadelphia, 1989). The following year Kivisto and Dag Blanck brought out a series of brilliant essays by leading scholars who had reevaluated Marcus Lee Hansen's thesis about third generation "return" and ethnic persistence, in *American Immigrants and Their Generations: Studies and Commentaries on the Hansen Thesis after Fifty Years* (Urbana, IL, 1990). Using, in part, extensive survey data from upstate New York, Richard D. Alba forcefully argued that European American ethnicity was fading (see, too, his essay in Milton Gordon's 1981 issue of the *Annals* cited above). He examines this in great detail in *Ethnic Identity: The Transformation of White America* (New Haven, CT, 1990). Another fine set of essays came to grips with some of the assimilationist arguments, evaluating the extent to which the data support one or the other position, or both, *Immigration and Ethnicity: American Society—'Melting Pot' or 'Salad Bowl'?* edited by Michael D. Innocenzo and Josef P. Sirefman (Westport, CT, 1992).

Herbert J. Gans had provided one of the principal arguments about the development of "symbolic ethnicity" and also investigated the relationship between class and ethnicity in his renowned study, *Urban Villagers: Group and Class in the Life of Italian Americans,* rev. ed. (New York, 1982). He reconsidered his position a decade later, finding more persistence than was at first evident, in "Ethnic Invention and Acculturation, A Bumpy-Line Approach," *Journal of American Ethnic History* 21.1 (Fall 1992): 42–52. A very interesting study that examined the elements of assimilation, persistence, and rejuvenation due to newcomers is Anny Bakalian, *Armenian-Americans: From Being to Feeling Armenian* (New Brunswick, NJ, 1993). Two other studies that illustrate the effects of renewed immigration are Steve J. Gold's excellent community explorations, *Refugee Communities: A Comparative Field Study*, of Soviet Jews and Vietnamese (Newbury Park, CA, 1992), and Susan Wiley Hardwick's analysis of the role of religion in binding several immigrant communities, *Russian Refuge: Religion, Migration, and Settlement on the North American Pacific Rim* (Chicago, 1993).

Several other works also provided platforms for scholars to examine and reevaluate the dynamics of the past three decades in terms of European origin groups and newer ones entering. A provocative set of essays attempting to make sense of the changes is in Nathan Glazer and Daniel P. Moynihan, eds., *Ethnicity: Theory and Experience* (Cambridge, MA, 1975). The drift toward a more conservative stance in Glazer's thinking could be seen in his own set of essays, *Ethnic Dilemmas, 1964–1982* (Cambridge, MA, 1983). Using 1980 census data, Stanley Lieberson and Mary C. Waters assessed some of the realities behind ethnic attitudes and behavior in *From Many Strands: Ethnic and Racial Groups in Contemporary America* (New York, 1988), and Waters then reported on her community studies in *Ethnic Options: Choosing Identities in America* (Berkeley, 1990). Two other collections of useful essays can be found in Vincent N. Parrillo, ed., *Rethinking Today's Minorities* (Westport, CT, 1991), and Charles H. Mindel, Robert W. Habenstein, and Roosevelt Wright, Jr., *Ethnic Families in America*, 3rd ed. (New York, 1988).

Other Works on Italians and Jews

In addition to the works already cited on Italian Americans (notably by Bayor, Avrich, Yans-McLaughlin, and Gans), others include: Humbert S. Nelli, *The Italians in Chicago, 1880–1930: A Study in Ethnic Mobility* (New York, 1970), with its last chapter on the 1920s; Irving L. Child, *Italian or American? The Second Generation in Conflict*, 2nd ed. (New York, 1970); Alexander DeConde, *Half Bitter, Half Sweet: An Excursion into Italian American History* (New York, 1971); Dino Cinel, *From Italy to San Francisco: The Immigrant Experience* (Stanford, 1982); Lydio F. Tomasi, ed., *Italian Americans: New Perspectives in Italian Immigration and Ethnicity* (Staten Island, NY, 1985); Gary Mormino and George E. Pozzetta's most readable account of Italians, Spaniards, and Cubans, in *The Immigrant World of Ybor City: Italians and Their Latin Neighbors in Tampa, 1885–1985* (Urbana, IL, 1987); Stephen Fox's breakthrough study, *The Unknown Internment: An Oral History of the Relocation of Italian Americans During World War Two* (Boston, 1990); and, edited by Paola A. Sensi-Isolani and Phylis Cancilla Martinelli, *Struggle and Success: An Anthology of the Italian Immigrant Experience in California* (Staten Island, NY, 1993).

Several books among many on Jewish Americans, in addition to those cited above by Bayor, Krause, Feingold, Dinnerstein, and Moore, have been useful. Charles Silberman, *A Certain People: American Jews and Their Lives Today* (New York, 1985), definitely emphasizes the extent of the Jews' success in overcoming rejections and self-doubt. Edward Shapiro's contribution to the recent five volumes on *The Jewish People in America*, edited by Feingold, is an outstanding analysis, *A Time for Healing: American Jewry Since World War Two* (Baltimore, 1992). Arthur Hertzberg's *The Jews in America: Four Centuries of an Uneasy Encounter* (New York, 1989) provides a good overview and interesting insights into the postwar period. Finally, a few essays of value are included in *A New Jewry? America Since the Second World War*, edited by Peter Y. Medding (New York, 1992).

Other Works on Latinos

The literature on Latino Americans has simply exploded in the last fifteen years, and only some can be cited, besides those by Deutsch, Sánchez, Zaragosa, Rieff, and Portes and Rumbaut. Although "Hispanic" is not the choice of self-labeling among most Latinos, authors having taken it from the U.S. Census and used it as the catch-all for the various Latino groups that have multiplied during the past four decades. See *The Hispanic Experience in the United States: Contemporary Issues and Perspectives*, edited by Edna Acosta-Belén and Barbara R. Sjostrom (New York, 1988); Joan Moore and Harry Pachon, *Hispanics in the United States* (Englewood Cliffs, NJ, 1985), expanding her volume on Mexican Americans but with little on Central and South Americans; and Frank D. Bean and Marta Tienda, *The Hispanic Population of the United States* (New York, 1987), a massive statistical, sociological study based on the 1980 census. Note, also, Alejandro Portes and Robert Bach's comparison of the two Latino populations, in *Latin Journey: Cuban and Mexican Immigrants in the United States* (Berkeley, 1985). F. Chris Garcia put together an excellent series of articles on *Latinos and the Political System* (Notre Dame, IN, 1988), although most are on Mexican Americans. In that regard, Juan Gómez-Quiñones provides an overview of the *Roots of Chicano Politics, 1600–1940* (Albuquerque, 1994); Mario T. García studied different classes of individual and organizational leaders in *Mexican Americans: Leadership, Ideology, and Identity, 1930–1960* (New Haven, CT, 1989); and David G. Gutiérrez has written an excellent analysis of Mexican American politics, especially since 1920, in *Walls and Mirrors: Mexican Americans, Mexican Immigrants, and the Politics of Ethnicity* (Berkeley, 1995). For many years, Carey McWilliams' *North From Mexico: The Spanish Speaking People of the United States*, rev. ed. (Westport CT, 1990) was one of the few histories of Mexican Americans, but originally it only brought the story up to 1940. Stan Steiner wrote an account in the late 1960s that remains one of the most readable histories of the group, *La Raza: The Mexican Americans* (New York, 1970). Rudolfo Acuña then authored one from an intensely angry perspective that calmed down with the second and third editions, as it also became far more detailed, *Occupied America: A History of Chicanos*, 3rd ed. (New York, 1988). Also presenting a Chicano perspective is John R. Chávez's *The Lost Land: The Chicano Image of the Southwest* (Albuquerque, 1984). Although marred in the last chapters by some questionable generalizations, a revised version of their own earlier history offers an up-to-date perspective, by Matt S. Meier and Feliciano Ribera, *Mexican Americans/American Mexicans: From Conquistadors to Chicanos* (New York, 1993). Walker Connor's collection of essays, *Mexican Americans in Comparative Perspective* (Washington, DC, 1985) contains an interesting selection of essays for the mid-1980s. Abraham Hoffman had written one of the first major studies of the repatriations of the 1930s, in *Unwanted Mexican-Americans in the Great Depression: Repatriation Pressures, 1929–1939* (Tucson, AZ, 1974). Among the more recent examinations of this is Camille Guerin-Gonzales, *Mexican Workers and American Dreams: Immigration, Repatriation, and California Farm Labor, 1900–1939* (New Brunswick, NJ, 1994). Arthur Corwin had attempted to untangle the complexities and incomplete data of migration in "Causes of Mexican Emigration to the United States," *Perspectives in American History* 7 (1973): 557–635. Lawrence A. Cardoso studied the early phase most carefully in *Mexican Emigration to the United States, 1897–1931* (Tucson, AZ, 1980), which is still regarded as the best treatment of the subject. Among other topics, David Montejano provides an outstanding portrait of the consequences of migration for Mexicans in Texas, and then their outmigration to other states, in *Anglos and Mexicans in the Making of Texas, 1836–1986* (Austin, 1987). One outcome could be seen in Felix M. Padilla's *Latino Ethnic Consciousness: The Case of Mexican Americans and Puerto Ricans in Chicago* (Notre Dame, IN, 1985). Representative of the innumerable studies of undocumented migration is that edited by Frank D. Bean, Barry Edmonston, and Jeffrey Passel, *Undocumented Migration to the United States: IRCA and the Experience of the 1980s* (Santa Monica, CA, and Washington, DC, 1990). The migration dynamics have been traced by Douglas Massey in various studies. See Massey, Rafael Alarcon, Jorge Durand, and Humberto Gonzalez, *Return to Aztlan: The Social Process of International Migration from Western Mexico* (Berkeley, 1987). (See also Wayne Cornelius' essay in Light and Bhachu, *Immigration and Entrepreneurship*, cited above.) The resulting interweaving of California and Mexico due to the massive migration streams is examined in a fine collection of essays edited by Abraham F. Lowenthal and Katrina Burgess, *The California-Mexico Connection* (Stanford, 1993). Finally, Juan Gómez-Quiñones has recently added still another volume addressing an important theme in Mexican American history: *Mexican American Labor, 1790–1990* (Albuquerque, 1994), with a large segment of it on the period since midcentury.

The studies of Miami by Alejandro Portes and Alex Stepick and by Guillermo Grenier and Stepick include Central and South Americans, as does the second part of Louise Lamphere's excellent analysis of *From Working Daughters to Working Mothers: Immigrant Women in a New England Industrial Community* (Ithaca, NY, 1987). An earlier set of essays on both the Caribbean and Central America is that edited by William F. Stinner, Klaus de Albuquerque, and Roy S. Bryce-Laporte, *Return Migration and Remittance: Developing a Caribbean Perspective*, RIIES Occasional Paper no. 3, Smithsonian (Washington, DC, 1982). A followup collection of very stimulating essays on the region was edited by Sergio Díaz-Briquets and Sidney Weintraub, *Determinants of Emigration from Mexico, Central America, and the Caribbean* (Boulder, CO, 1991). Two studies on Dominicans reveal the altered approaches over time but the consistent pressures on the island: Glen Hendricks, *The Dominican Diaspora: From the Dominican Republic to New York City—Villagers in Transition* (New York, 1974), and Sherri Grasmuck and Patricia R. Pessar, *Between Two Islands: Dominican International Migration* (Berkeley, 1991). For another new group fleeing chaos in parts of Central America, in addition to Hagan's book on Mayans, is a study of migration networking by Alan F. Burns, *Maya in Exile: Guatemalans in Florida* (Philadelphia, 1993). Finally, a profile of Latinos eager to fit in can be seen in Beatrice Rodríguez Owsley's New Orleans study, *The Hispanic American Entrepreneur: An Oral History of the American Dream* (New York, 1992).

Worthy of special mention is the long-overdue recognition of Latinos within the Catholic Church. Jay P. Dolan has put together three outstanding volumes on this topic for the Notre Dame History of Hispanics in the United States: with Gilbert M. Hinojosa, *Mexican Americans and the Catholic Church, 1900–1965* (1994); with Jaime R. Vidal, *Puerto Rican and Cuban Catholics in the U.S., 1900–1965* (1994); and, with Allan Figueroa Deck, S.J., *Hispanic Catholic Culture in the U.S.: Issues and Concerns* (1994).

Asians

A number of works by and about Asian Americans have been mentioned above, among them ones by Fawcett and Cariño, Daniels, Takaki, Chan, Lee, Mangiafico, Yung, Kikumura, Nakano, Kibria, and Welaratna. Particularly enlightening is a massive collection of articles, poetry, etc., in *Roots: An Asian American Reader*, edited by Amy Tachiki, Eddie Wong, Franklin Odo, and Buck Wong (Los Angeles, UCLA Asian Studies Center, 1971). The Center also sponsored a second volume, *Counterpoint: Perspectives on Asian Americans* (Los Angeles, 1976). Several works regarding Hawaii have proven most useful, in addition to the chapters in Ronald T. Takaki's *Strangers from a Different Shore.* Lawrence Fuch's *Hawaii Pono: A Social History of Hawaii* (New York, 1961) is considered a standard on the early years. Eleanor C. Nordyke's *The Peopling of Hawaii*, 2nd ed. (Honolulu, 1989) is a basic work for statistical data on the ethnic groups up through 1980. Eileen H. Tamura's *Americanization, Acculturation, and Ethnic Identity: The Nisei Generation in Hawaii* (Urbana, IL, 1994) provides an interesting history of second-generation Japanese Americans prior to World War II. Gary Y. Okihiro's *Cane Fires: The Anti-Japanese Movement in Hawaii, 1865–1945* (Philadelphia, 1991) is a fine, detailed history.

Roger Daniels is regarded as the one of the foremost scholars on Asian Americans, having written numerous books on them, including *Asian America: Chinese and Japanese in the United States since 1850* (Seattle, 1988); *The Decision to Relocate the Japanese Americans* (Malabar, FL, 1986); *Concentration Camps North America: Japanese in the United States and Canada during World War II* (Malabar, FL, 1981); *and Prisoners Without Trial: Japanese Americans in World War II* (New York, 1993). Bill Hosokawa wrote a very readable history of his generation, *Nisei: The Quiet Americans* (New York, 1969). Harry Kitano had written an excellent interdisciplinary text on *Japanese Americans: Evolution of a Subculture*, 2nd ed. (Englewood Cliffs, NJ, 1976), which he has now rewritten and updated as *Generations and Identity: The Japanese American* (Needham Heights, MA, 1993). A particularly good study that illuminates a prewar community in Oregon is Linda Tamura's *The Hood River Issei: An Oral History* (Urbana, IL, 1993).

With respect to the Chinese, Stanford Lyman's study in the Random House series was particularly good, *Chinese Americans* (New York, 1974). Also useful is Shih-shan Henry Tsai's *The Chinese Experience in America* (Bloomington, IN, 1986). For two different views of Chinatowns, the first one of San Francisco and the second of New York but both based on participant observations and interviews, compare Chalso Loo, editor, *Chinatown: Most Time, Hard Time* (New York, 1992), with Min Zhou, *Chinatown: The Socioeconomic Potential of an Urban Enclave* (Philadelphia, 1992). On Koreans an earlier work still of value is Hyung-chan Kim, ed., *The Korean Diaspora* (Santa Barbara, 1977). Koreans in three cities are examined, using three different approaches, by Won Moo Hurh, Hei Chu Kim, and Kwang Chung Kin, *Assimilation Patterns of Immigrants in the United States: A Case Study of Koreans in Chicago* (Washington, DC, 1979); Ilsoo Kim, *New Urban Immigrants: The Korean Community in New York* (Princeton, 1981); and Pyong Gap Min, *Ethnic Business Enterprise: Korean Small Business in Atlanta* (Staten Island, NY, 1988). On Filipinos, a good collection edited by Jesse Quinsaat for the early period is *Letters in Exile: A Reader on the History of Filipinos in America* (Los Angeles, 1976), as is Fred Cordova's *Filipinos: Forgotten Asian Americans—A Pictorial Essay/1763-Circa-1963* (Dubuque, IA, 1983). On Asian Indians, S. Chandrasekhar edited *From India to America* (La Jolla, CA, 1982). More complete is Joan Jensen's *Passage from India* (New Haven, CT, 1988).

Central to the Asian America story is the internment of Japanese Americans in concentration camps, for which there is now a vast body of literature, in addition to Daniels's work. One of the first to achieve great popularity was Michi Weglyn's *Years of Infamy: The Untold Story of America's Concentration Camps* (New York, 1976). The military story of the achievements of Japanese Americans was recounted vividly by Chester Tanaka, in *Go for Broke: A Pictorial History of the Japanese American 100th Battalion and the 442nd Regimental Combat Team* (Richmond, CA, 1982), but it is the tale of those left behind that culminated in the redress movement. Among the now numerous oral and first- person accounts are Estelle Ishigo, *Lone Heart Mountain* (Los Angeles, 1972); Jeanne Wakatsuki Houston and James D. Houston, *Farewell to Manzanar* (New York, 1973); *The Kikuchi Diary: Chronicle from an American Concentration Camp*, by Charles Kikuchi, edited by John Modell (Urbana, IL, 1993); and John Tateishi, *And Justice for All: An Oral History of the Japanese American Detention Camps* (New York, 1984). Several scholarly accounts immediately followed the war; here only four important, recent works can be noted: *Personal Justice Denied: Report of the Commission on Wartime Relocation and Internment of Civilians* (Washington, DC, 1982); Roger Daniels, Sandra Taylor, and Harry Kitano, eds., *Japanese Americans: From Re-*

location to Redress (Salt Lake City, 1986); Leslie T. Hatamiya, *Righting a Wrong: Japanese Americans and the Passage of the Civil Liberties Act of 1988* (Stanford, 1993); and Peter Irons, *Justice Delayed: The Record of the Japanese American Internment Cases* (Middletown, CT, 1989).

In terms of works dealing with more recent Asian American history, see Elliott R. Barkan, *Asian and Pacific Islander Migration to the United States*, cited above; Kitano and Daniels, *Asian Americans*, 2nd ed. (Englewood Cliffs, NJ, 1995), a very useful, updated, brief survey of the principal Asian American groups; and Herbert Barringer, Robert Gardner, and Michael J. Levin, *Asian And Pacific Islanders in the United States* (New York, 1993), a study, like Bean and Tienda's on Hispanics, based on the 1980 census. However, while extremely useful, it contains a number of errors. For different perspectives within a short time, compare Maxine Fisher, *The Indians of New York City: A Study in Immigrants from India* (New Delhi, 1980), with Arthur and Usha M. Helweg, *An Indian Success Story: East Indians in America* (Philadelphia, 1990), a very readable account of recent migration. Karen I. Leonard's *Making Ethnic Choices: California's Punjabi Mexican Americans* (Philadelphia, 1992) is an excellent interdisciplinary study of old immigrants and their children encountering the new ones.

Among the many analyses of Vietnamese adaptation to America, see Paul J. Strand and Woodrow Jones, Jr., *Indochinese Refugees in America: Problems of Adaptation and Assimilation* (Durham, NC, 1985); Nathan Caplan, John K. Whitmore, and Marcella H. Choy, *The Boat People and Achievement in America: A Study of Family Life, Hard Work, and Cultural Values* (Ann Arbor, MI, 1989); and Paul James Rutledge, *The Vietnamese Experience in America* (Bloomington, IN, 1992).

Four other works reflecting current trends are Timothy Fong's study of *The First Suburban Chinatown: The Remaking of Monterey Park, California* (Philadelphia, 1994); William Wei, *The Asian American Movement* (Philadelphia, 1993); and Franklin Ng, Judy Yung, Stephen Fugita, and Elaine H. Kim, *New Visions in Asian American Studies: Diversity, Community,*

Power (Pullman, WA, 1994); and Yen Le Espiritu, *Asian American Panethnicity: Bridging Institutions and Identities* (Philadelphia, 1992). Finally, Pyong Gap Min has edited a new collection of essays, with six chapters on contemporary issues of different Asian American populations, in *Asian Americans: Contemporary Trends and Issues* (Thousand Oaks, CA, 1995).

Other Current Trends

A number of final works highlight some of the new trends in terms of the examination of groups previously overlooked, the arrival in greater numbers of previously minor ones, the population shifts to the South, and the greater interest in the growing phenomenon of intermarriage across racial lines: Marilyn Halter, *Between Race and Ethnicity: Cape Verdean American Immigrants, 1860–1965* (Urbana, IL, 1993); Ron Kelley, ed., *Irangeles: Iranians in Los Angeles* (Berkeley, 1993), an excellent oral and photographic study; Raymond Mohl, ed., *Searching for the Sunbelt: Historical Perspectives on a Region* (Knoxville, 1990), with valuable articles on ethnic developments in the South due to in-migration and immigration by Ronald Bayor, Mohl, and Elliott Barkan; Paul R. Spikard, *Mixed Blood: Intermarriage and Ethnic Identity in Twentieth Century America* (Madison, 1989), and Maria P. P. Root, ed., *Racially Mixed People in America* (Newbury Park, CA, 1992).

INDEX

and urban riots, 1980–92, 190
awaiting visas, 1994, 3, 192
motives, contemporary, 3–4, 82,
    113, 119, 125
motives, of Mexican, 82–84, 125–
    26
motives, post-World War II, 82
spouses of military personnel, 75,
    93, 95
immigration
1920s and, 20
1945–65, regional distribution, 81
1951–65 vs. 1965–93, region of
    origin, 121
1966–93, 116, 203
Amerasian children, 139
and concept of a rimless world, 57,
    112–13
brain drain vs. remittances, 165–66
characteristics since 1965, 120–24,
debate over "costs" of, 186–89
Depression and, 45
during World War II, 66–67
early 1960s, 87
female, 1920s, 21
female, 1945–65, 93
female, since 1965, 128–29
growing opposition to, 1990s, 181–
    82, 185–86, 193–95
impact on women, 129–30
leading nations, 1950–90, 122, 202
public opinion concerning, 10–14,
    193–95
students, 164–65
war brides and grooms, 1946–50,
    73
Immigration Act of 1917, 10
Immigration Act of November 1990,
    116, 182–85
Immigration and Nationality Act of
    October 1965, 116
immigration and refugee policy
1929 vs. 1952 provisions, 77–78
1952 vs. 1965 provisions, 117

1965 vs. 1990 provisions, 184–85
Act of September 26, 1961, 79
Alien Registration Act, 1940, 59
and brain-drain controversy, 164–
    66
and Chinese, 67
and World War II, 66–67
anti-Communist emphasis, 134
Cuban and Haitian refugee policy
    changes, 1990s, 136–37
Cuban Refugee Adjustment Act
    of November 1966, 136–37
Displaced Persons Act, 1948, 75
Emergency Quota Act, 1921, 11
Immigration Act of 1917, 10
Immigration Act of November
    1990, 116, 182–85
Immigration and Nationality Act
    of October 1965, 116
Immigration Reform and Control
    Act of November 1986
    (IRCA), 118
Johnson-Reed Immigration Act,
    1924, 13
lottery/diversity visas, 118–19, 183,
    195–96
Married Women's Nationality Act
    (the Cable Act), 1922, 15
McCarran Internal Security Act,
    1950, 76
McCarran-Walter Immigration
    and Nationality Act, 1952, 77
Migration and Refugee Assistance
    Act [for Cubans], 1962, 137
National Origins System, 13–14,
    77, 80, 84, 116
Orderly Departure Program [for
    Vietnamese], 139
parole of Cubans and Southeast
    Asian refugees, 137
parole of Hungarian refugees, 79
parole of refugees, presidential
    power to, 77
political asylum, provisions for, 118

PHOTO CREDITS

All photos not otherwise credited are by Elliott Barkan

XV, YIVO Institute / Courtesy of the National Park Service, Liberty Island, U.S. Dept. of Interior / Courtesy of Muriel Petioni, New York; **XVI,** Hallahan, for the *Providence Evening Bulletin*, Library of Congress, 62-44049; **XVII,** Courtesy of the National Park Service, Liberty Island, U.S. Dept. of Interior / Bentley Historical Library, University of Michigan / Courtesy of the National Park Service, Harper's Ferry, Virginia, U.S. Dept. of Interior; **XVIII,** Photo by Roy Perry, 1937, Museum of the City of New York, 80.102.182; **XIX,** Brown Brothers, Sterling, PA., B0279 and B0710; **XX,** Both photos from the collection of Melvin Holli; **XXI,** From the collection of Melvin Holli / Visual Communications, Los Angeles; **XXII** UPI/Bettmann, New York / National Archives, W. & C., 780; **XXIII,** National Japanese American Historical Society / National Archives, Courtesy of the U.S. Holocaust Memorial Museum; **XXIV,** Top, Wide World; **XXV** Courtesy of the National Park Service, Harper's Ferry, Virginia, U.S. Dept. of the Interior / Courtesy of the National Park Service, Liberty Island, U.S. Dept. of the Interior, and the American Red Cross; **XXIX** Top, photo by Steve Gold; **XXX,** Courtesy of the Immigration and Naturalization Service / Forbes/ Life; **XXXI** Top, photo by Van Dongen, for the UN High Commission for Refugees. Courtesy of Thomas Kessner; **XXXIII** Bottom, photo by Steve Gold; **XXXIV** Top, photo by Steve Gold; **XXXVII** Wide World / Courtesy of Judy Chu; **XXXVIII** Cartoon by Steve Benson for the *Arizona Republic*, August 1993, Tribune Media Service

And Still They Come: Immigrants and American Society, 1920 to the 1990s

Project and copy editor, Maureen Hewitt
Production editor, Lucy Herz
Proofreader, Claudia Siler
Typesetter, City Desktop
Printing and binding by Thomson-Shore, Inc.

About the Author: Elliott Robert Barkan is Professor of History and Ethnic Studies at California State University, San Bernardino, and Assistant Dean of the School of Social and Behavioral Sciences. Professor Barkan is the book review editor for the *Journal of American Ethnic History*, and he has completed Fulbright lectureships to India, England, and Norway. His other writings include three books: *Edmund Burke and the American Revolution*, ed., *California's New Americans: A Manual for Analyzing History with Computers*, and *Asian and Pacific Islander Migration to the United States: A Model of New Global Patterns*.